An Approach to Indian Anthropology

An Approach to Indian Anthropology

P.V. Chandrashekara

2008

CYBER TECH PUBLICATIONS
4264/3, Ansari Road, Daryaganj, New Delhi-110002 (India)
Ph.: 011-23244078. Fax: 011-23280028
E-Mail: cyberpublicationsdelhi@yahoo.com

AN APPROACH TO INDIAN ANTHROPOLOGY

P.V. Chandrashekara

First Edition 2008

Published by :

G.S. Rawat for **Cyber Tech Publications**
4264/3, Ansari Road, Daryaganj, New Delhi-110002 (India)
Ph.: 011-23244078. Fax: 011-23280028
E-Mail: cyberpublicationsdelhi@yahoo.com

Printed at : **Amit Enterprises**, Maujpur, Delhi, (9810878184)

Preface

Anthropology cannot be treated as a general book or subject. It challenges people to exercise enormous flexibility, analytical capacity and thought, abilities that are especially important when sorting out the nuances of unfamiliar cultures. So, as I discuss the history and subject matter of anthropology. I could have stressed theory but much of the effective theory in anthropology is tied to specific areas, such as economics, poverty, ecology, health care, and conflict resolution. I want to give the reader a set of generalizable tools that can be used in various settings and domains. Students need to consider methods early in their training.

I frequently make use of case studies. The case study approach is often the best way to teach anthropology. Because anthropology currently covers so many domains, varied case studies can familiarize students with the many options for practice. At the same time, each case illustrates such principles as bottom-up perspectives in program evaluation or the corroboration of qualitative and quantitative methods.

The challenge of the global environmental crisis has generated rapid advances in environmental anthropology. Current work by political ecologists should stimulate the interest of students and illustrate how exceptionally relevant anthropology can be.

I have had some important help and influences in writing this book I heartily thank to them all. Although the book covers most of the significant principles but the valuable suggestions of the readers is always welcome.

—Author

Contents

1

History of Anthropology

The anthropologist Eric Wolf once characterized anthropology as the most scientific of the humanities, and the most humanistic of the social sciences. Understanding how anthropology developed contributes to understanding how it fits into other academic disciplines.

Contemporary anthropologists claim a number of earlier thinkers as their forebearers and the discipline itself has many sources. However, anthropology can best be understood as an outgrowth of the Age of Enlightenment. It was during this period that Europeans attempted systematically to study human behavior. Traditions of jurisprudence, history, philology and sociology developed during this time and informed the development of the social sciences of which anthropology was a part. At the same time, the romantic reaction to the Enlightenment produced thinkers such as Herder and later Wilhelm Dilthey whose work formed the basis for the culture concept which is central to the discipline.

These intellectual movements in part grappled with one of the greatest paradoxes of modernity: as the world is becoming smaller and more integrated, people's experience of the world is increasingly atomized and dispersed. As Karl Marx and Friedrich Engels observed in the 1840s:

All old-established national industries have been destroyed or are daily being destroyed. They are dislodged by new industries, whose introduction becomes a life and death question for all civilized nations, by industries that no longer work up indigenous raw material but raw material drawn from the remotest zones; industries whose products are consumed, not only at home, but in every quarter of the globe. In place of the old wants, satisfied by the production of the country, we find new wants, requiring for their satisfaction the products of distant lands and climes. In place of the old local and national seclusion and self-sufficiency, we have intercourse in every direction, universal interdependence of nations.

Ironically, this universal interdependence, rather than leading to greater human solidarity, has coincided with increasing racial, ethnic, religious, and class divisions, and new-and to some confusing or disturbing-cultural expressions. These are the conditions of life with which people today must contend, but they have their origins in processes that began in the 16th century and accelerated in the 19th century.

Institutionally anthropology emerged from natural history (expounded by authors such as Buffon). This was the study of human beings-typically people living in European colonies. Thus studying the language, culture, physiology, and artifacts of European colonies was more or less equivalent to studying the flora and fauna of those places. It was for this reason, for instance, that Lewis Henry Morgan could write monographs on both The League of the Iroquois and The American Beaver and His Works. This is also why the material culture of 'civilized' nations such as China have historically been displayed in fine arts museums alongside European art while artifacts from Africa or Native North American cultures were displayed in Natural History Museums with dinosaur bones and nature dioramas. This being said, curatorial practice has changed dramatically in recent years, and it would be wrong to see anthropology as merely an extension of colonial rule and European chauvinism, since its relationship to imperialism was and is complex.

Museums such as the British Museum weren't the only site of anthropological studies: with the New Imperialism period, starting in the 1870s, zoos became unattended "laboratories", especially the so-called "ethnological exhibitions" or "Negro villages". Thus, "savages" from the colonies were displayed, often nudes, in cages, in what has been called "human zoos". For example, in 1906, Congolese pygmy Ota Benga was put by anthropologist Madison Grant in a cage in the Bronx Zoo, labelled "the missing link" between an orangutan and the "white race"-Grant, a renowned eugenicist, was also the author of The Passing of the Great Race (1916). Such exhibitions were attempts to illustrate and prove in the same movement the validity of scientific racism, which first formulation may be found in Arthur de Gobineau's An Essay on the Inequality of Human Races (1853-55). In 1931, the Colonial Exhibition in Paris still displayed Kanaks from New Caledonia in the "indigenous village"; it received 24 million visitors in six months, thus demonstrating the popularity of such "human zoos".

GROWTH AND DEVELOPMENT

Anthropology grew increasingly distinct from natural history and by the end of the nineteenth century the discipline began to crystallize into its modern form-by 1935, for example, it was possible for T.K. Penniman to write a history of the discipline entitled A Hundred Years of Anthropology. At the time, the field was dominated by 'the comparative method'. It was assumed that all societies passed through a single evolutionary process from the most primitive to most advanced. Non-European societies were thus seen as evolutionary 'living fossils' that could be studied in order to understand the European past. Scholars wrote histories of prehistoric migrations which were sometimes valuable but often also fanciful. It was during this time that Eurcpeans first accurately traced Polynesian migrations across the Pacific Ocean for instance-although some of them believed it originated in Egypt. Finally, the concept of race was actively discussed as a way to classify-and rank-human beings based on inherent biological difference.

In the twentieth century academic disciplines began to organize around three main domains. The "sciences" seeks to derive natural laws through reproducible and falsifiable experiments. The "humanities" reflected an attempt to study different national traditions, in the form of history and the arts, as an attempt to provide people in emerging nation-states with a sense of coherence. The "social sciences" emerged at this time as an attempt to develop scientific methods to address social phenomena, in an attempt to provide a universal basis for social knowledge. Anthropology does not easily fit into one of these categories, and different branches of anthropology draw on one or more of these domains.

Drawing on the methods of the natural sciences as well as developing new techniques involving not only structured interviews but unstructured "participant-observation"-and drawing on the new theory of evolution through natural selection, they proposed the scientific study of a new object: "humankind," conceived of as a whole.

Crucial to this study is the concept "culture," which anthropologists defined both as a universal capacity and propensity for social learning, thinking, and acting (which they see as a product of human evolution and something that distinguishes Homo sapiens-and perhaps all species of genus Homo-from other species), and as a particular adaptation to local conditions that takes the form of highly variable beliefs and practices. Thus, "culture" not only transcends the opposition between nature and nurture; it transcends and absorbs the peculiarly European distinction between politics, religion, kinship, and the economy as autonomous domains. Anthropology thus transcends the divisions between the natural sciences, social sciences, and humanities to explore the biological, linguistic, material, and symbolic dimensions of humankind in all forms.

In the mid-Twentieth century American anthropology began to methodologically study its own history. In 1967 Marvin Harris published his, The Rise of Anthropological Theory presenting argumentative examinations of anthropology's historical developments, and George W. Stocking Jr., established the historicist school, examining the historical contexts of anthropological movements.

STUDY OF ANTHROPOLOGY

Anthropology consists of the study of humanity. It is holistic in two senses: it is concerned with all human beings at all times and with all dimensions of humanity.

In principle, it is concerned with all institutions of all societies. Since the work of Franz Boas and Bronislaw Malinowski in the late 19th-and early 20th-centuries, anthropology has been distinguished from other social science disciplines by its emphasis on cultural relativity, in-depth examination of context, cross-cultural comparisons, and the importance it places on long-term, experiential immersion in the area of research, often known as participant-observation.

In the United States, and to a lesser extent in Britain and other English-speaking countries, anthropology has often been traditionally conceived as comprising four related fields of study:

- Biological or physical anthropology seeks to understand the physical human being through the study of genetics, inherited traits and variations thereof, evolution, adaptation, etc. Subfields or related fields include primatology, nutritional anthropology, and human and population genetics.
- Socio-cultural anthropology is the investigation, often through long term, intensive field studies, of the culture and social organization of a particular people: language, economic and political organization, kinship, gender relations, religion, mythology, symbolism, etc. (U.S. universities more often use the term cultural anthropology; British universities have tended to call the corresponding field social anthropology, and for much of the 20th century emphasized the analysis of social organization more than cultural symbolism.) In some European countries, socio-cultural anthropology is known as ethnology (a term also used in English-speaking countries to denote the comparative aspect of socio-cultural anthropology.) Subfields and related fields include psychological anthropology, folklore, anthropology of religion, ethnic studies, and cultural studies.
- Linguistic anthropology seeks to understand the processes of human communications, verbal and non-verbal; it identifies the many subtle elements of the world's languages and documents their structure, function and history. Linguistic anthropologists often draw on related fields including semeiotics, cognitive linguistics, discourse analysis, and narrative analysis.

- Archaeology is the study of the human past through the exploration, discovery, excavation, dating, and methodological analysis of material remains left by past humans; it includes prehistoric cultures and their development as well as historically documented cultures.

In countries of the British Commonwealth, social anthropology has often been institutionally separate from physical anthropology and primatology, which may be connected with departments of biology or zoology; and from archaeology, which may be connected with departments of Classics, Egyptology, and the like. In various times and places, anthropologists have also found themselves institutionally linked with scholars of folklore, museum studies, geography, sociology, social relations, ethnic studies, and cultural studies.

Some anthropologists have used anthropological studies to frame cultural critiques. This has been particularly prominent in America, from the popular critiques of Victorianism by Margaret Mead and Ruth Benedict through contemporary attacks on post-colonialism under the heading of postmodernism.

Anthropology is a methodologically diverse discipline, incorporating both qualitative methods and quantitative methods. Ethnographies-intensive case studies based on field research-have historically had a central place in the literature of the discipline. Currently, advancements across the scientific disciplines such as in physics and chemistry have aided anthropologists in their efforts to better understand all of humanity. Radiocarbon dating is just one of many technologies used regularly in the field of anthropology.

HISTORICAL AND INSTITUTIONAL CONTEXT

The anthropologist Eric Wolf once described anthropology as "the most scientific of the humanities, and the most humanistic of the sciences." Contemporary anthropologists claim a number of earlier thinkers as their forebears, and the discipline has several sources; Claude Lévi-Strauss, for example, claimed Montaigne and Rousseau as important influences. Anthropology can best be understood as an outgrowth of the Age of Enlightenment, a period when Europeans attempted systematically to study human behavior. The traditions of jurisprudence, history, philology, and sociology then evolved into something more closely resembling the modern views of these disciplines and informed the development of the social sciences, of which anthropology was a part. At the same time, the romantic reaction to the Enlightenment produced thinkers, such as Johann Gottfried Herder and later Wilhelm Dilthey, whose work formed the basis for the "culture concept," which is central to the discipline.

Institutionally, anthropology emerged from the development of natural history (expounded by authors such as Buffon) that occurred during the European colonization of the 17th, 18th, 19th and 20th centuries. Programs of ethnographic study originated in this era as the study of the "human primitives" overseen by colonial administrations. There was a tendency in late 18th century Enlightenment thought to understand human society as natural phenomena that behaved in accordance with certain principles and that could be observed empirically. In some ways, studying the language, culture, physiology, and artifacts of European colonies was not unlike studying the flora and fauna of those places. Saartje Baartman, a Namaqua woman, was examined by anatomist Georges Cuvier. This being said, curatorial practice has changed dramatically in recent years, and it would be inaccurate to see anthropology as merely an extension of colonial rule and European chauvinism, since its relationship to imperialism was and is complex.

Anthropology grew increasingly distinct from natural history, and by the end of the nineteenth century, it had begun to crystallize into its modern form; by 1935, for example, it was possible for T. K. Penniman to write a history of the discipline entitled "A Hundred Years of Anthropology." Early anthropology was dominated by proponents of unilinealism, who argued that all societies passed through a single evolutionary process, from the most primitive to the most advanced. Non-European societies were thus seen as evolutionary "living fossils," which could be studied in order to understand the European past. Scholars wrote histories of prehistoric migrations that were sometimes valuable but often also fanciful. It was during this time that Europeans, such as Paul Rivet, first accurately traced Polynesian migrations across the Pacific Ocean-though some of them believed those emigrations had originated in Egypt. Finally, concepts of race were developed with a view to better understanding the nature of the biological variation within the Human species, and tools such as Anthropometry were devised as a means of measuring and categorizing this variation, not just within the genus Homo, but in fossil Hominids and primates as well. Racialistic concepts were advocated by a few and gave rise to theories of Scientific racism.

Anténor Firmin wrote De l'égalité des races humaines (1885) as a direct rebuttal to Count Arthur de Gobineau's polemical four-volume work Essai sur l'inegalite des Races Humaines (1853-1855), which asserted the superiority of the Aryan race and the inferiority of blacks and other people of color. Firmin's work argued the opposite, that "all men are endowed with the same qualities and the same faults, without distinction of color or anatomical form. The races are equal" (pp. 450). Firmin grew up in Haiti, and was admitted to the Societé d' Anthropologie de Paris in 1884 while serving as a diplomat. His persuasive critique and rigorous analysis of many of that society's leading scholars made him an early pioneer in the so-called vindicationist struggle in anthropology. Many scholars also associate his work with the very first ideas of Pan-Africanism. Many modern anthropologists no longer refer to races as biological realities and may instead refer to the idea of clines.

In the twentieth century, academic disciplines began to organize around three main domains. The domain of the sciences seeks to derive natural laws through reproducible and falsifiable experiments; that of the humanities reflects an attempt to study different national traditions, in the form of history and the arts, as an attempt to provide people in emerging nation-states with a sense of coherence; the social sciences emerged at this time as an attempt to develop scientific methods to address social phenomena and provide a universal basis for social knowledge. Anthropology does not easily fit into one of these categories, and different branches of anthropology draw on one or more of these domains.

Drawing on the methods of the natural sciences and developing new techniques involving not only structured interviews, but unstructured participant observation, and drawing on the new theory of evolution through natural selection, the branches of anthropology proposed the scientific study of a new object: humankind, conceived of as a whole. Crucial to this study is the concept of culture, which anthropologists defined both as a universal capacity and a propensity for social learning, thinking, and acting (which they saw as a product of human evolution and something that distinguishes Homo sapiens-and perhaps all species of genus Homo-from other species), and as a particular adaptation to local conditions, which takes the form of highly variable beliefs and practices. Thus, culture not only transcends the opposition between nature and nurture, but absorbs the peculiarly European distinction among politics, religion, kinship, and the economy as autonomous domains. Anthropology thus transcends the divisions between the natural sciences, social sciences, and humanities to explore the biological, linguistic, material, and symbolic dimensions of humankind in all forms.

Anthropology in the United States

Anthropology in the United States was influenced by the availability of Native American societies as ethnographic subjects and the political debates around the definition of humanity and citizenship.

Jacksonian America and Polygenism

Late eighteenth century ethnology established the scientific foundation for the field, which began to mature when Andrew Jackson was President of the United States (1829-1837). Jackson was responsible for implementing the Indian Removal Act, the coerced and forced removal of an estimated 100,000 American Indians during the 1830s to Indian Territory in present-day Oklahoma; for insuring that the franchise was extended to all white men, irrespective of financial means while denying virtually all black men the right to vote; and, for suppressing abolitionists' efforts to end slavery while vigorously defending that institution. Finally, he was responsible for appointing Chief Justice Roger B. Taney who would decide, in Scott v. Sandford (1857), that Negroes were "beings of an inferior order, and altogether unfit to associate with the white race... and so far inferior that they had no rights which the white man was bound to respect." As a result of this decision, black people, whether free or enslaved, could never become citizens of the United States.

It was in this context that the so-called American School of Anthropology thrived as the champion of polygenism or the doctrine of multiple origins-sparking a debate between those influenced by the Bible who believed in the unity of humanity and those who argued from a scientific standpoint for the plurality of origins and the antiquity of distinct types. Like the monogenists, these theories were not monolithic and often used words like races, species, hybrid, and mongrel interchangeably. A scientific consensus began to emerge during this period "that there exists a Genus Homo, embracing many primordial types of 'species.'" Charles Caldwell, Samuel George Morton, Samuel A. Cartwright, George Gliddon, Josiah C. Nott, and Louis Agassiz, and even South Carolina Governor James Henry Hammond were all influential proponents of this school. While some were disinterested scientists, others were passionate advocates who used science to promote slavery in a period of increasing sectional strife. All were complicity in establishing the putative science that justified slavery, informed the Dred Scott decision, underpinned miscegenation laws, and eventually fueled Jim Crow. Samuel G. Morton, for example, claimed to be just a scientist but he did not hesitate to provide evidence of Negro inferiority to John C. Calhoun, the prominent pro-slavery Secretary of State to help him negotiate the annexation of Texas as a slave state.

TYPES OF MANKIND, 1854

The high-water mark of polygenitic theories was Josiah Nott and Gliddon's voluminous eight-hundred page tome titled Types of Mankind, published in 1854. Reproducing the work of Louis Agassiz and Samuel Morton, the authors spread the virulent and explicitly racist views to a wider, more popular audience. The first printing sold out quickly and by the end of the century it had undergone nine editions. Although many Southerners felt that all the justification for slavery they needed was found in the Bible, others used the new science to defend slavery and the repression of American Indians. Abolitionists, however, felt they had to take this science on its own terms.

And for the first time, African American intellectuals waded into the contentious debate.

In the immediate wake of Types of Mankind and during the pitched political battles that led to Civil War, Frederick Douglass (1818-1895), the statesman and persuasive abolitionist, directly attacked the leading theorists of the American School of Anthropology. In an 1854 address, entitled "The Claims of the Negro Ethnologically Considered," Douglass argued that "by making the enslaved a character fit only for slavery, [slaveowners] excuse themselves for refusing to make the slave a freeman.... For let it be once granted that the human race are of multitudinous origin, naturally different in their moral, physical, and intellectual capacities... a chance is left for slavery, as a necessary institution.... There is no doubt that Messrs. Nott, Glidden, Morton, Smith and Agassiz were duly consulted by our slavery propagating statesmen" (p. 287).

Boasian Anthropology

Cultural anthropology in the United States was influenced greatly by the ready availability of Native American societies as ethnographic subjects. The field was pioneered by staff of the Bureau of Indian Affairs and the Smithsonian Institution's Bureau of American Ethnology, men such as John Wesley Powell and Frank Hamilton Cushing. Lewis Henry Morgan (1818-1881), a lawyer from Rochester, New York, became an advocate for and ethnological scholar of the Iroquois. His comparative analyses of religion, government, material culture, and especially kinship patterns proved to be influential contributions to the field of anthropology. Like other scholars of his day (such as Edward Tylor), Morgan argued that human societies could be classified into categories of cultural evolution on a scale of progression that ranged from savagery, to barbarism, to civilization. Generally, Morgan used technology (such as bowmaking or pottery) as an indicator of position on this scale.

Franz Boas established academic anthropology in the United States in opposition to this sort of evolutionary perspective. Boasian anthropology was politically active and suspicious of research dictated by the U.S. government and wealthy patrons.

It was rigorously empirical and skeptical of overgeneralizations and attempts to establish universal laws. Boas studied immigrant children to demonstrate that biological race was not immutable, and that human conduct and behavior resulted from nurture, rather than nature.

Influenced by the German tradition, Boas argued that the world was full of distinct cultures, rather than societies whose evolution could be measured by how much or how little "civilization" they had. He believed that each culture has to be studied in its particularity, and argued that cross-cultural generalizations, like those made in the natural sciences, were not possible. In doing so, he fought discrimination against immigrants, African Americans, and Native North Americans. Many American anthropologists adopted his agenda for social reform, and theories of race continue to be popular targets for anthropologists today. The so-called "Four Field Approach" has its origins in Boasian Anthropology, dividing the discipline in the four crucial and interrelated fields of sociocultural, biological, linguistic, and prehistoric anthropology.

Boas used his positions at Columbia University and the American Museum of Natural History to train and develop multiple generations of students. His first generation of students included Alfred Kroeber, Robert Lowie, Edward Sapir and Ruth Benedict, all of whom produced richly detailed studies of indigenous North American cultures. They provided a wealth of details used to attack the theory of a single evolutionary process. Kroeber and Sapir's focus on Native American languages helped establish linguistics as a truly general science and free it from its historical focus on Indo-European languages.

The publication of Alfred Kroeber's textbook, Anthropology, marked a turning point in American anthropology. After three decades of amassing material, Boasians felt a growing urge to generalize. This was most obvious in the 'Culture and Personality' studies carried out by younger Boasians such as Margaret Mead and Ruth Benedict. Influenced by psychoanalytic psychologists such as Sigmund Freud and Carl Jung, these authors sought to understand the way that individual personalities were shaped by the wider cultural and social forces in which they grew up. Though such works as Coming of Age in Samoa and The Chrysanthemum and the Sword remain popular with the American public, Mead and Benedict never had the impact on the discipline of anthropology that some expected. Boas had planned for Ruth Benedict to succeed him as chair of Columbia's anthropology department, but she was sidelined by Ralph Linton, and Mead was limited to her offices at the AMNH.

Anthropology in Britain

Whereas Boas picked his opponents to pieces through attention to detail, modern anthropology in Britain was formed by rejecting historical reconstruction in the name of a science of society that focused on analyzing how societies held together in the present.

The two most important scholars in this tradition were Alfred Reginald Radcliffe-Brown and Bronislaw Malinowski, both of whom released seminal works in 1922. Radcliffe-Brown's initial fieldwork, in the Andaman Islands, was carried out in the old style of historical reconstruction. After reading the work of French sociologists Émile Durkheim and Marcel Mauss, Radcliffe-Brown published an account of his research (entitled simply The Andaman Islanders) that paid close attention to the meaning and purpose of rituals and myths. Over time, he developed an approach known as structural-functionalism, which focused on how institutions in societies worked to balance out or create an equilibrium in the social system to keep it functioning harmoniously. Malinowski, in contrast, advocated an unhyphenated functionalism, which examined how society functioned to meet individual needs. He is better known, however, for his detailed ethnography and advances in methodology. His classic ethnography, Argonauts of the Western Pacific, advocated getting "the native's point of view" and an approach to fieldwork that became standard in the field.

Malinowski and Radcliffe-Brown's influence stemmed from the fact that they, like Boas, actively trained students and aggressively built up institutions that furthered their programmatic ambitions. This was particularly the case with Radcliffe-Brown, who spread his agenda for "Social Anthropology" by teaching at universities across the

Commonwealth. From the late 1930s until the postwar period appeared a string of monographs and edited volumes that cemented the paradigm of British Social Anthropology. Famous ethnographies include The Nuer, by Edward· Evan Evans-Pritchard, and The Dynamics of Clanship Among the Tallensi, by Meyer Fortes; well-known edited volumes include African Systems of Kinship and Marriage and African Political Systems. Contemporary social anthropology is international and has branched in many directions.

Anthropology in France

Anthropology in France has a less clear genealogy than the British and American traditions. Most commentators consider Marcel Mauss to be the founder of the French anthropological tradition. Mauss was a member of Durkheim's Année Sociologique group, and while Durkheim and others examined the state of modern societies, Mauss and his collaborators (such as Henri Hubert and Robert Hertz) drew on ethnography and philology to analyze societies which were not as 'differentiated' as European nation states. In particular, Mauss's Essay on the Gift was to prove of enduring relevance in anthropological studies of exchange and reciprocity.

Throughout the interwar years, French interest in anthropology often dovetailed with wider cultural movements such as surrealism and primitivism which drew on ethnography for inspiration. Marcel Griaule and Michel Leiris are examples of people who combined anthropology with the French avant-garde. During this time most of what is known as ethnologie was restricted to museums, such as the Musée de l'Homme founded by Paul Rivet, and anthropology had a close relationship with studies of folklore.

Above all, however, it was Claude Lévi-Strauss who helped institutionalize anthropology in France. In addition to the enormous influence his structuralism exerted across multiple disciplines, Lévi-Strauss established ties with American and British anthropologists. At the same time he established centers and laboratories within France to provide an institutional context within anthropology while training influential students such as Maurice Godelier and Françoise Héritier who would prove influential in the world of French anthropology. Much of the distinct character of France's anthropology today is a result of the fact that most anthropology is carried out in nationally funded research laboratories (CNRS) rather than academic departments in universities.

Other influential writers in the 1970s include Pierre Clastres, who explains in his books on the Guayaki tribe in Paraguay that "primitive societies" actively oppose the institution of the state. Therefore, these stateless societies are not less evolved than societies with states, but took the active choice of conjuring the institution of authority as a separate function from society. The leader is only a spokeperson for the group when it has to deal with other groups ("international relations") but has no inside authority, and may be violently removed if he attempts to abuse this position.

Canadian Anthropology

Canadian anthropology began, as in other parts of the Colonial world, as ethnological data in the records of travellers and missionaries. In Canada, Jesuit Missionaries such as Fathers LeClercq, Le Jeune and Sagard, in the 1600s, provide the oldest ethnographic records of First Nations in what was then the Domain of Canada.

True anthropology began with a Government department: the Geological Survey of Canada, and George Mercer Dawson (director in 1895). Dawson's support for anthropology created impetus for the profession in Canada. This was expanded upon by Prime Minister Wilfrid Laurier, who established a Division of Anthropology within the Geological Survey in 1810. Anthropologists were recruited from England and the USA, setting the foundation for the unique Canadian style of anthropology.

Early scholars include the brilliant linguist and Boasian, Edward Sapir, also Oxford graduates Marius Barbeau and Diamond Jenness. Born in rural Québec, Barbeau became a Rhodes scholar and eventually a classmate of Jenness. The two studied under Tylor and Marett at Oxford. In Canada, Barbeau and Jenness worked at the National Museum (as it became known later). In 1944, Canada's first home-grown anthropologist established the archive which has become an key source of ethnographic and folklore material.

Following George Mercer Dawson (of McGill, Montreal) and Franz Boas, Sapir and Barbeau conducted ethnographic research and collected material culture from the peoples of the Northwest Coast, especially Haida. Jenness is best known for his research in the Arctic among the Copper Inuit. However, in actuality, they all worked in a variety of areas in Canada, recording traditions and songs, studying languages, and collecting artifacts for the museum. They essentially had sole responsibility for the development of the profession in Canada from 1910 until 1925 when Sapir left. The development was slow relative to expansion (due to the colonizing needs) of Britain and the USA. The first academic position in anthropology at a Canadian university was awarded to Thomas McIlwraith. The next universities to hire anthropologists, UBC and McGill, did so only in 1947. The first PhD in anthropology was granted in 1956, with only a few more being granted until the late 1960s. The 1970s brought a boom in university development and in professional anthropology, and by 1980 about 400 people with doctorates in anthropology were employed in Canada, and many more with a master's degree. Harry Hawthorne built the department at UBC and set a standard for the use of anthropological research as a guide to public policy in his classic report to the federal government, coauthored by M.-A. Tremblay, "A Survey of the Contemporary Indians of Canada" (1966, 1967).

Canadian Anthropology is characterized by a combination of Americanist Boasian-influenced interest in First Nations, British Anthropological concerns with social function and process, and Francophone concerns with small, rural and ethnically isolated community studies. Issues of disparity, continuity and change, political-economy, environment and cultural ecology, and personality, culture and symbolism predominated the discourse from World War I to the Vietnam War era.

Post World War Anthropology

Before second World War British 'social anthropology' and American 'cultural anthropology' were still distinct traditions.

It was after the war that the two would blend to create a 'sociocultural' anthropology.

In the 1950s and mid-1960s anthropology tended increasingly to model itself after the natural sciences. Some anthropologists, such as Lloyd Fallers and Clifford Geertz, focused on processes of modernization by which newly independent states could develop.

Others, such as Julian Steward and Leslie White, focused on how societies evolve and fit their ecological niche-an approach popularized by Marvin Harris. Economic anthropology as influenced by Karl Polanyi and practiced by Marshall Sahlins and George Dalton focused on how traditional economics ignored cultural and social factors. In England, British Social Anthropology's paradigm began to fragment as Max Gluckman and Peter Worsley experimented with Marxism and authors such as Rodney Needham and Edmund Leach incorporated Lévi-Strauss's structuralism into their work.

Structuralism also influenced a number of developments in 1960s and 1970s, including cognitive anthropology and componential analysis. Authors such as David Schneider, Clifford Geertz, and Marshall Sahlins developed a more fleshed-out concept of culture as a web of meaning or signification, which proved very popular within and beyond the discipline.

In keeping with the times, much of anthropology became politicized through the Algerian War of Independence and opposition to the Vietnam War; Marxism became a more and more popular theoretical approach in the discipline. By the 1970s the authors of volumes such as Reinventing Anthropology worried about anthropology's relevance.

In the 1980s issues of power, such as those examined in Eric Wolf's Europe and the People Without History, were central to the discipline. Books like Anthropology and the Colonial Encounter pondered anthropology's ties to colonial inequality, while the immense popularity of theorists such as Antonio Gramsci and Michel Foucault moved issues of power and hegemony into the spotlight. Gender and sexuality became popular topics, as did the relationship between history and anthropology, influenced by Marshall Sahlins (again), who drew on Lévi-Strauss and Fernand Braudel to examine the relationship between social structure and individual agency.

In the late 1980s and 1990s authors such as George Marcus and James Clifford pondered ethnographic authority, particularly how and why anthropological knowledge was possible and authoritative. They were reflecting trends in research and discourse initiated by Feminists in the academy, although they excused themselves from commenting specifically on those pioneering critics. Nevertheless, key aspects of feminist theorsing and methods became de rigeur as part of the 'post-modern moment' in anthropology: Ethnographies became more reflexive, explicitly addressing the author's methodology, cultural, gender and racial positioning, and their influence on his or her ethnographic analysis. This was part of a more general trend of postmodernism that was popular contemporaneously. Currently anthropologists have begun to pay attention to globalization, medicine and biotechnology, indigenous rights, and the anthropology of industrialized societies.

they argue, can gain yet more power by exploiting knowledge and artifacts of the people they study while the people they study gain nothing, or even lose, in the exchange (for example, Deloria). Little critical writing has been published in response to these wide-ranging claims, themselves the product of the political concerns and atmosphere of their own times.

- It is claimed the discipline was ahistorical, and dealt with its "objects" (sic) "out of time," to their detriment (Fabian). It is often claimed that anthropologists regularly "exoticized 'the Other,'" or, with equal assurance, that they inappropriately universalized "Others" and "human nature."
- Other more explicitly political concerns have to do with anthropologists' entanglements with government intelligence agencies, on the one hand, and anti-war politics on the other. Franz Boas publicly objected to US participation in World War I, and after the war he published a brief expose and condemnation of the participation of several American archeologists in espionage in Mexico under their cover as scientists. But by the 1940s, many of Boas' anthropologist contemporaries were active in the allied war effort against the "Axis" (Nazi Germany, Fascist Italy, and Imperial Japan). Many served in the armed forces but others worked in intelligence (for example, Office of Strategic Services [OSS] and the Office of War Information). David H. Price's work on American anthropology during the Cold War provides detailed accounts of the pursuit and dismissal of several anthropologists for their vocal left-wing sympathies. On the other hand, attempts to accuse anthropologists of complicity with the CIA and government intelligence activities during the Vietnam War years have turned up surprisingly little. (Anthropologists did not participate in the stillborn Project Camelot, for example) On the contrary, many anthropologists (students and teachers) were active in the antiwar movement and a great many resolutions condemning the war in all its aspects were

2

Politics of Anthropology

American cultural anthropology developed during the first four decades of the 20th century under the powerful influence of Franz Boas and his students and their struggle against racial determinism and the ethnocentrism of 19th century cultural evolutionism. With the additional impact of the Great Depression and World War II, American anthropology developed a pronounced liberal-left tone by the 1950s. However, the discipline's deep involvement with nonwestern cultures put it in a vulnerable position during the campus upheavals of the late 1960s and in the subsequent "culture wars." The "politics of anthropology" has become a pervasive concern since then. Whatever the realities, the notion of anthropology as somehow complicity in morally unacceptable projects has become a significant topic both within the discipline and in "cultural studies" and "post-colonialism," etc. A few of the central elements in this discourse are the following:

- The claim that the discipline grew out of colonialism, perhaps was in league with it, and derived some of its key notions from it, consciously or not. It is often assumed that an example of this exploitative relationship can be seen in the relationship between British anthropologists and colonial forces in Africa, yet this assumption has not been supported by much evidence.
- The idea that social and political problems must arise because anthropologists usually have more power than the people they study; it is a form of colonialist theft in which the anthropologist gains power at the expense of subjects (Rabinow, Dwyer, McGrane). Anthropologists,

> passed overwhelmingly at the annual meetings of the American Anthropological Association (AAA). In the decades since the Vietnam war the tone of cultural and social anthropology, at least, has been increasingly politicized, with the dominant liberal tone of earlier generations replaced with one more radical, a mix of, and varying degrees of, Marxist, feminist, anarchist, post-colonial, post-modern, Saidian, Foucaultian, identity-based, and more.

Professional anthropological bodies often object to the use of anthropology for the benefit of the state. Their codes of ethics or statements may proscribe anthropologists from giving secret briefings. The Association of Social Anthropologists of the UK and Commonwealth (ASA) has called certain scholarships ethically dangerous. The AAA's current 'Statement of Professional Responsibility' clearly states that "in relation with their own government and with host governments... no secret research, no secret reports or debriefings of any kind should be agreed to or given."

More recently, there have been concerns expressed about bioprospecting, along with struggles for self-representation for native peoples and the repatriation of indigenous remains and material culture, with anthropologists often in the lead on these issues.

Other political controversies come from the emphasis in American anthropology on cultural relativism and its long-standing antipathy to the concept of race. The development of sociobiology in the late 1960s was opposed by cultural anthropologists such as Marshall Sahlins, who argued that these positions were reductive. While authors such John Randal Baker continued to develop the biological concept of race into the 1970s, the rise of genetics has proven to be central to developments on this front.

As genetics continues to advance as a science some anthropologists such as Luca Cavalli-Sforza have continued to transform and advance notions of race through the use of recent developments in genetics, such as tracing past migrations of peoples through their mitochondrial and Y-chromosomal DNA, and ancestry-informative markers.

BRANCHES OF ANTHROPOLOGY

In North America, anthropology is traditionally divided into four sub-disciplines:

- Physical anthropology, or biological anthropology, which studies primate behavior, human evolution, osteology, forensics, and population genetics;
- Cultural anthropology (called social anthropology and now often known as socio-cultural anthropology in the United Kingdom, and both terms are used in Canada with limited distinction), which studies social networks, diffusion, social behavior, kinship patterns, law, politics, ideology, religion, beliefs, patterns in production and consumption, exchange, socialization, gender, and other expressions of culture, with strong emphasis on the importance of fieldwork or participant observation (that is, living among the social group being studied for an extended period of time);
- Linguistic anthropology, which studies variation in language across time and space, the social uses of language, and the relationship between language and culture, and
- Archaeology, which studies the material remains of human societies. Archaeology itself is normally treated as a separate (but related) field in the rest of the world, although closely related to the anthropological field of material culture, which deals with physical objects created or used within a living or past group as a means of understanding its cultural values.

A number of subfield or modes of anthropology cut across these divisions, however. For example, medical anthropology is often considered a subfield of socio-cultural anthropology; however, many anthropologists who study medical topics also look at biological variation in populations or the interaction of culture and biology. They may also use linguistic analysis. Similarly, forensic anthropologists may use both techniques from both physical anthropology and archaeology, and may also practice as medical anthropologists. Applied anthropology is perhaps better considered an emphasis than a subfield in the same sense as the standard four; applied anthropologists may work for government agencies, nongovernmental agencies, or private industry, using techniques from any of the subfields to address matters such as policy implementation, impact assessments, education, marketing research, or product development.

More recently, some anthropology programs began dividing the field into two, one emphasizing the humanities and critical theory, the other emphasizing the natural sciences and empirical observation.

HUMANITY

Humanity the all humans and they deeds in past now and future. Deeds, some forgotten some over glorified, of the continuous tree of human life, whose all branches, just by its existence, add undivided part to Humanity as whole.

Humans create complex social structures composed of cooperating and competing groups, ranging in scale from nations to individual families, and social interaction between humans has established a variety of social norms, rituals, traditions, values, laws, and ethics which form the basis of human society. Humans also have an appreciation for beauty and aesthetics which, combined with the human desire for self-expression, has led to cultural innovations such as art, literature and music.

ANTHROPOLOGICAL THEORIES OF VALUE

Anthropological theories of value attempt to expand on the traditional theories of value used by economists or ethicists. They are often broader in scope than the theories of value of Adam Smith, David Ricardo, John Stuart Mill, Karl Marx, etc. usually including sociological, political, institutional, and historical perspectives (transdisciplinarity). Some have influenced feminist economics.

The basic premise is that economic activities can only be fully understood in the context of the society that creates them. The concept of "value" is a social construct, and as such is defined by the culture using the concept. Yet we can gain some insights into modern patterns of exchange, value, and wealth by examining previous societies. An anthropological approach to economic processes allows us to critically examine the cultural biases inherent in the principles of modern economics. Anthropological linguistics is a related field which looks at the terms we use to describe economic relations and the ecologies they are set within. Many anthropological economists (or economic anthropologists) are reacting against what they see as the portrayal of modern society as an economic machine that merely produces and consumes.

Marcel Mauss and Bronislaw Malinowski for example wrote about objects that circulate in society without being consumed. Georges Bataille wrote about objects which are destroyed, but not consumed. Bruce Owens talks about objects of value that are neither circulating nor consumed (e.g. gold reserves, warehoused paintings, family heirlooms).

David Graeber attempts to synthesize the insights of Karl Marx and Marcel Mauss. He sees value as a model for human "meaning-making". Starting with Marxist definitions of consumption and production, he introduces Mauss's idea of "objects that are not consumed" and constructs a list of things that are neither consumption nor production. Graeber's list includes those human activities that are not consumption, in the narrow sense of simply purchasing something, and are not production, in the sense of creating or modifying something intended for sale or exchange. It includes:

- cooking a meal,
- extinguishing a fire,
- dressing and undressing,
- applying makeup,
- watching television,
- playing in a band,
- falling in love,
- reading,
- listening to music,
- going to a museum or gallery,
- taking a photograph,

- gardening,
- writing,
- conducting a coming of age ceremony,
- going window shopping,
- doing sports,
- acting,
- teaching,
- having an argument,
- playing games,
- having sex,
- attending a religious service,
- looking at old photos.

Criticisms

Economists typically use the term consumption in a way that is far broader than merely purchasing something and then tossing it. It is quite common to talk about the consumption of time. Many of the items on his list would be considered either production or consumption by most economists. Also Gary Becker's household production functions and similar topics note that people often purchase goods and then combine them with time to produce something that has meaning or practicality to them (which produce utility).

ANTHROPOLOGY OF MEDIA

Anthropology of media (also anthropology of mass media, media anthropology) is an area of study within social or cultural anthropology that emphasizes ethnographic studies as a means of understanding producers, audiences, and other cultural and social aspects of mass media.

Methodology

What is distinctive about anthropology of media is the use of ethnography. Within media studies, media ethnographies have been of increasing interest. However these have often not followed anthropological approaches to ethnography like participant observation and long term fieldwork. These differences mean that anthropologists who take an interest in the media see themselves as a subfield distinct from ethnographic approaches in media studies and cultural studies.

Theory

The anthropology of media is a fairly inter-disciplinary area, with a wide range of other influences. The theories used in the anthropology of media range from practice approaches, attributable to theorists such as Pierre Bourdieu, as well as discussions of the appropriation and adaptation of new technologies and practices. Theoretical approaches have also been picked up from visual anthropology and from film theory as well as from studies of ritual and performance studies (e.g. dance and theatre). Theoretical discussions have also been picked up from studies of consumption, audience reception in media studies, new media and network theories, theories of globalisation, theories of international civil society, and discussions of participatory communications, and governance from development studies.

ETHNOGRAPHIC CONTEXTS

The types of ethnographic contexts explored in the anthropology of media range from the production of media: ethnographies of newsrooms in newspapers, journalists in the field, film production and so on, as well as reception studies, following audiences in their responses to media. Other types include cyber anthropology (a relatively new area of internet research, as well as ethnographies of other contexts which happen to include media, such as development work, social movements, health education. This is in addition to many classic ethnographic contexts, where media such as radio, the press, new media and television have started to make their presences felt.

3

Religious and Cultural Anthropology

The anthropology of religion involves the study of religious institutions in relation to other social institutions, and the comparison of religious beliefs and practices across cultures. In the 19th century, cultural anthropology was dominated by an interest in cultural evolution; most anthropologists assumed that there was a simple distinction between "primitive" and "modern" religion and tried to provide accounts of how the former evolved into the latter. In the 20th century most anthropologists rejected this approach. Today the anthropology of religion reflects the influence of, or an engagement with, such theorists as Karl Marx, Sigmund Freud, Émile Durkheim, and Max Weber. They are especially concerned with how religious beliefs and practices may reflect political or economic forces; or the social functions of religious beliefs and practices.

Anthropological approaches to religion reflect a more general tension within anthropology: the discipline defines itself as a science in that all anthropologists base their interpretations and explanations on empirical evidence (and many anthropologists are concerned with developing universal models of human behavior), and the discipline also defines itself in terms of the seriousness with which it takes local beliefs and practices, and its commitment to understanding different cultures in their own terms through participant observation. Thus, although many Westerners (including anthropologists) have rejected "religion" out of hand as being unscientific, virtually all anthropologists assume that there must be good reasons for the endurance and importance of religion and, by implication, assume that religious beliefs and practices are in some sense "reasonable." In order to determine the reasons for the importance of religion, however, anthropologists generally move beyond the literal claims of any religion to look at its metaphorical meaning or latent social functions.

One major problem in the anthropology of religion is the definition of religion itself. At one time anthropologists believed that certain religious practices and beliefs were more or less universal to all cultures at some point in their development, such as a belief in spirits or ghosts, the use of magic as a means of controlling the supernatural, the use of divination as a means of discovering occult knowledge, and the performance of rituals such as prayer and sacrifice as a means of influencing the outcome of various events through a supernatural agency, sometimes taking the form of shamanism or ancestor worship.

According to Clifford Geertz, religion is a system of symbols, beliefs, and patterns of behaviors by which human beings control that which is beyond their control. Today, anthropologists debate, and many reject, the cross-cultural validity of these categories (often viewing them as examples of European primitivism). Anthropologists have considered various criteria for defining religion-such as a belief in the supernatural or the reliance on ritual-but few claim that these criteria are universally valid.

In Western culture, religion has become more or less synonymous with monotheism and the various moral codes that monotheism prescribes. Moral codes have also evolved in conjunction with Hindu and Buddhist beliefs, independent of monotheism. However, prescriptive moral codes or even normative ethical codes are not a necessary component of religious beliefs or practices any more than they are a necessary component of science and the scientific method.

Anthony F.C. Wallace proposes four categories of religion, each subsequent category subsuming the previous. These are, however, synthetic categories and do not necessarily encompass all religions.

1. Individualistic: most basic; simplest. Example: vision quest.

2. Shamanistic: part-time religious practitioner, uses religion to heal, to divine, usually on the behalf of a client. The Tillamook have four categories of shaman. Examples of shamans: spiritualists, faith healers, palm readers. One who has acquired religious authority through one's own means.
3. Communal: elaborate set of beliefs and practices; group of people arranged in clans by lineage, age group, or some religious societies; people take on roles based on knowledge.
4. Ecclesiastical: Most complex. Incorporates elements of the previous three.

VISUAL ANTHROPOLOGY

Visual anthropology is a subfield of cultural anthropology that developed out of the study and production of ethnographic photography, film and since the mid-1990s, new media. While the term is sometimes used interchangeably with ethnographic film, visual anthropology also encompasses the anthropological study of representation, including areas such as performance, museums, art, and the production and reception of mass media.

History

Even before the emergence of anthropology as an academic discipline in the 1880s, ethnologists were using photography as a tool of research. Anthropologists and non-anthropologists conducted much of this work in the spirit of salvage ethnography or attempts to record for posterity the ways-of-life of societies assumed doomed to extinction.

The history of anthropological filmmaking is intertwined with that of non-fiction and documentary filmmaking. Some of the first motion pictures of the ethnographic other were made with Lumière equipment (Promenades des Éléphants à Phnom Penh, 1901). Robert Flaherty, probably best known for his films chronicling the lives of Arctic peoples (Nanook of the North, 1922), became a filmmaker in 1913 when his supervisor suggested that he take a camera and equipment with him on an expedition north. Flaherty focused on "traditional" Eskimo ways of life, omitting to that end any signs of modernity among his film subjects (even to the point of refusing to use a rifle to help kill a walrus his informants had harpooned as he filmed them, according to Barnouw; this scene made it into Nanook where it served as evidence of their "pristine" culture). This pattern would persist in many ethnographic films to follow.

By the 1940s, anthropologists such as Hortense Powdermaker, Gregory Bateson and Margaret Mead (Trance and Dance in Bali, 1952) were bringing anthropological perspectives to bear on mass media and visual representation. The work of Bateson and Mead as well as that of anthropologically-minded filmmakers such as Tim Asch, Robert Gardner and John Marshall led to the realization there existed a need to systematically study, understand and produce ethnographic films in a scholarly manner. Visual anthropology first found purchase in an academic setting in 1958 with the creation of the Film Study Center at Harvard's Peabody Museum of Archaeology and Ethnology.

At present, the Society for Visual Anthropology (SVA) represents the subfield in the United States as a section of the American Anthropological Association.

4

Physical Anthropology

BIOLOGICAL ANTHROPOLOGY

Biological anthropology, or physical anthropology, studies the mechanisms of biological evolution, genetic inheritance, human adaptability and variation, primatology, primate morphology, and the fossil record of human evolution.

Physical anthropology developed in the 19th century, prior to the rise of Alfred Wallace and Charles Darwin's theory of natural selection, and Gregor Mendel's work on genetics. Physical anthropology was so called because all of its data was physical (fossils, especially human bones). With the rise of Darwinian theory and the modern synthesis, anthropologists had access to new forms of data, and many began to call themselves "biological anthropologists."

Some of the early branches of physical anthropology, such as early anthropometry, are now rejected as pseudoscience. Metrics such as the cephalic index were used to derive behavioral characteristics. Two of the earliest founders of scientific physical anthropology were Paul Broca and Franz Boas.

Branches

- Primatology, the study of primates,
- Population genetics, the study of biological human variability and diversity (related to evolutionary biology)
- Human adaptation, the study of human adaptive responses (physiological, developmental, and genetic) to environmental stress and variation.

- Human anatomy the study of the anatomy and physiology of humans and their ancestors.
- Human evolution including:
  - o Paleoanthropology, the study of fossil evidence for human evolution.
  - o Human behavioral ecology, the study of behavioral adaptations such as foraging, reproduction, and ontogeny from an evolutionary ecological perspective.
- Neuroanthropology, the study of the evolution of the human brain, and of culture as a neurological adaptation of the species to its environment.

The study of human evolution often involves other specializations:

- Human osteology, the study of skeletal material. Experts in osteology are able to apply their skills and knowledge to other areas:
  - o Paleopathology, which studies the traces of disease and injury in human skeletons
  - o Forensic anthropology, the analysis and identification of human remains in the service of coroners or medical examiners. This research often provides law enforcement with important evidence.

EVOLUTION

In biology, evolution is the change from generation to generation in a population's inherited characteristics, or traits. Minor random changes in the genes that encode these traits produces new traits, and variations on old ones, within every generation. While random chance can intervene and cause even the most beneficial trait to be lost, organisms with traits that help them to survive and reproduce tend to have more offspring. In doing so, they will pass more copies of these beneficial traits on to the next generation, leading, on average, to advantageous traits becoming more common in each generation, while disadvantageous traits become rarer. Given enough time, this passive process result in varied adaptations to changing environmental conditions. Furthermore, because newly discovered beneficial traits are conserved (for as long as they remain beneficial), natural selection allows for the gradual accumulation of improvements which continuously build upon each other, potentially resulting in very high levels of optimisation over time. As differences in and between populations accumulate, new species can evolve from prior ones. All known species are descended from a single ancestor through this process of gradual divergence.

The theory of evolution by natural selection was first put forth in detail in Charles Darwin's 1859 book On the Origin of Species. In the 1930s, Darwinian natural selection was combined with Mendelian inheritance to form the modern evolutionary synthesis. With its enormous explanatory and predictive power, this theory has become the central organizing principle of modern biology, providing a unifying explanation for the diversity of life on Earth.

Basic Processes

Evolution consists of two basic types of processes: those that introduce new genetic variation into a population, and those that affect the frequencies of existing genes. Random copying errors in genetic material (mutations), migration between populations (gene flow), and the reshuffling of genes during sexual reproduction (genetic recombination) create variation in organisms. In some organisms, like bacteria and plants, variation is also produced through horizontal gene transfer (the transfer of genetic material between organisms that are not directly related) and the mixing of genetic material by hybridization (interbreeding between species).

Genetic drift and natural selection act on this variation by increasing or decreasing the frequency of traits: genetic drift does so randomly, while natural selection does so based on whether a trait is beneficial, or conducive to reproduction.

Variation

The variation in a population's apparent traits, or phenotypes, is primarily the result of the specific genetic makeup, or genotypes, encoded on DNA molecules called chromosomes. A specific location on a chromosome is known as a locus; a variant of a DNA sequence at a given locus is an allele. The modern evolutionary synthesis defines evolution as the change in the relative frequencies of alleles in a population. The variation between different DNA codings (alleles) at various loci is thus considered responsible for evolutionary change.

Genetic variation is often the result of a new mutation in a single individual; in subsequent generations, the frequency of that variant may fluctuate in the population, becoming more or less prevalent relative to other alleles at the site. All evolutionary forces act by driving this change in allele frequency in one direction or another. Variation disappears when an allele reaches the point of fixation-when it either reaches a frequency of zero and disappears from the population, or reaches a frequency of one and replaces the ancestral allele entirely.

Most sites in the complete DNA sequence, or genome, of a species are identical in all individuals in the population. Consequently, relatively small genotypic changes can lead to dramatic phenotypic ones. Sites with more than one allele are called polymorphic, or segregating, sites. Polymorphism leads to distinct groups of traits arising within the same species, such as different hair colors or sexes. Interactions between a genotype and the environment may also affect the phenotype, as reflected in developmental and phenotypic plasticity.

Heredity

Gregor Mendel's work provided the first firm basis to the idea that heredity occurred in discrete units. He noticed several traits in peas that occur in only one of two forms (e.g., the peas were either "round" or "wrinkled"), and was able to show that the traits were: heritable (passed from parent to offspring); discrete (i.e., if one parent had round peas and the other wrinkled, the progeny were not intermediate, but either round or wrinkled); and distributed to progeny in a well-defined and predictable manner (Mendelian inheritance). His research laid the foundation for the concept of discrete heritable traits, known today as genes. After Mendel's work was "rediscovered" in 1900, the concepts involved were found to have wide applicability, and it was found that most complex traits were polygenetic and not controlled by single-unit characters.

Later research gave a physical basis to the notion of genes, and eventually identified DNA as the genetic material, with genes functioning as discrete elements within DNA. DNA is not perfectly copied, and rare mistakes (mutations) in genes can affect traits that the genes control (e.g., pea shape).

A gene can have modifications such as DNA methylation, which do not change the nucleotide sequence of a gene, but do result in the epigenetic inheritance of a change in the expression of that gene in a trait. Another epigenetic mechanism is via micro RNA and RNA interference, which serve regulatory roles in gene transcription and translation.

Non-DNA based forms of heritable variation exist, such as transmission of the secondary structures of prions or structural inheritance of patterns in the rows of cilia in protozoans such as Paramecium and Tetrahymena. Investigations continue into whether these mechanisms allow for the production of specific beneficial heritable variation in response to environmental signals. If this were shown to be the case, then some instances of evolution would lie outside of the typical Darwinian framework, which avoids any connection between environmental signals and the production of heritable variation. However, the processes that produce these variations are rather rare, often reversible, and leave the genetic information intact.

Mutation

Genetic variation arises due to random mutations that occur at a certain rate in the genomes of all organisms. Mutations are permanent, transmissible changes to the genetic material (usually DNA or RNA) of a cell, and can be caused by: "copying errors" in the genetic material during cell division; by exposure to radiation, chemicals, or viruses. In multicellular organisms, mutations can be subdivided into germline mutations that occur in the gametes and thus can be passed on to progeny, and somatic mutations that can lead to the malfunction or death of a cell and can cause cancer.

Mutations that are not affected by natural selection are called neutral mutations. Their frequency in the population is governed by mutation rate, genetic drift and selective pressure on linked alleles. It is understood that most of a species' genome, in the absence of selection, undergoes a steady accumulation of neutral mutations.

Individual genes can be affected by point mutations, also known as SNPs, in which a single base pair is altered. The substitution of a single base pair may or may not affect the function of the gene, while deletions and insertions of base pairs usually results in a non-functional gene.

Mobile elements, transposons, make up a major fraction of the genomes of plants and animals and appear to have played a significant role in the evolution of genomes. These mobile insertional elements can jump within a genome and alter existing genes and gene networks to produce evolutionary change and diversity.

On the other hand, gene duplications, which may occur via a number of mechanisms, are believed to bc one major source of raw material for evolving new genes as tens to hundreds of genes are duplicated in animal genomes every million years. Most genes belong to larger "families" of genes derived from a common ancestral gene (two genes from a species that are in the same family are dubbed "paralogs").

Another mechanism causing gene duplication is intergenic recombination, particularly "exon shuffling", i.e., an aberrant recombination that joins the "upstream" part of one gene with the "downstream" part of another. Genome duplications and chromosome duplications also appear to have served a significant role in evolution. Genome duplication has been the driving force in the Teleostei genome evolution, where up to four genome duplications are thought to have happened, resulting in species with more than 250 chromosomes.

Large chromosomal rearrangements do not necessarily change gene function, but do generally result in reproductive isolation, and, by definition, speciation; in sexual organisms, species are usually defined by the ability to interbreed). An example of this mechanism is the fusion of two chromosomes in the Homo genus that produced human chromosome 2; this fusion did not occur in the chimpanzee lineage, resulting in two separate chromosomes in extant chimpanzees.

Horizontal gene Transfer

Horizontal gene transfer (HGT) is any process in which an organism transfers genetic material to another organism that is not its offspring. This mechanism allows for the transfer of genetic material between unrelated organisms and is a form of gene flow.

Many mechanisms for horizontal gene transfer have been observed, such as antigenic shift, reassortment, and hybridization. Viruses can transfer genes between species via transduction. Bacteria can incorporate genes from other dead bacteria or plasmids via transformation, exchange genes with living bacteria via conjugation, and have plasmids "set up residence separate from the host's genome". Hybridization is highly significant in plant speciation, and one out of ten species of birds are known to hybridize. There are also examples of hybridization in mammals and insects; however, this most often results in sterile offspring.

Horizontal gene transfer has been shown to result in the spread of antibiotic resistance across bacterial populations. Furthermore, findings indicate that HGT has been a major mechanism for prokaryotic and eukaryotic evolution.

Horizontal gene transfer complicates the inference of the phylogeny of life, as the original metaphor of a tree of life no longer fits. Rather, since genetic information is passed to other organisms and other species in addition to being passed from parent to offspring, "biologists [should] use the metaphor of a mosaic to describe the different histories combined in individual genomes and use [the] metaphor of a net to visualize the rich exchange and cooperative effects of HGT among microbes".

EVOLUTIONARY MECHANISMS

Selection and Adaptation

Natural selection comes from differences in survival and reproduction. Differential mortality is the survival rate of individuals to their reproductive age. Differential fertility is the total genetic contribution to the next generation. Note that, whereas mutations and genetic drift are random, natural selection is not, as it preferentially selects for different mutations based on differential fitnesses. For example, rolling dice is random, but always picking the higher number on two rolled dice is not random. The central role of natural selection in evolutionary theory has given rise to a strong connection between that field and the study of ecology.

Natural selection can be subdivided into two categories: ecological selection occurs when organisms that survive and reproduce increase the frequency of their genes in the gene pool over those that do not survive; and sexual selection occurs when organisms which are more attractive to the opposite sex because of their features reproduce more and thus increase the frequency of those features in the gene pool.

Natural selection operates on mutations in a number of different ways. Arguably the most common form of selection is stabilizing selection, which decreases the frequency of harmful mutations; "living fossils" may be a result of this. Other forms of natural selection include directional selection, which increases the frequency of a beneficial mutation, and artificial selection, the purposeful breeding of a species.

Through the process of natural selection, organisms become better adapted to their environments. Adaptation is any evolutionary process that increases the fitness of the individual, or sometimes the trait that confers increased fitness, e.g., a stronger prehensile tail or greater visual acuity. Note that adaptation is context-sensitive; a trait that increases fitness in one environment may decrease it in another.

Most biologists believe that adaptation occurs through the accumulation of many mutations of small effect. However, macromutation is an alternative process for adaptation that involves a single, very large-scale mutation.

Recombination

In asexual organisms, variants in genes on the same chromosome will always be inherited together-they are linked, by virtue of being on the same DNA molecule. However, sexual organisms, in the production of gametes, shuffle linked alleles on homologous chromosomes inherited from the parents via meiotic recombination. This shuffling allows independent assortment of alleles (mutations) in genes to be propagated in the population independently. This allows bad mutations to be purged and beneficial mutations to be retained more efficiently than in asexual populations.

However, the meitoic recombination rate is not very high-on the order of one crossover (recombination event between homologous chromosomes) per chromosome arm per generation. Therefore, linked alleles are not perfectly shuffled away from each other, but tend to be inherited together. This tendency may be measured by comparing the co-occurrence of two alleles, usually quantified as linkage disequilibrium (LD). A set of alleles that are often co-propagated is called a haplotype. Strong haplotype blocks can be a product of strong positive selection.

Recombination is mildly mutagenic, which is one of the proposed reasons why it occurs with limited frequency. Recombination also breaks up gene combinations that have been successful in previous generations, and hence should be opposed by selection. However, recombination could be favoured by negative frequency-dependent selection (this is when rare variants increase in frequency) because it leads to more individuals with new and rare gene combinations being produced.

When alleles cannot be separated by recombination (for example in mammalian Y chromosomes), there is an observable reduction in effective population size, known as the Hill-Robertson effect, and the successive establishment of bad mutations, known as Muller's ratchet.

Genetic Drift

Genetic drift is the change in allele frequency from one generation to the next as a result of the statistical effect of chance. The frequency of an allele in the offspring generation will vary according to a probability distribution of the frequency of the allele in the parent generation. Thus, over time even in the absence of selection upon the alleles, allele frequencies tend to "drift" upward or downward, eventually becoming "fixed"-that is, going to 0% or 100% frequency. Thus, fluctuations in allele frequency between successive generations may result in some alleles disappearing from the population due to chance alone. Two separate populations that begin with the same allele frequencies therefore might drift apart by random fluctuation into two divergent populations with different allele sets (for example, alleles present in one population could be absent in the other, or vice versa).

Gene Flow and Population Structure

Gene flow, also called migration, is the exchange of genetic variation between populations, when geography and culture are not obstacles. Ernst Mayr thought that gene flow is likely to be homogenising, and therefore counteracting selective adaptation. Obstacles to gene flow result in reproductive isolation, a necessary condition for speciation.

The free movement of alleles through a population may also be impeded by population structure, the size and geographical distribution of a population. For example, most real-world populations are not actually fully interbreeding; geographic proximity has a strong influence on the movement of alleles within the population. Population structure has profound effects on possible mechanisms of evolution. The effect of genetic drift depends strongly on the size of the population: drift is important in small mating populations, where chance fluctuations from generation to generation can be large. The relative importance of natural selection and genetic drift in determining the fate of new mutations also depends on the population size and the strength of selection. Natural selection is predominant in large populations, while genetic drift is in small populations. Finally, the time for an allele to become fixed in the population by genetic drift (that is, for all individuals in the population to carry that allele) depends on population size-smaller populations require a shorter time for fixation.

An example of the effect of population structure is the founder effect, in which a population temporarily has very few individuals as a result of a migration or population bottleneck, and therefore loses much genetic variation. In this case, a single, rare allele may suddenly increase very rapidly in frequency within a specific population if it happened to be prevalent in a small number of "founder" individuals. The frequency of the allele in the resulting population can be much higher than otherwise expected, especially for deleterious, disease-causing alleles. Since population size has a profound effect on the relative strengths of genetic drift and natural selection, changes in population size can alter the dynamics of these processes considerably.

Speciation and Extinction

Speciation is the process by which new biological species arise. This may take place by various mechanisms. Allopatric speciation occurs in populations that become isolated geographically, such as by habitat fragmentation or migration. Sympatric speciation occurs when new species emerge in the same geographic area. Ernst Mayr's peripatric speciation is a type of speciation that exists in between the extremes of allopatry and sympatry. Peripatric speciation is a critical underpinning of the theory of punctuated equilibrium. An example of rapid sympatric speciation can be clearly observed in the triangle of U, where new species of Brassica sp. have been made by the fusing of separate genomes from related plants.

Extinction is the disappearance of species (i.e., gene pools). The moment of extinction is generally defined as occurring at the death of the last individual of that species. Extinction is not an unusual event on a geological time scale-species regularly appear through speciation, and disappear through extinction. The Permian-Triassic extinction event was the Earth's most severe extinction event, rendering extinct 90% of all marine species and 70% of all terrestrial vertebrate species. In the Cretaceous-Tertiary extinction event, many forms of life perished (including approximately 50% of all genera), the most commonly mentioned among them being the non-avian dinosaurs. The Holocene extinction event is a current mass extinction, involving the rapid extinction of tens or hundreds of thousands of species each year. Scientists consider human activities to be the primary cause of the ongoing extinction event, as well as the related influence of climate change.

Cooperation

Generally mathematical models incorporating mutation and natural selection have been used to model adaptation and evolution. Recent trends now incorporate "game theory" as more applicable to generating reliable models. This work and others studies have focused attention on cooperation as a fundamental property needed for evolution to construct new levels of organization. Selfish replicators sacrificing their own reproductive potential to cooperate seems paradoxical in a competitive world. However a number of mechanisms have demonstrated the capacity to generate cooperation, and even altruism, such as kin selection, direct reciprocity, indirect reciprocity, network reciprocity, and group selection. The ubiquity of cooperation in the natural world and studies from the last twenty years reveal cooperation as a significant principle in constructive evolution.

Evidence of Evolution

Evolution has left numerous signs of the histories of different species. Fossils, along with the comparative anatomy of present-day organisms, constitute the morphological, or anatomical, record. By comparing the anatomies of both modern and extinct species, paleontologists can infer the lineages of those species.

The development of molecular genetics, and particularly of DNA sequencing, has allowed biologists to study the record of evolution left in organisms' genetic structures. The degrees of similarity and difference in the DNA sequences of modern species allows geneticists to reconstruct their lineages. It is from DNA sequence comparisons that figures such as the 96% genotypic similarity between humans and chimpanzees are obtained.

Other evidence used to demonstrate evolutionary lineages includes the geographical distribution of species. For instance, monotremes and most marsupials are found only in Australia, showing that their common ancestor with placental mammals lived before the submerging of the ancient land bridge between Australia and Asia.

Scientists correlate all of the above evidence, drawn from paleontology, anatomy, genetics, and geography, with other information about the history of Earth. For instance, paleoclimatology attests to periodic ice ages during which the world's climate was much cooler, and these are often found to match up with the spread of species which are better-equipped to deal with the cold, such as the woolly mammoth.

Morphological Evidence

Fossils are critical evidence for estimating when various lineages originated. Since fossilization of an organism is an uncommon occurrence, usually requiring hard parts (like teeth, bone, or pollen), the fossil record provides only sparse and intermittent information about ancestral lineages.

The fossil record provides several types of data important to the study of evolution. First, the fossil record contains the earliest known examples of life itself, as well as the earliest occurrences of individual lineages. For example, the first complex animals date from the early Cambrian period, approximately 520 million years ago. Second, the records of individual species yield information regarding the patterns and rates of evolution, showing whether, for example, speciation occurs gradually and incrementally, or in relatively brief intervals of geologic time. Thirdly, the fossil record is a document of large-scale patterns and events in the history of life. For example, mass extinctions frequently resulted in the loss of entire groups of species, while leaving others relatively unscathed. Recently, molecular biologists have used the time since divergence of related lineages to calibrate the rate at which mutations accumulate, and at which the genomes of different lineages evolve.

Phylogenetics, the study of the ancestry of species, has revealed that structures with similar internal organization may perform divergent functions. Vertebrate limbs are a common example of such homologous structures. The appendages on bat wings, for example, are very structurally similar to human hands, and may constitute a vestigial structure. Vestigial structures are idiosyncratic anatomical features such as the panda's "thumb", which indicate how an organism's evolutionary lineage constrains its adaptive development. Other examples of vestigial structures include the degenerate eyes of blind cave-dwelling fish, and the presence of hip bones in whales and snakes. Such structures may exist with little or no function in a more current organism, yet have a clear function in an ancestral species. Examples of vestigial structures in humans include wisdom teeth, the coccyx and the vermiform appendix.

These anatomical similarities in extant and fossil organisms can give evidence of the relationships between different groups of organisms. Important fossil evidence includes the connection of distinct classes of organisms by so-called "transitional" species, such as the Archaeopteryx, which provided early evidence for intermediate species between dinosaurs and birds, and the recently-discovered Tiktaalik, which clarifies the development from fish to animals with four limbs.

Molecular Evidence

By comparing the DNA sequences of species, we can discern their evolutionary relationships. The resultant phylogenetic trees are typically congruent with traditional taxonomy, and are often used to either strengthen or correct taxonomic classifications. Sequence comparison is considered a measure robust enough to be used to correct erroneous assumptions in the phylogenetic tree in instances where other evidence is scarce.

For example, neutral human DNA sequences are approximately 1.2% divergent (based on substitutions) from those of their nearest genetic relative, the chimpanzee, 1.6% from gorillas, and 6.6% from baboons. Genetic sequence evidence thus allows inference and quantification of genetic relatedness between humans and other apes. The sequence of the 16S rRNA gene, a vital gene encoding a part of the ribosome, was used to find the broad phylogenetic relationships between all extant life. This analysis, originally done by Carl Woese, resulted in the three-domain system, arguing for two major splits in the early evolution of life. The first split led to modern bacteria, and the subsequent split led to modern archaea and eukaryotes.

Since metabolic processes do not leave fossils, research into the evolution of the basic cellular processes is done largely by comparison of existing organisms. Many lineages diverged when new metabolic processes appeared, and it is theoretically possible to determine when certain metabolic processes appeared by comparing the traits of the descendants of a common ancestor or by detecting their physical manifestations. As an example, the appearance of oxygen in the earth's atmosphere is linked to the evolution of photosynthesis.

The proteomic evidence also supports the universal ancestry of life. Vital proteins, such as the ribosome, DNA polymerase, and RNA polymerase, are found in everything from the most primitive bacteria to the most complex mammals. The core part of the protein is conserved across all lineages of life, serving similar functions. Higher organisms have evolved additional protein subunits, largely affecting the regulation and protein-protein interaction of the core. Other overarching similarities between all lineages of extant organisms, such as DNA, RNA, amino acids, and the lipid bilayer, give support to the theory of common descent. The chirality of DNA, RNA, and amino acids is conserved across all known life. As there is no functional advantage to right-or left-handed molecular chirality, the simplest hypothesis is that the choice was made randomly by early organisms and passed on to all extant life through common descent. Further evidence for reconstructing ancestral lineages comes from junk DNA such as pseudogenes, "dead" genes which steadily accumulate mutations.

There is also a large body of molecular evidence for a number of different mechanisms for large evolutionary changes, among them: genome and gene duplication, which facilitates rapid evolution by providing substantial quantities of genetic material under weak or no selective constraints; horizontal gene transfer, the process of transferring genetic material to another cell that is not an organism's offspring, allowing for species to acquire beneficial genes from each other; recombination, capable of reassorting large numbers of different alleles and of establishing reproductive isolation; and endosymbiosis, the incorporation of genetic material and biochemical composition of a separate species, a process observed in organisms such as the protist hatena and used to explain the origin of organelles such as mitochondria and plastids as the absorption of ancient prokaryotic cells into ancient eukaryotic ones.

Ancestry of Organisms

The theory of universal common descent proposes that all organisms on Earth are descended from a common ancestor or ancestral gene pool. Evidence for common descent is inferred from traits shared between all living organisms. In Darwin's day, the evidence of shared traits was based solely on visible observation of morphologic similarities, such as the fact that all birds, even those which do not fly, have wings. Today, there is strong evidence from genetics that all organisms have a common ancestor. For example, every living cell makes use of nucleic acids as its genetic material, and uses the same 20 amino acids as the building blocks for proteins. The universality of these traits strongly suggests common ancestry, because the selection of many of these traits seems arbitrary.

History of Life

The origin of life from self-catalytic chemical reactions is not a part of biological evolution, but rather of pre-evolutionary abiogenesis. However, disputes over what defines life make the point at which such increasingly complex sets of reactions became true organisms unclear. Not much is yet known about the earliest developments in life. There is no scientific consensus regarding the relationship of the three domains of organisms (Archaea, Bacteria, and Eukaryota) or regarding the precise reactions involved in abiogenesis. Attempts to shed light on the origin of life generally focus on the behavior of macromolecules-particularly RNA-and the behavior of complex systems.

Fossil evidence indicates that the diversity and complexity of modern life has developed over much of the 4.57 billion year history of Earth. Oxygenic photosynthesis emerged around 3 billion years ago, and the subsequent emergence of an oxygen-rich atmosphere made the development of aerobic cellular respiration possible around 2 billion years ago. In the last billion years, simple multicellular plants and animals began to appear in the oceans. Soon after the emergence of the first animals, the Cambrian explosion, a geologically brief period of remarkable biological diversity, originated all the major body plans, or phyla, of modern animals. This event is now believed to have been triggered by the development of the Hox genes.

About 500 million years ago (mya), plants and fungi colonized the land, and were soon followed by arthropods and other animals. Amphibians first appeared around 300 mya, followed by reptiles, then mammals around 200 mya and birds around 100 mya. The human genus arose around 2 mya, while the earliest modern humans lived 200 thousand years ago.

STUDY OF EVOLUTION

History of Modern Evolutionary Thought

Although the idea of evolution has existed since classical antiquity, being first discussed by Greek philosophers such as Anaximander, the first convincing exposition of a mechanism by which evolutionary change could occur was not proposed until Charles Darwin and Alfred Russel Wallace jointly presented the theory of evolution by natural selection to the Linnean Society of London in separate papers in 1858. Shortly after, the publication of Darwin's On the Origin of Species popularized and provided detailed support for the theory.

However, Darwin had no working mechanism for inheritance. This was provided by Gregor Mendel, whose research revealed that distinct traits were inherited in a well-defined and predictable manner.

In the 1930s, Darwinian natural selection and Mendelian inheritance were combined to form the modern evolutionary synthesis. In the 1940s, the identification of DNA as the genetic material by Oswald Avery and colleagues, and the articulation of the double-helical structure of DNA by James Watson and Francis Crick, provided a physical basis for the notion that genes were encoded in DNA. Since then, the role of genetics in evolutionary biology has become increasingly central.

Academic Disciplines

Scholars in a number of academic disciplines continue to document examples of evolution, contributing to a deeper understanding of its underlying mechanisms. Every subdiscipline within biology both informs and is informed by knowledge of the details of evolution, such as in ecological genetics, human evolution, molecular evolution, and phylogenetics. Areas of mathematics (such as bioinformatics), physics, chemistry, and other fields all make important contributions to current understanding of evolutionary mechanisms. Even disciplines as far removed as geology and sociology play a part, since the process of biological evolution has coincided in time and space with the development of both the Earth and human civilization.

Evolutionary biology is a subdiscipline of biology concerned with the origin and descent of species, as well as their changes over time. It was originally an interdisciplinary field including scientists from many traditional taxonomically-oriented disciplines. For example, it generally includes scientists who may have a specialist training in particular organisms, such as mammalogy, ornithology, or herpetology, but who use those organisms to answer general questions in evolution. Evolutionary biology as an academic discipline in its own right emerged as a result of the modern evolutionary synthesis in the 1930s and 1940s. It was not until the 1970s and 1980s, however, that a significant number of universities had departments that specifically included the term evolutionary biology in their titles.

Evolutionary developmental biology (informally, evo-devo) is a field of biology that compares the developmental processes of different animals in an attempt to determine the ancestral relationship between organisms and how developmental processes evolved. The discovery of genes regulating development in model organisms allowed for comparisons to be made with genes and genetic networks of related organisms.

Physical anthropology emerged in the late 19th century as the study of human osteology, and the fossilized skeletal remains of other hominids. At that time, anthropologists debated whether their evidence supported Darwin's claims, because skeletal remains revealed temporal and spatial variation among hominids, but Darwin had not offered an explanation of the specific mechanisms that produce variation. With the recognition of Mendelian genetics and the rise of the modern synthesis, however, evolution became both the fundamental conceptual framework for, and the object of study of, physical anthropologists. In addition to studying skeletal remains, they began to study genetic variation among human populations (population genetics); thus, some physical anthropologists began calling themselves biological anthropologists.

The capability of evolution through selection to produce designs optimized for a particular environment has greatly interested mathematicians, scientists and engineers. There has been some recent success in implementing these ideas for artificial uses, including genetic algorithms, which can find the solution to a multi-dimensional problem more quickly than standard software produced by human intelligent designers, and the use of evolutionary fitness landscapes to optimize the design of a system Evolutionary optimization techniques are particularly useful in situations in which it is easy to determine the quality of a single solution, but hard to go through all possible solutions one by one.

Misunderstandings

There are a number of common misunderstandings about evolution, some of which have hindered its general acceptance and form the basis of various objections to evolution. Critics of evolution frequently assert that evolution is "just a theory", a misunderstanding of the meaning of theory in a scientific context: whereas in colloquial speech a theory is a conjecture or guess, in science a theory is "a model of the universe, or a restricted part of it, and a set of rules that relate quantities in the model to observations that we make". Critics also state that evolution is not a fact, although from a scientific viewpoint evolution is considered both a theory and a fact.

Another common misunderstanding is the idea that one species, such as humans, can be more "highly evolved" or "advanced" than another. It is often assumed that evolution must lead to greater complexity, or that devolution ("backwards" evolution) can occur. Scientists consider evolution a non-directional process that does not proceed toward any ultimate goal; advancements are only situational, and organisms' complexity can either increase, decrease, or stay the same, depending on which is advantageous, and thus selected for.

Evolution is also frequently misinterpreted as stating that humans evolved from monkeys; based on this, some critics argue that monkeys should no longer exist. This misunderstands speciation, which frequently involves a subset of a population cladogenetically splitting off before speciating, rather than an entire species simply turning into a new one. Additionally, biologists have never claimed that humans evolved from monkeys-only that humans and monkeys share a common ancestor, as do all organisms.

It is also frequently claimed that speciation has only been inferred, never directly observed. In reality, the evolution of numerous new species has been observed. A similar claim is that only microevolution, not macroevolution, has been observed; however, macroevolution has been observed as well, and modern evolutionary synthesis draws little distinction between the two, considering macroevolution to simply be microevolution on a larger scale.

Evolution is sometimes misrepresented as being guided solely by "chance" or "randomness". This leads to expressions of disbelief that "pure chance" might generate the remarkable complexity of living beings, and probability arguments are sometimes used to criticize evolution by assessing the probability that a certain highly complex feature might occur "by chance". Darwinian evolution, however, is emphatically not random in its direction. Mutation is random; but natural selection, which determines whether or not those mutations are preserved and propagated throughout the population, is extremely non-random, in that only those features which are adaptive will be preserved. At any time, the evolutionary process encounters a multitude of possible directions, each being proposed by different, random mutations; but only those directions which prove to be adaptive will actually be "taken", and thus be used as a starting point for further exploration. In time, this highly biased (and therefore non-random) preservation allows evolution to reach arbitrary levels of adaptive complexity: the gradual accumulation of small, "plausibly lucky" improvements creates a final result which would have been highly implausible by purely random assembly.

Social and Religious Controversies

Ever since the publication of The Origin of Species in 1859, evolution has been a source of nearly constant controversy. In general, controversy has centered on the philosophical, social, and religious implications of evolution, not on the science of evolution itself; the proposition that biological evolution occurs through the mechanism of natural selection is completely uncontested within the scientific community.

As Darwin recognized early on, perhaps the most controversial aspect of evolutionary thought is its applicability to human beings. Specifically, many object to the idea that all diversity in life, including human beings, arose through natural processes without a need for supernatural intervention. Although many religions, such as Catholicism, have reconciled their beliefs with evolution through theistic evolution, creationists argue against evolution on the basis that it contradicts their theistic origin beliefs. In some countries-notably the United States-these tensions between scientific and religious teachings have fueled the ongoing creation-evolution controversy, a social and religious conflict especially centering on public education. While many other fields of science, such as cosmology and earth science also conflict with a literal interpretation of many religious texts, evolutionary biology has borne the brunt of these debates. Some also argue that evolutionary common descent "degrades" human beings by placing them on the same level as other animals, in contrast with past views of a great chain of being in which humans are "above" animals.

Evolution has been used to support philosophical and ethical choices which most contemporary scientists consider were neither mandated by evolution nor supported by science. For example, the eugenic ideas of Francis Galton were developed into arguments that the human gene pool should be improved by selective breeding policies, including incentives for reproduction for those of "good stock" and disincentives, such as compulsory sterilization, "euthanasia", and later, prenatal testing, birth control, and genetic engineering, for those of "bad stock". Another example of an extension of evolutionary theory that is now widely regarded as unwarranted is "Social Darwinism", a term given to the 19th century Whig Malthusian theory developed by Herbert Spencer into ideas about "survival of the fittest" in commerce and human societies as a whole, and by others into claims that social inequality, racism, and imperialism were justified.

5

Genetics

Genetics (from the Greek genno = give birth) is the science of genes, heredity, and the variation of organisms. The word "genetics" was first suggested to describe the study of inheritance and the science of variation by the prominent British scientist William Bateson in a personal letter to Adam Sedgwick, dated April 18, 1905. Bateson first used the term "genetics" publicly at the Third International Conference on Plant Hybridization (London, England) in 1906.

Heredity and variations form the basis of genetics. Humans applied knowledge of genetics in prehistory with the domestication and breeding of plants and animals. In modern research, genetics provides important tools for the investigation of the function of a particular gene, e.g., analysis of genetic interactions. Within organisms, genetic information generally is carried in chromosomes, where it is represented in the chemical structure of particular DNA (deoxyribonucleic acid) molecules. Genes encode the information necessary for synthesizing the amino-acid sequences in proteins, which in turn play a large role in determining the final phenotype, or physical appearance, of the organism.

In diploid organisms, a dominant allele on one chromosome will mask the expression of a recessive gene on the other. The only way that a recessive allele can be seen as a trait is if both parents contained that same recessive allele. Codominance is when both alleles for the same gene are considered dominant, in which case, both alleles will be present as traits.

The phrase to code for is often used to mean a gene contains the instructions about how to build a particular protein, as in the gene codes for the protein. The "one gene, one protein" concept is now known to be simplistic. For example, a single gene may produce multiple products, depending on how its transcription is regulated. Genes code for the nucleotide sequences in mRNA, tRNA and rRNA, required for protein synthesis.

Genetics determines much (but not all) of the appearance of organisms, including humans, and possibly how they act. Environmental differences and random factors also play a part. Monozygotic ("identical") twins, a clone resulting from the early splitting of an embryo, have the same DNA, but different personalities and fingerprints. Genetically-identical plants grown in colder climates incorporate shorter and less-saturated fatty acids to avoid stiffness.

HISTORY

In his paper "Versuche über Pflanzenhybriden" ("Experiments in Plant Hybridization"), presented in 1865 to the Brunn Natural History Society, Gregor Mendel traced the inheritance patterns of certain traits in pea plants and showed that they could be described mathematically. Although not all features show these patterns of Mendelian inheritance, his work suggested the utility of the application of statistics to the study of inheritance. Since that time many more complex forms of inheritance have been demonstrated.

The significance of Mendel's work was not understood until early in the twentieth century, after his death, when his research was re-discovered by other scientists working on similar problems.

Mendel did not understand the nature of inheritance. We now know that some heritable information is carried in DNA. (Retroviruses, including influenza, oncoviruses and HIV, and many plant viruses, carry information as RNA.) Manipulation of DNA can in turn alter the inheritance and features of various organisms.

TIMELINE OF NOTABLE DISCOVERIES

- 1865: Gregor Mendel's paper, Experiments on Plant Hybridization

- 1869: Friedrich Miescher discovers a weak acid in the nuclei of white blood cells that today we call DNA (Hartl and Jones).
- 1880-1890: Walther Flemming, Eduard Strasburger, and Edouard van Beneden elucidate chromosome distribution during cell division
- 1903: Chromosomes are discovered to be hereditary units
- 1906: The term "genetics" is first introduced publicly by the British biologist William Bateson at the Third International Conference on Plant Hybridization in London, England.
- 1910: Thomas Hunt Morgan shows that genes reside on chromosomes, and discovered linked genes on chromosomes that do not follow Mendel's law of independent allele segregation
- 1913: Alfred Sturtevant makes the first genetic map of a chromosome
- 1913: Gene maps show chromosomes containing linear arranged genes
- 1918: Ronald Fisher publishes On the correlation between relatives on the supposition of Mendelian inheritance-the modern synthesis starts.
- 1927: Physical changes in genes are called mutations
- 1928: Frederick Griffith discovers a hereditary molecule that is transmissible between bacteria.
- 1931: Crossing over is the cause of recombination.
- 1941: Edward Lawrie Tatum and George Wells Beadle show that genes code for proteins; see the original central dogma of genetics
- 1944: Oswald Theodore Avery, Colin McLeod and Maclyn McCarty isolate DNA as the genetic material (at that time called transforming principle)
- 1950: Erwin Chargaff shows that the four nucleotides are not present in nucleic acids in stable proportions, but that some general rules appear to hold (e.g., the

nucleotide bases Adenine-Thymine and Cytosine-Guanine always remain in equal proportions). Barbara McClintock discovers transposons in maize

- 1952: The Hershey-Chase experiment proves the genetic information of phages (and all other organisms) to be DNA
- 1953: DNA structure is resolved to be a double helix by James D. Watson and Francis Crick, with the help of Rosalind Franklin
- 1956: Jo Hin Tjio and Albert Levan established the correct chromosome number in humans to be 46
- 1958: The Meselson-Stahl experiment demonstrates that DNA is semiconservatively replicated
- 1961: The genetic code is arranged in triplets
- 1964: Howard Temin showed using RNA viruses that Watson's central dogma is not always true
- 1970: Restriction enzymes were discovered in studies of a bacterium, Haemophilus influenzae, enabling scientists to cut and paste DNA
- 1972: Walter Fiers and his team at the Laboratory of Molecular Biology of the University of Ghent (Ghent, Belgium) were the first to determine the sequence of a gene: the gene for Bacteriophage MS2 coat protein.
- 1976: Walter Fiers and his team determine the complete nucleotide-sequence of Bacteriophage MS2-RNA
- 1977: DNA is sequenced for the first time by Fred Sanger, Walter Gilbert, and Allan Maxam working independently. Sanger's lab complete the entire genome of sequence of Bacteriophage F-X174.
- 1983: Kary Banks Mullis discovers the polymerase chain reaction enabling the easy amplification of DNA
- 1985: Alec Jeffreys discovers genetic finger printing.
- 1989: The first human gene is sequenced by Francis Collins and Lap-Chee Tsui. It encodes the CFTR protein. Defects in this gene cause cystic fibrosis

- 1995: The genome of Haemophilus influenzae is the first genome of a free living organism to be sequenced.
- 1996: Saccharomyces cerevisiae is the first eukaryote genome sequence to be released
- 1998: The first genome sequence for a multicellular eukaryote, C. elegans is released.
- 2001: First draft sequences of the human genome are released simultaneously by the Human Genome Project and Celera Genomics.
- 2003: (14 April) Successful completion of Human Genome Project with 98% of the genome sequenced to a 99.99% accuracy.
- 2006: Marcus Pembrey and Olov Bygren publish Sex-specific, male-line transgenerational responses in humans, a proof of epigenetics.

AREAS OF GENETICS

Classical Genetics

Classical genetics consists of the techniques and methodologies of genetics that predate the advent of molecular biology. After the discovery of the genetic code and such tools of cloning as restriction enzymes, the avenues of investigation open to geneticists were greatly broadened. Some classical genetic ideas have been supplanted with the mechanistic understanding brought by molecular discoveries, but many remain intact and in use, such as Mendel's laws and Muller's morphs. Patterns of inheritance still remain a useful tool for the study of genetic diseases.

Behavioral Genetics

Behavioral genetics studies the influence of varying genetics on animal behavior. Behavioral genetics studies the effects of human disorders as well as its causes. Behavioral genetics has yielded some very interesting questions about the evolution of various behaviors, and even some fundamental principles of evolution in general. For example, guppies and meerkats seem to be genetically driven to post a lookout to watch for predators. This lookout stands a significantly slimmer chance of survival than the others, so because of the mechanism of natural selection, it would seem that this trait would be lost after a few generations. However, the gene has remained, leading evolutionary philosopher/scientists such as Richard Dawkins and W. D. Hamilton to propose explanations, including the theories of kin selection and reciprocal altruism. The interactions and behaviors of gregarious creatures is partially genetic in cause and must therefore be approached by evolutionary theory.

Clinical Genetics

Physicians who are trained as Geneticists diagnose, treat, and counsel patients with genetic disorders or syndromes. These doctors are typically trained in a genetics residency and/or fellowship. Clinical genetics is also the study of genetic causes of clinical diseases.

Molecular Genetics

Molecular genetics builds upon the foundation of classical genetics but focuses on the structure and function of genes at a molecular level. Molecular genetics employs the methods of both classical genetics (such as hybridization) and molecular biology. It is so-called to differentiate it from other sub fields of genetics such as ecological genetics and population genetics. An important area within molecular genetics is the use of molecular information to determine the patterns of descent, and therefore the correct scientific classification of organisms: this is called molecular systematics. The study of inherited features not strictly associated with changes in the DNA sequence is called epigenetics.

Some take the view that life can be defined, in molecular terms, as the set of strategies which RNA polynucleotides have used and continue to use to perpetuate themselves. This definition grows out of work on the origin of life, specifically the RNA world hypothesis.

Population, Quantitative and Ecological Genetics

Population, quantitative and ecological genetics are all very closely related subfields and also build upon classical genetics (supplemented with modern molecular genetics). They are chiefly distinguished by a common theme of studying populations of organisms drawn from nature but differ somewhat in the choice of which aspect of the organism on which they focus. The foundational discipline is population genetics which studies the distribution of and change in allele frequencies of genes under the influence of the four evolutionary forces: natural selection, genetic drift, mutation and migration. It is the theory that attempts to explain such phenomena as adaptation and speciation. The related subfield of quantitative genetics, which builds on population genetics, aims to predict the response to selection given data on the phenotype and relationships of individuals. A more recent development of quantitative genetics is the analysis of quantitative trait loci. Traits that are under the influence of a large number of genes are known as quantitative traits, and their mapping to a location on the chromosome requires accurate phenotypic, pedigree and marker data from a large number of related individuals.

Ecological genetics again builds upon the basic principles of population genetics but is more explicitly focused on ecological issues. While molecular genetics studies the structure and function of genes at a molecular level, ecological genetics focuses on wild populations of organisms, and attempts to collect data on the ecological aspects of individuals as well as molecular markers from those individuals. Population genetics is closely linked with the methods of genetic epidemiology. One method to study gene-disease associations is using the principle of Mendelian randomization.

Genomics

A more recent development is the rise of genomics, which attempts the study of large-scale genetic patterns across the genome for (and in principle, all the DNA in) a given species. The field typically depends on the availability of whole genome sequences, computational tools and Sequence profiling tool using bioinformatics approaches for analysis of large sets of data.

CLOSELY-RELATED FIELDS

The science which grew out of the union of biochemistry and genetics is widely known as molecular biology. The term "genetics" is often widely conflated with the notion of genetic engineering, where the DNA of an organism is modified for some kind of practical end, but most research in genetics is aimed at understanding and explaining the effect of genes on phenotypes and in the role of genes in populations, rather than genetic engineering.

POPULATION GENETICS

Population genetics is the study of the allele frequency distribution and change under the influence of the four evolutionary forces: natural selection, genetic drift, mutation, and gene flow. It also takes account of population subdivision and population structure in space. As such, it attempts to explain such phenomena as adaptation and speciation. Population genetics was a vital ingredient in the modern evolutionary synthesis, its primary founders were Sewall Wright, J. B. S. Haldane and R. A. Fisher, who also laid the foundations for the related discipline of quantitative genetics.

Scope and Theoretical Considerations

Perhaps the most significant "formal" achievement of the modern evolutionary synthesis has been the framework of mathematical population genetics. Indeed some authors (Beatty 1986) would argue that it does define the core of the modern synthesis.

Lewontin (1974) outlined the theoretical task for population genetics. He imagined two spaces: a "genotypic space" and a "phenotypic space". The challenge of a complete theory of population genetics is to provide a set of laws that predictably map a population of genotypes (G1) to a phenotype space (P1), where selection takes place, and another set of laws that map the resulting population (P2) back to genotype space (G2) where Mendelian genetics can predict the next generation of genotypes, thus completing the cycle. Even leaving aside for the moment the non-Mendelian aspects revealed by molecular genetics, this is clearly a gargantuan task. Visualizing this transformation schematically:

T1 represents the genetic and epigenetic laws, the aspects of functional biology, or development, that transform a genotype into phenotype. We will refer to this as the "genotype-phenotype map". T2 is the transformation due to natural selection, T3 are epigenetic relations that predict genotypes based on the selected phenotypes and finally T4 the rules of Mendelian genetics.

In practice, there are two bodies of evolutionary theory that exist in parallel, traditional population genetics operating in the genotype space and the biometric theory used in plant and animal breeding, operating in phenotype space. The missing part is the mapping between the genotype and phenotype space. This leads to a "sleight of hand" (as Lewontin terms it) whereby variables in the equations of one domain, are considered parameters or constants, where, in a full-treatment they would be transformed themselves by the evolutionary process and are in reality functions of the state variables in the other domain. The "sleight of hand" is assuming that we know this mapping. Proceeding as if we do understand it is enough to analyze many cases of interest. For example, if the phenotype is almost one-to-one with genotype (sickle-cell disease) or the time-scale is sufficiently short, the "constants" can be treated as such; however, there are many situations where it is inaccurate.

Population Geneticists

The three founders of population genetics were the Britons R.A. Fisher and J.B.S. Haldane and the American Sewall Wright. Fisher and Wright had some fundamental disagreements and a controversy about the relative roles of selection and drift continued for much of the century between the Americans and the British. The Frenchman Gustave Malécot was also important early in the development of the discipline. John Maynard Smith was Haldane's pupil, whilst W.D. Hamilton was heavily influenced by the writings of Fisher. The American George R. Price worked with both Hamilton and Maynard Smith. On the American side, Richard Lewontin and the Japanese Motoo Kimura were heavily influenced by Wright. Luigi Luca Cavalli-Sforza is a Stanford-based population geneticist particularly interested in human population genetics.

ADAPTATION

A biological adaptation is an anatomical structure, physiological process or behavioral trait of an organism that has evolved over a period of time by the process of natural selection such that it increases the expected long-term reproductive success of the organism. The term adaptation is also sometimes used as a synonym for natural selection, but most biologists discourage this usage. Organisms that are adapted to their environment are able to:

- get air, water, food and nutrients
- cope with physical conditions such as temperature, light and heat
- defend themselves from their natural enemies
- reproduce
- respond to changes around them

Adaptations enable living organisms to cope with environmental stresses and pressures. One common form of physical adaptation is acclimatization. Acclimatization allows the organism to survive in a new environment. Adaptation can be structural or behavioural. Structural adaptations are special body parts of an organism that help it to survive in its natural habitat (e.g., skin color, shape, body covering). Behavioral adaptations are special ways a particular organism behaves to survive in its natural habitat. Physiological adaptations are systems present in an organism that allow it to perform certain biochemical reactions (e.g., making venom, secreting slime, being able to keep a constant body temperature).

Organisms that are not suitably adapted to their environment will either have to move out of the habitat or die out. The term die out in the context of adaptation simply means that the death rate over the entire species (population, gene pool...) exceeds the birth rate for a long enough period for the species to disappear; due to individual phenotypic plasticity, individuals will be more or less successful.

It is possible for an adaptation to be poorly selected, the advantage it confers over generations decreasing, up to and including the adaptation becoming a hindrance to the species' long-term survival. This is known as maladaptation and can apply to both humans and animals in such fields as biology, psychology (where it applies to behaviors and other learned survival mechanisms) and other fields. There is a great difference between adaptation and acclimation. Adaptation occurs over many generations; it is generally a slow process caused by natural selection. Acclimation generally occurs within a single lifetime and copes with issues that are less threatening. For example, if a human was to move to a higher altitude, respiration and physical exertion would become a problem, but after spending time in high altitude conditions one may acclimate to the pressure and function and no longer notice the change.

The theory of adaptation was first put forth by Jean-Baptiste Lamarck. His theories are also referred to as the inheritance of acquired traits.

Lamarck's theory was for a time held as an alternative scientific explanation for evolutionary change observed by Charles Darwin in the The Origin of Species. The classic giraffe analogy offers the best delineation between the two.

- According to Darwin, more long-necked giraffes reproduce than short-necked giraffes and as such giraffes today have long necks.
- According to Lamarck, it was giraffes stretching their necks in response to higher leaves that resulted in giraffes having long necks. (This trait being passed on to the next generation)

Although neither theory in its conception could provide a complete description of the mechanism of transmission of trait variation (i.e., particulate inheritance), many recognized Darwin's theory immediately upon publication as a more complete and empirically supported theory. Modern genetics have since established the fundamental implausibility of Lamarckian inheritance, due to the one-way nature of transcription. However, see epigenetics and Baldwinian evolution for analogous processes in modern evolutionary theory.

PRIMATOLOGY

Primatology is the study of non-human primates. It is a diverse discipline and primatologists can be found in departments of biology, anthropology, psychology and many others. It is closely related to physical anthropology, which is the primatology of the genus Homo, especially Homo sapiens. The fields cross over in the study of the hominids, which includes all ape-like ancestors of man and the other great apes.

Modern primatology is an extremely diverse science. It ranges from anatomical studies of primate ancestors and field studies of primates in their natural habitat, to experiments in animal psychology and ape language. It has cast an immense amount of light on basic human behaviors and ancient ancestry of these behaviors.

Disciplines

Primatology as a science has many different disciplines that stem from the differing cultural backgrounds of the founders of the field. Indeed, the study itself seems to change throughout different areas of the world, as different approaches, theories and methods are used in the researching of primates and their relationships and links with humans.

There are two main disciplines within the field of primatology, Western primatology and Japanese primatology. These two divergent disciplines stem from their unique cultural backgrounds and philosophies that went into their founding. Though, fundamentally, both Western and Japanese primatology share many of the same principles, the areas of their focus in primate research and their methods of obtaining data differ widely.

WESTERN PRIMATOLOGY

Origins

Western primatology stems primarily from colonial research into primate behaviour, especially by French colonial scientists. Early primate study focused primarily in medical research, but some scientists also conducted "civilizing" experiments on chimpanzees in order to gauge both primate intelligence and the limits of their brainpower.

Theory

The Western study of primatology looks at the more biological and psychological aspects of their subjects. Their focus is on studying the common links between humans and primates, past our shield of 'society' and into the nature we share with our ancestors. We will better understand our primitive selves, by understanding our closest animal relatives. Obviously, there have been some cultural and religious issues with the field of primatology, especially as it pertains to the Theory of Evolution.

The discipline of Western primatology is affected by the Judeo-Christian background of European and American science. As such, researchers tend to have a "steward" mentality towards their subjects, much like that of a park ranger or a guardian. Subjects should be unharmed by study, and protected both from and by the research that is done.

Methods

Western primatology is a very hard objective science. The general belief is that human interaction with nature must be either extremely limited, or completely controlled. Either way, the observers must be totally neutral to their subjects. This allows for data to be unbiased and for the subjects to be uninfluenced by human interference.

This focus relies on two major areas of study; field study-which is the more limited approach-and laboratory study-the more controlled approach.

Field study is done in fully natural environments, in which scientific observers literally watch primates exist in their natural habitat.

Laboratory study is done in totally controlled lab settings. In this area of study, scientists are able to perform controlled experimentation on the learning capabilities and behavioural patterns of the animals.

Both types of primate study in the Western methodology are meant to be very neutral. Though there are certain Western primatologists who do more subjective research, the emphasis in this discipline is on the objective.

Western primatology tends to focus on individual researchers and their exploits. Stories of researchers such as Dian Fossey and Jane Goodall are extreme examples of this.

Long term sites of research tend to be best associated with their founders, and this leads to some tension between younger primatologists and the veterans in the field.

Notable Western Primatologists

- C. R. Carpenter
- Frans de Waal
- Dian Fossey
- Birute Galdikas
- Jane Goodall
- Craig Stanford
- Robert Sapolsky

Japanese Primatology

Origins

The discipline of Japanese primatology was developed out of animal ecology. It is mainly credited to Kinji Imanishi and Junichiro Itani. Imanishi was an animal ecologist who began studying wild horses before focusing more on primate ecology. He helped found the Primate Research Group in 1950. Junichiro was a renowned anthropologist and a professor at Kyoto University. He is a co-founder of the Primate Research Institute and the Centre for African Area Studies.

Unlike Western Primatology, the Japanese discipline is a male dominated science.

Theory

The Japanese discipline of primatology tends to be more interested in the social aspects of primates. Social evolution and anthropology are of primary interest to them. The Japanese theory believes that studying primates will give us insight into the duality of human nature: individual self vs. social self.

The traditional and cultural aspects of Japanese science lend themselves to an "older sibling" mentality. It is believed that animals should be treated with respect, but also a firm authority. This is not to say that the Japanese study of primatology is cruel-far from it-just that it doesn't feel that their subjects should be given reverential treatment.

One particular Japanese primatologist, Kawai Masao, introduced the concept of kyokan. This was the theory that the only way to attain reliable scientific knowledge was to attain a mutual relation, personal attachment and shared life with the animal subjects. Though Kawai is the only Japanese primatologist associated with the use of this term, the underlying principle is part of the foundation of Japanese primate research.

Methods

Japanese primatology is a carefully disciplined subjective science. It is believed that the best data comes through identification with your subject. Neutrality is eschewed in favour of a more casual atmosphere, where researcher and subject can mingle more freely. Domestication of nature is not only desirable, but necessary for study. Japanese primatologists are renowned for their ability to recognise animals by sight, and indeed most primates in a research group are usually named and numbered. Comprehensive data on every single subject in a group is uniquely Japanese trait of primate research. Each member of the primate community has a part to play, and the Japanese researchers are interested in this complex interaction.

For Japanese researchers in primatology, the findings of the team are emphasised over the individual. The study of primates is a group effort, and the group will get the credit for it. It is also not unusual to see a team of researches observing the same group of primates for several years in order to get very detailed demographic and social histories.

Notable Japanese Primatologists

- Imanishi, Kinji
- Junichiro, Itani
- Masao, Kawai

Primatology in Sociobiology

Where sociobiology attempts to understand the actions of all animal species within the context of advantageous and disadvantageous behaviors, primatology takes an exclusive look at the family Primates, which includes Homo sapiens. The interface between primatology and sociobiology examines in detail the evolution of primate behavioral processes, and what studying our closest living primate relatives can tell about our own minds. The meeting point of these two disciplines has become a nexus of discussion on key issues concerning the evolution of sociality, the development and purpose of language and deceit, and the development and propagation of culture. Additionally, this interface is of particular interest to the science watchers in science and technology studies, who examine the social conditions which incite, mould, and eventually react to scientific discoveries and knowledge. The STS approach to primatology and sociobiology stretches beyond studying the apes, into the realm of observing the people studying the apes.

Taxonomic Basis

Before molecular biology, the father of modern taxonomy, Carolus Linnaeus, organized natural objects into kinds. He sorted these kinds by morphology, the shape of the object. As it happens, animals such as chimpanzees and orangutans resemble humans very closely, so Linnaeus placed Homo sapiens together with all the other similar-looking organisms into the taxonomic order Primates. Modern techniques in molecular biology have reinforced humanity's place within the Primate order. Humans and simians share the vast majority of their DNA, with chimpanzees sharing between 97-99% genetic identity with humans.

From Grooming to Speaking

Although grooming is observed in many animal species, the grooming activities undertaken by primates are not strictly for the elimination of parasites. In primates, grooming is a social activity that strengthens relationships. The amount of grooming taking place between members of a troop is a potent indicator of alliance formation or troop solidarity. Robin Dunbar suggests a link between primate grooming and the development of human language. The size of the neocortex in a primate's brain correlates directly to the number of individuals it can keep track of socially, be it a troop of chimps or a tribe of humans.

This number is referred to as the monkeysphere. If a population exceeds the size outlined by its cognitive limitations, the group undergoes a schism. Set into an evolutionary context, the Dunbar number shows a drive for the development of a method of bonding that is less labor intensive than grooming: language. As the monkeysphere grows, the amount of time that would need to be spent grooming troopmates soon becomes unmanageable. Furthermore, it is only possible to bond with one troopmate at a time while grooming. The evolution of vocal communication solves both the time constraint and the one-on-one problem, but at a price.

Language allows for bonding with multiple people at the same time at a distance, but the bonding produced by language is less intense. This view of language evolution covers the general biological trends needed for language development, but it takes another hypothesis to uncover the evolution of the cognitive processes necessary for language.

Modularity of the Primate Mind

Noam Chomsky's concept of innate language addresses the existence of universal grammar, which suggests a special kind of "device" all humans are born with whose sole purpose is language. Fodor's modular mind hypothesis expands on this concept, suggesting the existence of preprogrammed modules for dealing with many, or all aspects of cognition. Although these modules do not need to be physically distinct, they must be functionally distinct. Orangutans are currently being taught language at the Smithsonian National Zoo using a computer system developed by primatologist Dr. Francine Neago in conjunction with IBM.

The massive modularity theory thesis posits that there are a huge number of tremendously interlinked but specialized modules running programs called Darwinian algorithms, or DA. DA can be selected for just as a gene can, eventually improving cognition. The contrary theory, of generalist mind, suggests that the brain is just a big computer that runs one program, the mind. If the mind is a general computer, for instance, the ability to use reasoning should be identical regardless of the context. This is not what is observed. When faced with abstract numbers and letters with no "real world" significance, respondents of the Wason card test generally do very poorly. However, when exposed to a test with an identical rule set but socially relevant content, respondents score markedly higher. The difference is especially pronounced when the content is about reward and payment. This test strongly suggests that human logic is based on a module originally developed in a social environment to root out cheaters, and that either the module is at a huge disadvantage where abstract thinking is involved, or that other less effective modules are used when faced with abstract logic.

Further evidence supporting the modular mind has steadily emerged with some startling revelations concerning primates. A very recent study indicated that human babies and grown monkeys approach and process numbers in a similar fashion, suggesting an evolved set of DA for mathematics (Jordan). The conceptualization of both human infants and primate adults is cross-sensory, meaning that they can add 15 red dots to 20 beeps and approximate the answer to be 35 grey squares. As more evidence of basic cognitive modules are uncovered, they will undoubtedly form a more solid foundation upon which the more complex behaviors can be understood.

Primate Theory of Mind

Primate behavior, like human behavior, is highly social and ripe with the intrigue of kingmaking, powerplays, deception, cuckoldry, and apology. In order to understand the staggeringly complex nature of primate interactions, we look to theory of mind. Theory of mind asks whether or not an individual recognizes and can keep track of information asymmetry amongst individuals in the group, and whether or not they can attribute folk psychological states to their peers. If some primates can tell what others know and want and act accordingly, they can gain advantage and status.

Recently, chimpanzee theory of mind has been advanced by Felix Warneken of the Max Planck Institute. His studies have shown that chimpanzees can recognize whether a researcher desires a dropped object, and act accordingly by picking it up. Even more compelling is the observation that chimps will only act if the object is dropped in an accidental-looking manner: if the researcher drops the object in a way that appears intentional, the chimp will ignore the object.

In a related experiment, groups of chimps were given rope-pulling problems they could not solve individually. Warneken's subjects rapidly figured out which individual in the group was the best rope puller and assigned it the bulk of the task. This research is highly indicative of the ability of chimps to detect the folk psychological state of "desire", as well as the ability to recognize that other individuals are better at certain tasks than they are.

Criticisms

Scientific studies concerning primate and human behavior have been subject to the same set of political and social complications, or biases, as every other scientific discipline. The borderline and multidisciplinary nature of primatology and sociobiology make them ripe fields of study because they are amalgams of objective and subjective sciences. Current scientific practice, especially in the hard sciences, requires a total dissociation of personal experience from the finished scientific product (Bauchspies 8). This is a strategy that is incompatible with observational field studies, and weakens them in the eyes of hard science. As mentioned above, the Western school of primatology tries to minimize or control subjectivity to the greatest degree possible, while the Japanese school of primatology tends to embrace the closeness inherent in studying nature.

Social critics of science, some operating from within the field, cry foul when reviewing the young disciplines of primatology and sociobiology. Claims are made that researchers form opinions on issues concerning human sociality prior to doing their studies, and then seek evidence that agrees with their worldview or otherwise furthers a sociopolitical agenda. In particular, the use of primatological studies to assert gender roles, and promote or subvert feminism has been a serious point of contention.

An example of this is Zuckerman's 1932 study of captive hamadryas baboons, as critiqued in Sturm and Fedigan's

Changing Views on Primate Societies. Zuckerman observed male baboons kill each other off in great number in their captive environment. Whether intended or not, the study served to reinforce images of the male as the sole competitor in an often violent race to secure dominance and access to a harem of females. Despite wildly unrealistic overcrowding and completely incorrect male to female ratio, Zuckerman's paper was viewed as good science at the time. These ideas justified the status quo of human male dominance, and consequently, the studies were widely supported and assumed to be the basis of a primate-wide template for behavior, including that of humans. Incidentally, the hamadryas baboon females are among the most submissive and most gender-unequal of all primates, although primates and humans share a tremendous variation in troop structure (Hrdy 101, Stone).

PRIMATE

A primate (L. prima, first) is any member of the biological order Primates, the group that contains all the species commonly related to the lemurs, monkeys, and apes, with the latter category including humans. The English singular primate is a back-formation from the Latin name Primates, which itself was the plural of the Latin primas ("one of the first, excellent, noble"). Primates are found all over the world. Non-human primates occur mostly in Central and South America, Africa, and southern Asia. A few species exist as far north in the Americas as southern Mexico, and as far north in Asia as northern Japan.

The Primates order is divided informally into three main groupings: prosimians, monkeys of the New World, and monkeys and apes of the Old World. The prosimians are species whose bodies most closely resemble that of the early proto-primates. The most well known of the prosimians, the lemurs, are located on the island of Madagascar and to a lesser extent on the Comoros Islands, isolated from the rest of the world. The New World monkeys include the familiar capuchin, howler, and squirrel monkeys. They live exclusively in the Americas. Discounting humans, the rest of the simians, the Old World monkeys and the apes, inhabit Africa and southern and central

Asia, although fossil evidence shows many species existed in Europe as well.

Physical description

All primates have five fingers (pentadactyly), a generalized dental pattern, and a primitive (unspecialized) body plan. Another distinguishing feature of primates is fingernails. Opposing thumbs are also a characteristic primate feature, but are not limited to this order; opossums, for example, also have opposing thumbs. In primates, the combination of opposing thumbs, short fingernails (rather than claws) and long, inward-closing fingers is a relic of the ancestral practice of gripping branches, and has, in part, allowed some species to develop brachiation as a significant means of transportation. Forward-facing color binocular vision was also useful for the brachiating ancestors of humans, particularly for finding and collecting food, although recent studies suggest it was more useful in courtship. All primates, even those that lack the features typical of other primates (like lorises), share eye orbit characteristics, such as a postorbital bar, that distinguish them from other taxonomic orders. Old World species (apes and some monkeys) tend to have significant sexual dimorphism. This is characterized most in size difference, with males being up to a bit more than twice as heavy as females. This dimorphism is a result of a polygynous mating system where there is significant pressure to attract and defend multiple mates. New World species form pair bonds, and so these species (including tamarins and marmosets) generally do not show a significant size difference between the sexes.

Habitat

Primates evolved from arboreal animals and many modern species live mostly in trees and hardly ever come to the ground. Other species are partially terrestrial, such as baboons and the Patas Monkey. Only a few species are fully terrestrial, such as the Gelada and Humans. Primates live in a diverse number of forested habitats, including rain forests, mangrove forests, and mountain forests to altitudes of over 3000 m. Although most species are generally shy of water, a few are fine swimmers and are comfortable in swamps and watery areas, including the

Proboscis Monkey, De Brazza's Monkey and Allen's Swamp Monkey, which even developed small webbing between its fingers. Some primates, such the Rhesus Macaque and the Hanuman Langur, are hemerophile species and cities and villages have become their typical habitat.

Classification and Evolution

Close Relations

The Primate order lies in a tight clustering of related orders (the Euarchontoglires) within the Eutheria, a subclass of Mammalia. Recent molecular genetic research on primates, flying lemurs, and treeshrews has shown that the two species of flying lemur (Dermoptera) are more closely related to the primates than the treeshrews of the order Scandentia, even though the treeshrews were at one time considered primates. These three orders make up the Euarchonta clade. This clade combines with the Glires clade (made up of the Rodentia and Lagomorpha) to form the Euarchontoglires clade. Variously, both Euarchonta and Euarchontoglires are ranked as superorders. Also, some scientists consider Dermoptera a suborder of Primates and call the "true" primates the suborder Euprimates.

Classification

In older classifications, the Primates were divided into two superfamilies: Prosimii and Anthropoidea. The Prosimii included all of the prosimians: all of Strepsirrhini plus the tarsiers. The Anthropoidea contained all of the simians.

In modern, cladistic reckonings, the Primate order is also a true clade. The suborder Strepsirrhini, the "wet-nosed" primates, split off from the primitive primate line about 63 million years ago (mya). The seven strepsirhine families are the four related lemur families and the three remaining families that include the lorises, the Aye-aye, the galagos, and the pottos. Some classification schemes wrap the Lepilemuridae into the Lemuridae and the Galagidae into the Lorisidae, yielding a three-two family split instead of the four-three split as presented here. Other lineages of lower primates inhabited Earth. During the Eocene, most of the northern continents were dominated by two dominant groups, the adapids and the omomyids. The former is considered a member of Strepsirrhini, but it does not have a tooth-comb like modern lemurs. The latter was related closely to tarsiers, monkeys, and apes. Adapids survived until 10 mya; omomyids on the other hand perished 20 million years earlier. The Aye-aye is difficult to place in Strepsirrhini. Its family, Daubentoniidae, could be a lemuriform primate and its ancestors split from lemur line more recently than the lemurs and lorises split, about 50 mya. Otherwise it is sister to all of the other strepsirrhines, in which case in evolved away from the main strepsirrhine line between 50 and 63 mya.

The suborder Haplorrhini, the "dry-nosed" primates, is composed of two sister clades. The prosimian tarsiers in family Tarsiidae (monotypic in its own infraorder Tarsiiformes), represent the most primitive division at about 58 mya. The Simiiformes infraorder contains the two parvorders: the New World monkeys in one, and the Old World monkeys, humans and the other apes in the other. This division happened about 40 mya. However about 30 mya, three groups split from the main haplorrhine lineage. One group stayed in Asia and are closest in kin to the "dawn monkey" Eosimias. The second stayed in Africa, where they developed into the Old World primates. The third rafted to South America to become the New World monkeys. Mysteriously the aboriginal Asian Haplorrhini vanished from record once Africa collided with Eurasia 24 mya. Apes and monkeys spread into Europe and Asia. Close behind came lorises and tarsiers, also African castaways. The first hominid fossils were discovered in Northern Africa and date back 7 mya. Modern humans did not appear until 0.2 mya, eventually becoming the most prevalent primate and mammal on Earth.

The discovery of new species happens at a rate of a few new species each year, and the evaluation of current populations as distinct species is in flux. Colin Groves lists about 350 species of primates in Primate Taxonomy in 2001. The recently published third edition of Mammal Species of the World (2005) lists 376 species. But even MSW3's list falls short of current understanding as its collection cutoff was in 2003, and a number publications since MSW3 push the number of species up to 404.

Extant Primate Families

- Order Primates
  - o Suborder Strepsirrhini: non-tarsier prosimians
- Infraorder Lemuriformes
- Superfamily Cheirogaleoidea
- Family Cheirogaleidae: dwarf lemurs and mouse-lemurs (30 species)
- Superfamily Lemuroidea
- Family Lemuridae: lemurs (19 species)
- Family Lepilemuridae: sportive lemurs (22 species)
- Family Indriidae: woolly lemurs and allies (14 species)
- Infraorder Chiromyiformes
- Family Daubentoniidae: Aye-aye (1 species)
- Infraorder Lorisiformes
- Family Lorisidae: lorises, pottos and allies (9 species)
- Family Galagidae: galagos (19 species)
  - o Suborder Haplorrhini: tarsiers, monkeys and apes
- Infraorder Tarsiiformes
- Family Tarsiidae: tarsiers (8 species)
- Infraorder Simiiformes
- Parvorder Platyrrhini: New World monkeys
- Family Cebidae: marmosets, tamarins, capuchins and squirrel monkeys (56 species)
- Family Aotidae: night or owl monkeys (douroucoulis) (7 species)
- Family Pitheciidae: titis, sakis and uakaris (41 species)
- Family Atelidae: howler, spider and woolly monkeys (24 species)
- Parvorder Catarrhini
- Superfamily Cercopithecoidea
- Family Cercopithecidae: Old World monkeys (134 species)

- Superfamily Hominoidea
- Family Hylobatidae: gibbons or "lesser apes" (13 species)
- Family Hominidae: humans and other great apes (7 species)

Some Prehistoric Primates

- Adapis, an adapid
- Australopithecus, ape-like human ancestor
- Branisella boliviana, an early New World monkey
- Dryopithecus, an early ape
- Eosimias, an early catarrhine
- Sahelanthropus tchadensis, a possible ancestor of humans
- Aegyptopithecus zeuxis, an early haplorrhine
- Pliopithecus, ancestor of the modern gibbons
- Gigantopithecus, the largest ape
- Godinotia, an adapid
- Megaladapis, a giant lemur
- Notharctus, an adapid
- Plesiopithecus teras, a relative of lorises and galagos
- Protopithecus brasiliensis, a giant New World monkey
- Sivapithecus, an early ape
- Tielhardina, the earliest haplorrhines
- Victoriapithecus, an early Old World monkey
- Pierolapithecus catalaunicus, a possible ancestor of large apes

Primate Hybrids

In The Variation Of Animals And Plants Under Domestication Charles Darwin noted: "Several members of the family of Lemurs have produced hybrids in the Zoological Gardens."

Many gibbons are hard to identify based on fur coloration and are identified either by song or genetics. These morphological ambiguities have led to hybrids in zoos. Zoo gibbons usually come from the black market pet trade in Southeast Asia, which transported gibbons across countries all over the region. As a result, perhaps as much as 95% of zoo gibbons are of unknown geographic origin.

As most zoos rely on morphological variation or labels that are impossible to verify to assign species and subspecies names, it is unfortunately common for gibbons to be misidentified and housed together. For example, some collections' supposedly pure breeding pairs were actually mixed pairs or hybrids from previous mixed pairs. The hybrid offspring were sent to other gibbon breeders and led to further hybridization in captive gibbons. Within-genus hybrids also occur in wild gibbons where the ranges overlap (Agile Gibbons and Pileated Gibbons x Lar Gibbons, Agile Gibbons x Müller's Bornean Gibbon, Yellow-cheeked Gibbons x Northern White-cheeked Gibbons).

Intergeneric gibbon hybridizations have only occurred in captivity. Silvery Gibbons (Hylobates moloch) and Müller's Bornean Gibbon (H. muelleri) have hybridized with Siamangs (Symphalangus syndactylus) in captivity-a female Siamang produced hybrid "Siabon" offspring on 2 occasions when housed with a male gibbon; only one hybrid survived.

Anubis Baboons and Hamadryas Baboons have hybridized in the wild where their ranges meet. A Rheboon is a captive-bred Rhesus Macaque/Hamadryas Baboon hybrid with a baboon-like body shape and macaque-like tail.

Different macaque species can interbreed. In "The Variation Of Animals And Plants Under Domestication" Charles Darwin wrote: A Macacus, according to Flourens, bred in Paris; and more than one species of this genus has produced young in London, especially the Macacus rhesus, which everywhere shows a special capacity to breed under confinement. Hybrids have been produced both in Paris and London from this same genus. The Japanese Macaque (Macaca fuscata) has interbred with the introduced Taiwanese Macacque (M. cyclopis) when the latter escaped into the wild from private zoos.

Various hybrid monkeys are bred within the pet trade, for example:

- Hybrid capuchin monkeys e.g. Tufted Capuchin (Cebus apella) x Weeper Capuchin (C. olivaceus)
- Liontail Macaque x Pigtail Macaque hybrids
- Rhesus Macaque x Stumptail Macaque hybrids.

Among Old World monkeys, natural hybridization is not uncommon. There numerous field reports of hybrid monkeys and detailed studies of zones where species overlap and hybrids occur.

Among the great apes, Sumatran and Bornean orangutans are considered separate species with anatomical differences, producing sterile or poorly fertile hybrids. Hybrid orangutans are genetically weaker, with lower survival rates than pure animals.

Legal Status

Humans are recognized as persons and protected in law by the United Nations Universal Declaration of Human Rights and by all governments, though to varying degrees. Non-human primates are not classified as persons, which means their individual interests have no formal recognition or protection. The status of non-human primates has generated much debate, particularly through the Great Ape Project which argues for their personhood.

Thousands of primates are used every year around the world in scientific experiments because of their psychological and physiological similarity to humans. Chimpanzees, baboons, marmosets, macaques, and green monkeys are most commonly used in these experiments. In the European Union, around 10,000 were used in 2004, with 4,652 experiments conducted on 3,115 non-human primates in the UK alone in 2005. As of 2004, 3,100 non-human primates were living in captivity in the United States, in zoos, circuses, and laboratories, 1,280 of them being used in experiments. European campaign groups such as the BUAV are seeking a ban on all primate use in experiments as part of the European Union's current review of existing law on animal experimentation.

Laughter in Primates

Laughter might not be confined or unique to humans, despite Aristotle's observation that "only the human animal laughs". The differences between chimpanzee and human laughter may be the result of adaptations that have evolved to enable human speech. However, some behavioural psychologists argue that self-awareness of one's situation, or the ability to identify with somebody else's predicament, are prerequisites for laughter, so animals are not really laughing in the same way that we do.

Chimpanzees, gorillas, and orangutans show laughter-like vocalizations in response to physical contact, such as wrestling, play chasing, or tickling. This is documented in wild and captive chimpanzees. Chimpanzee laughter is not readily recognizable to humans as such, because it is generated by alternating inhalations and exhalations that sound more like breathing and panting. The differences between chimpanzee and human laughter may be the result of adaptations that have evolved to enable human speech. There are instances in which non-human primates have been reported to have expressed joy. One study analyzed and recorded sounds made by human babies and bonobos also known as pygmy chimpanzees were tickled. It found although the bonobo's laugh was a higher frequency, the laugh followed the same spectrographic pattern of human babies to include as similar facial expressions. Humans and chimpanzees share similar ticklish areas of the body such as the armpits and belly. The enjoyment of tickling in chimpanzees does not diminish with age.

6

Human Evolution

Human evolution is that part of biological evolution concerning the emergence of humans as a distinct species. It is the subject of a broad scientific inquiry that seeks to understand and describe how this change and development occurred. The study of human evolution encompasses many scientific disciplines, most notably physical anthropology, linguistics and genetics. The term "human", in the context of human evolution, refers to the genus Homo, but studies of human evolution usually include other hominins, such as the australopithecines.

History of Paleoanthropology

The modern field of paleoanthropology began in the 19th century with the discovery of "Neanderthal man" (the eponymous skeleton was found in 1856, but there had been finds elsewhere since 1830), and with evidence of so-called cave men. The idea that humans are similar to certain great apes had been obvious to people for some time, but the idea of the biological evolution of species in general was not legitimized until after Charles Darwin published On the Origin of Species in 1859. Though Darwin's first book on evolution did not address the specific question of human evolution-"light will be thrown on the origin of man and his history," was all Darwin wrote on the subject-the implications of evolutionary theory were clear to contemporary readers. Debates between Thomas Huxley and Richard Owen focused on the idea of human evolution. Huxley convincingly illustrated many of the similarities and differences between humans and apes in his 1863 book Evidence as to Man's Place in Nature. By the time Darwin published his own book on the subject, Descent of Man, it was already a well-known interpretation of his theory-and the interpretation which made the theory highly controversial. Even many of Darwin's original supporters (such as Alfred Russel Wallace and Charles Lyell) balked at the idea that human beings could have evolved their apparently boundless mental capacities and moral sensibilities through natural selection.

Since the time of Carolus Linnaeus, the great apes were considered the closest relatives of human beings, based on morphological similarity. In the 19th century, it was speculated that their closest living relatives were chimpanzees and gorillas, and based on the natural range of these creatures, it was surmised humans share a common ancestor with other African apes and that fossils of these ancestors would ultimately be found in Africa.

It was not until the 1920s that hominin fossils were discovered in Africa. In 1924, Raymond Dart described Australopithecus africanus. The type specimen was the Taung Child, an australopithecine infant discovered in a cave deposit being mined for concrete at Taung, South Africa. The remains were a remarkably well-preserved tiny skull and an endocranial cast of the individual's brain. Although the brain was small (410 cm^3), its shape was rounded, unlike that of chimpanzees and gorillas, and more like a modern human brain. Also, the specimen exhibited short canine teeth, and the position of the foramen magnum was evidence of bipedal locomotion. All of these traits convinced Dart that the Taung baby was a bipedal human ancestor, a transitional form between apes and humans. Another 20 years would pass before Dart's claims were taken seriously, following the discovery of more fossils that resembled his find. The prevailing view of the time was that a large brain evolved before bipedality. It was thought that intelligence on par with modern humans was a prerequisite to bipedalism.

The australopithecines are now thought to be immediate ancestors of the genus Homo, the group to which modern humans belong. Both australopithecines and Homo sapiens are part of the tribe Hominini, but recent data has brought into doubt the position of A. africanus as a direct ancestor of modern humans; it may well have been a dead-end cousin. The australopithecines were originally classified as either gracile or robust. The robust variety of Australopithecus has since been reclassified as Paranthropus. In the 1930s, when the robust specimens were first described, the Paranthropus genus was used. During the 1960s, the robust variety was moved into Australopithecus. The recent trend has been back to the original classification as a separate genus.

Before Homo

The evolutionary history of the primates can be traced back for some 60 million years, as one of the oldest of all surviving placental mammal groups. Most paleontologists consider that primates share a common ancestor with the bats, another extremely ancient lineage, and that this ancestor probably lived during the late Cretaceous together with the last dinosaurs. The oldest known primates come from North America, but they were widespread in Eurasia and Africa as well, during the tropical conditions of the Paleocene and Eocene. With the beginning of modern climates, marked by the formation of the first Antarctic ice in the early Oligocene around 40 million years ago, primates went extinct everywhere but Africa and southern Asia.

Fossil evidence found in Germany 20 years ago (Begun, Journal of Human Evolution, 2001) was determined to be about 16.5 million years old, some 1.5 million years older than similar species from East Africa. It suggests that the great ape and human lineage first appeared in Eurasia and not Africa. The discoveries suggest that the early ancestors of the hominids (the family of great apes and humans) migrated to Eurasia from Africa about 17 million years ago, just before these two continents were cut off from each other by an expansion of the Mediterranean Sea. Begun says that the great apes flourished in Eurasia and that their lineage leading to the African apes and humans-Dryopithecus-migrated south from Europe or Western Asia into Africa.

The surviving tropical population, which is seen most completely in the upper Eocene and lowermost Oligocene fossil beds of the Fayum depression southwest of Cairo, gave rise to all living primates-lemurs of Madagascar, lorises of Southeast

Asia, galagos or "bush babies" of Africa, and the anthropoids; platyrrhines or New World monkeys, and catarrhines or Old World monkeys and the great apes and humans.

The earliest known catarrhine is Kamoyapithecus from uppermost Oligocene at Eragaleit in the northern Kenya rift valley, dated to 24 Ma (millions of years before present). Its ancestry is generally thought to be close to such genera as Aegyptopithecus, Propliopithecus, and Parapithecus from the Fayum, at around 35 Ma. There are no fossils from the intervening 11 million years. No near ancestor to South American platyrrhines, whose fossil record begins at around 30 Ma, can be identified among the North African fossil species, and possibly lies in other forms that lived in West Africa that were caught up in the still-mysterious transatlantic sweepstakes that sent primates, rodents, boa constrictors, and cichlid fishes from Africa to South America sometime in the Oligocene.

In the early Miocene, after 22 Ma, many kinds of arboreally adapted primitive catarrhines from East Africa suggest a long history of prior diversification. Because the fossils at 20 Ma include fragments attributed to Victoriapithecus, the earliest cercopithecoid, the other forms are (by default) grouped as hominoids, without clear evidence as to which are closest to living apes and humans. Among the presently recognized genera in this group, which ranges up to 13 Ma, we find Proconsul, Rangwapithecus, Dendropithecus, Limnopithecus, Nacholapithecus, Equatorius, Nyanzapithecus, Afropithecus, Heliopithecus, and Kenyapithecus, all from East Africa. The presence of other generalized non-cercopithecids of middle Miocene age from sites far distant--Otavipithecus from cave deposits in Namibia, and Pieroloapithecus and Dryopithecus from France, Spain and Austria--is evidence of a wide diversity of forms across Africa and the Mediterranean basin during the relatively warm and equable climatic regimes of the early and middle Miocene. The youngest of the Miocene hominoids, Oreopithecus, is from 9-Ma coal beds in Italy.

"Modern humans are actually hybrids created by millennia of interbreeding between early hominids and chimpanzees," according to geneticist James Mallet and other MIT and Harvard scientists, as quoted in the newsmagazine This Week, June 9,

2006. The interbreeding began about 6.3 million years ago. Then, for a million years, the ancestors of the human race "continued to acquire chromosomes from chimps until a second and final break about 5.3 million years ago."

Molecular evidence indicates that the lineage of gibbons (family Hylobatidae) became distinct between 18 and 12 Ma, and that of orangutans (subfamily Ponginae) at about 12 Ma; we have no fossils that clearly document the ancestry of gibbons, which may have originated in a so far unknown SE-Asian hominoid population, but fossil proto-orangutans may be represented by Ramapithecus from India and Griphopithecus from Turkey, dated to around 10 Ma.

Molecular evidence further suggests that between 8 and 4 MYA, first the gorillas, and then the chimpanzee (genus Pan) split off from the line leading to the humans; we have no fossil record, however, of either group of African great apes, possibly because bones do not fossilize in rain forest environments. Hominines, however, seem to have been one of the mammal groups (as well as antelopes, hyaenas, dogs, pigs, elephants, and horses) that adapted to the open grasslands as soon as this biome appeared, due to increasingly seasonal climates, about 8 Ma, and their fossils are relatively well known. The earliest are Sahelanthropus tchadensis (7-6 MYA) and Orrorin tugenensis (6 MYA), followed by:

- Ardipithecus (5.5-4.4 MYA), with species Ar. kadabba and Ar. ramidus;
- Australopithecus (4-2 MYA), with species Au. anamensis, Au. afarensis, Au. africanus, Au. bahrelghazali, and Au. garhi;
- Paranthropus (3-1.2 MYA), with species P. aethiopicus, P. boisei, and P. robustus;
- Homo (2 MYA-present).

THE GENUS HOMO

In modern taxonomy, Homo sapiens is the only extant species of its genus, Homo. Likewise, the ongoing study of the origins of Homo sapiens often demonstrates that there were other Homo species, all of which are now extinct. While some of these other species might have been ancestors of H. sapiens, many were likely our "cousins", having speciated away from our ancestral line. There is not yet a consensus as to which of these groups should count as separate species and which as subspecies of another species. In some cases this is due to the paucity of fossils, in other cases it is due to the slight differences used to classify species in the Homo genus. The Sahara pump theory provides an explanation of the early variation in the genus Homo.

The word homo is Latin for "person", chosen originally by Carolus Linnaeus in his classification system. It is often translated as "man", although this can lead to confusion, given that the English word "man" can be generic like homo, but can also specifically refer to males. Latin for "man" in the gender-specific sense is vir, cognate with "virile" and "werewolf". The word "human" is from humanus, the adjectival form of homo.

HOMO HABILIS

H. habilis lived from about 2.4 to 1.5 million years ago (MYA). H. habilis, the first species of the genus Homo, evolved in South and East Africa in the late Pliocene or early Pleistocene, 2.5-2 MYA, when it diverged from the Australopithecines. H. habilis had smaller molars and larger brains than the Australopithecines, and made tools from stone and perhaps animal bones. One of the first known hominids, it was nicknamed 'handy man' by its discoverer, Louis Leakey. Some scientists have proposed moving this species out of Homo and into Australopithecus.

HOMO RUDOLFENSIS AND HOMO GEORGICUS

These are proposed species names for fossils from about 1.9-1.6 MYA, the relation of which with H. habilis is not yet clear.

- H. rudolfensis refers to a single, incomplete skull from Kenya.
- H.georgicus, from Georgia, may be an intermediate form between H. habilis and H. erectus.

HOMO ERGASTER AND HOMO ERECTUS

The first fossils of Homo erectus were discovered by Dutch physician Eugene Dubois in 1891 on the Indonesian island of Java. He originally gave the material the name Pithecanthropus erectus based on its morphology that he considered to be intermediate between that of humans and apes.

H. erectus lived from about 1.8 MYA to 70,000 years ago. Often the early phase, from 1.8 to 1.25 MYA, is considered to be a separate species, H. ergaster, or it is seen as a subspecies of erectus, Homo erectus ergaster.

In the Early Pleistocene, 1.5-1 MYA, in Africa, Asia, and Europe, presumably, Homo habilis evolved larger brains and made more elaborate stone tools; these differences and others are sufficient for anthropologists to classify them as a new species, H. erectus. In addition H. erectus was the first human ancestor to walk truly upright. This was made possible by the evolution of locking knees and a different location of the foramen magnum (the hole in the skull where the spine enters). They may have used fire to cook their meat. A famous example of Homo erectus is Peking Man; others were found in Asia (notably in Indonesia), Africa, and Europe. Many paleoanthropologists are now using the term Homo ergaster for the non-Asian forms of this group, and reserving H. erectus only for those fossils found in the Asian region and meeting certain skeletal and dental requirements which differ slightly from ergaster.

HOMO CEPRANENSIS AND HOMO ANTECESSOR

These are proposed as species that may be intermediate between H. erectus and H. heidelbergensis.

- H. cepranensis refers to a single skull cap from Italy, estimated to be about 800,000 years old.
- H. antecessor is known from fossils from Spain and England that are 800,000-500,000 years old.

HOMO HEIDELBERGENSIS

H. heidelbergensis (Heidelberg Man) lived from about 800,000 to about 300,000 years ago. Also proposed as Homo sapiens heidelbergensis or Homo sapiens paleohungaricus.

HOMO NEANDERTHALENSIS

H. neanderthalensis lived from about 250,000 to as recent as 30,000 years ago. Also proposed as Homo sapiens neanderthalensis: there is ongoing debate over whether the 'Neanderthal Man' was a separate species, Homo neanderthalensis, or a subspecies of H. sapiens. While the debate remains unsettled, the prevailing view of evidence, collected by examining mitochondrial DNA and Y-chromosomal DNA, currently indicates that little or no gene flow occurred between H. neanderthalensis and H. sapiens, and, therefore, the two were separate species. In 1997, Dr. Mark Stoneking, then an associate professor of anthropology at Pennsylvania State University, stated: "These results [based on mitochondrial DNA extracted from Neanderthal bone] indicate that Neanderthals did not contribute mitochondrial DNA to modern humans... Neanderthals are not our ancestors." Subsequent investigation of a second source of Neanderthal DNA confirmed these findings. However, supporters of the multiregional hypothesis point to recent studies indicating non-African nuclear DNA heritage dating to one MYA, as well as apparent hybrid fossils found in Portugal and elsewhere, in rebuttal to the prevailing view.

HOMO RHODESIENSIS, AND THE GAWIS CRANIUM

- H. rhodesiensis, estimated to be 300,000-125,000 years old, most current experts believe Rhodesian Man to be within the group of Homo heidelbergensis though other designations such as Archaic Homo sapiens and Homo sapiens rhodesiensis have also been proposed.
- In February 2006 a fossil, the Gawis cranium, was found which might possibly be a species intermediate between H. erectus and H. sapiens or one of many evolutionary dead ends. The skull from Gawis, Ethiopia, is believed to be 500,000-250,000 years old. Only summary details are known, and no peer reviewed studies have been released by the finding team. Gawis man's facial features suggest its being either an intermediate species and an example of a "Bodo man" female.

HOMO SAPIENS

H. sapiens ("sapiens" means wise or intelligent) has lived from about 250,000 years ago to the present. Between 400,000 years ago and the second interglacial period in the Middle Pleistocene, around 250,000 years ago, the trend in cranial expansion and the elaboration of stone tool technologies developed, providing evidence for a transition from H. erectus to H. sapiens.

The direct evidence suggests there was a migration of H. erectus out of Africa, then a further speciation of H. sapiens from H. erectus in Africa (there is little evidence that this speciation occurred elsewhere). Then a subsequent migration within and out of Africa eventually replaced the earlier dispersed H. erectus. This migration and origin theory is usually referred to as the single-origin theory. However, the current evidence does not preclude multiregional speciation, either. This is a hotly debated area in paleoanthropology.

Current research establishes that human beings are highly genetically homogenous, meaning that the DNA of individual Homo sapiens is more alike than usual for most species, a result of their relatively recent evolution. Distinctive genetic characteristics have arisen, however, primarily as the result of small groups of people moving into new environmental circumstances.

Such small groups are initially highly inbred, allowing the relatively rapid transmission of traits favorable to the new environment. These adapted traits are a very small component of the Homo sapiens genome and include such outward "racial" characteristics as skin color and nose form in addition to internal characteristics such as the ability to breathe more efficiently in high altitudes.

H. sapiens idaltu, from Ethiopia, lived from about 160,000 years ago (proposed subspecies). It is the oldest known anatomically modern human.

Homo Floresiensis

H. floresiensis, which lived about 100,000-12,000 years ago (announced 28 October 2004 in the science journal Nature), has been nicknamed hobbit for its small size, probably a result of insular (island) dwarfism.

H. floresiensis is intriguing both for its size and its age, being a concrete example of a recent species of the genus Homo that exhibits derived traits not shared with modern humans. In other words, H. floresiensis share a common ancestor with modern humans, but split from the modern human lineage and followed a distinct evolutionary path.

The main find was a fossil believed to be a woman of about 30 years of age. Found in 2003 it has been dated to approximately 18,000 years old. Her brain size was only 380 cm^3 (which can be considered small even for a chimpanzee). She was only 1 meter in height. However, there is an ongoing debate over whether H. floresiensis is indeed a separate species.

Some scientists presently believe that H. floresiensis was a modern H. sapiens suffering from pathological dwarfism. This hypothesis is supported in part, because the modern humans who live on Flores, the island where the fossil was found, are pygmies. This coupled with pathological dwarfism could indeed create a hobbit-like human. The other major attack on H. floresiensis is that it was found with tools only associated with H. sapiens.

Use of Tools

Using tools is not only a sign of intelligence, it also may have acted as a stimulus for human evolution. Over the past 3 or 2 million years, human brain size has increased threefold. A brain needs a lot of energy: the brain of modern man uses about 20 Watts (about 400 calories per day), one fifth of total human energy consumption. Early hominoids, like apes, were essentially plant eaters (fruit, leaves, roots), their diet only occasionally supplemented by meat (often from scavenging). However, plant food in general yields considerably less energy and nutritive value than meat. Therefore, being able to hunt for large animals, which was only possible by using tools such as spears, made it possible for humans to sustain larger and more complex brains, which in turn allowed them to develop yet more intelligent and efficient tools.

Precisely when early man started to use tools is difficult to determine, because the more primitive these tools are (for example, sharp-edged stones) the more difficult it is to decide whether they are natural objects or human artifacts. There is some evidence that the australopithecines (4 MYA) may have used broken bones as tools, but this is debated.

Stone Tools

Stone tools are first attested around 2.6 million years ago, when H. habilis in Eastern Africa used so-called pebble tools, choppers made out of round pebbles that had been split by simple strikes.

This marks the beginning of the Paleolithic, or Old Stone Age; its end is taken to be the end of the last Ice Age, around 10,000 years ago. The Paleolithic is subdivided into the Lower Paleolithic (Early Stone Age, ending around 350,000-300,000 years ago), the Middle Paleolithic (Middle Stone Age, until 50,000-30,000 years ago), and the Upper Paleolithic.

The period from 700,000-300,000 years ago is also known as the Acheulean, when H. ergaster (or erectus) made large stone hand-axes out of flint and quartzite, at first quite rough (Early Acheulian), later "retouched" by additional, more subtle strikes at the sides of the flakes.

After 350,000 BP (Before Present) the more refined so-called Levallois technique was developed. It consisted of series of consecutive strikes, by which scrapers, slicers ("racloirs"), needles, and flattened needles were made. Finally, after about 50,000 BP, ever more refined and specialized flint tools were made by the Neanderthals and the immigrant Cro-Magnons (knives, blades, skimmers). In this period they also started to make tools out of bone.

The "Modern Man" Debate and the Great Leap Forward

Until about 50,000-40,000 years ago the use of stone tools seems to have progressed stepwise: each phase (habilis, ergaster, neanderthal) started at a higher level than the previous one, but once that phase had started further development was slow.

In other words, one might call these Homo species culturally conservative. After 50,000 BP, what Jared Diamond, author of The Third Chimpanzee, and other anthropologists characterize as a Great Leap Forward, human culture apparently started to change at much greater speed: "modern" humans started to bury their dead carefully, made clothing out of hides, developed sophisticated hunting techniques (such as pitfall traps, or driving animals to fall off cliffs), and made cave paintings. This speed-up of cultural change seems connected with the arrival of modern humans, homo sapiens sapiens. Additionally, human culture began to become more advanced, in that, different populations of humans begin to create novelty in existing technologies.

Artifacts such as fish hooks, buttons and bone needles begin to show signs of variation among different population of humans, something that has not been seen in human cultures prior to 50,000 BP. Typically, neanderthalenis populations are found with technology similar to other contemporary neanderthalensis populations.

Theoretically, modern human behaviour is taken to include four ingredient capabilities: abstract thinking (concepts free from specific examples), planning (taking steps to achieve a farther goal), innovation (finding new solutions), and symbolic behaviour (such as images, or rituals).

Among concrete examples of modern human behaviour, anthropologists include specialization of tools, use of jewelry and images (such as cave drawings), organization of living space, rituals (for example, burials with grave gifts), specialized hunting techniques, exploration of less hospitable geographical areas, and barter trade networks. Debate continues whether there was indeed a "Revolution" leading to modern man ("the big bang of human consciousness"), or a more gradual evolution.

THE AQUATIC APE THEORY

The aquatic ape hypothesis of human evolution sought to answer some of the most basic questions about human evolution: Why do humans walk upright? Why are they naked? Why does human sexual behavior differ from other primates?

Why are humans the only primate to acquire spoken language? Why are humans the only primate to shed tears? Why are human babies plump and other primates skinny? Why are humans the only land mammal to have subcutaneous fat attached to the skin? Sir Alister Hardy, an eminent marine biologist, identified many anatomical and physiological characteristics found only in man among primates, but which are characteristically found in marine mammals.

The examination of human biology in the light of a speculated marine phase in human evolution answers many of the questions. The assumption is that at some time in evolution humans were coastal dwelling primates. The proposition was taken up by the Welsh popular science writer Elaine Morgan in a series of persuasive books. The theory is largely dismissed by mainstream anthropologists but raises a number of intriguing questions as to why human biology is as it is.

7

Osteology

Osteology is the scientific study of bones. A subdiscipline of anthropology (US) archeology (EU), osteology is a detailed study of the structure of bones, skeletal elements, teeth, morphology, function, disease, pathology, the process of ossification (from cartilaginous molds), the resistance and hardness of bones (biophysics), etc. Often used by scientists with identification of human remains with regard to age, death, gender, growth, and development in a biocultural context.

METHODS

A typical analysis will include:

- an inventory of the skeletal elements present
- a dental inventory
- ageing data, based upon epiphyseal fusion, dental eruption and tooth wear
- sexing data, based upon bone morphology
- stature and other metric data
- race
- non-metric traits
- pathology and/or cultural modifications
- taphonomy, including weathering, gnawing, butchery, burning and related processes

APPLICATIONS

Osteological approaches are frequently applied to investigations in disciplines such as forensic science, physical anthropology and archaeology, and has a place in research on topics including:

- health
- demography
- diet
- disease
- activity patterns
- physique
- genetics of early populations
- population migration
- ancient warfare
- social inequality
- identification of unknown remains
- criminal investigations
- war crimes.

FORENSIC SCIENCE

Forensic science (often shortened to forensics) is the application of a broad spectrum of sciences to answer questions of interest to the legal system. This may be in relation to a crime or to a civil action. The use of the term "forensics" in place of "forensic science" could be considered incorrect; the term "forensic" is effectively a synonym for "legal" or "related to courts" (from Latin, it means "before the forum"). However, it is now so closely associated with the scientific field that many dictionaries include the meaning that equates the word "forensics" with "forensic science."

"Forensic" comes from the Latin word "forensis" meaning forum. During the time of the Romans, a criminal charge meant presenting the case before a group of public individuals. Both the person accused of the crime and the accuser would give speeches based on their side of the story. The individual with the best argumentation and delivery would determine the outcome of the case. In other words, the person with the best forensis skills would win.

SUBDIVISIONS

- Forensic accounting is the study and interpretation of accounting evidence.
- Forensic anthropology is the application of physical anthropology in a legal setting, usually for the recovery and identification of skeletonized human remains.
- Forensic economics is the study and interpretation of economic damage evidence to include present day calculations of lost earnings and benefits, the lost value of a business, lost business profits, lost value of household service, replacement labor costs and future medical care costs.
- Forensic engineering studies the causes of failure of devices and structures.
- Forensic epistemology deals with philosophical knowledge in a legal setting, typically for understanding behavior of states.
- Forensic linguistics deals with anything in the legal system that requires linguistic expertise.
- Forensic psychology and forensic psychiatry deal with the legal aspects of human behavior.
- Forensics science using science to create an argument in places such as court.
- Forensic biology performs serological and DNA analysis of physiological fluids for the purpose of identification and individualization.
- Forensic serology is the application of the study of blood, semen, saliva and other body fluids to legal matters.

APPLICATIONS

Criminalistics is the application of various sciences to answer questions relating to examination and comparison of biological evidence, trace evidence, impression evidence (such as fingerprints, footwear impressions, and tire tracks), controlled substances, firearms, and other evidence in criminal investigations. Typically, evidence is processed in a crime lab.

This is the division of forensic science most often reported in the media and depicted in popular fiction.

Some of the other forensic science disciplines are:

Forensic entomology deals with the examination of insects in, on, and around human remains to assist in determination of time or location of death. It is also possible to determine if the body was moved after death.

Forensic geology deals with trace evidence in the form of soils, minerals and petroleums.

Forensic odontology is the study of the uniqueness of dentition better known as the study of teeth.

Forensic photography is the art of producing an accurate photographic reproduction of a crime scene for the benefit of a court.

Forensic toxicology is the study of the effect of drugs and poisons on the human body.

Forensic firearms examination is the science dealing with the investigation of use of firearms and ammunition.

Questioned document examination is the study and interpretation of evidence that takes the form of a document, including handwriting and printmaking.

HISTORY

The "Eureka" legend of Archimedes (287-212 BC) can be considered an early account of the use of forensic science. In this case, by examining the principles of water displacement, Archimedes was able to prove that a crown was not made of gold (as it was fraudulently claimed) by its density and buoyancy.

The earliest account of fingerprint use to establish identity was during the 7th century. According to Soleiman, an Arabic merchant, a debtor's fingerprints were affixed to a bill, which would then be given to the lender. This bill was legally recognized as proof of the validity of the debt.

The first written account of using medicine and entomology to solve (separate) criminal cases is attributed to the book Xi Yuan Ji Lu, written in 1248 China by Song Ci. In one of the accounts, the case of a person murdered with a sickle was solved by a death investigator who instructed everyone to bring their sickles to one location. Flies, attracted by the smell of blood, eventually gathered on a single sickle. In light of this, the murderer confessed. The book also offered advice on how to distinguish between a drowning (water in the lungs) and strangulation (broken neck cartilage).

In sixteenth century Europe, medical practitioners in army and university settings began to gather information on cause and manner of death. Ambroise Paré, a French army surgeon, systematically studied the effects of violent death on internal organs. Two Italian surgeons, Fortunato Fidelis and Paolo Zacchia, laid the foundation of modern pathology by studying changes which occurred in the structure of the body as the result of disease. In the late 1700s, writings on these topics began to appear. These included: "A Treatise on Forensic Medicine and Public Health" by the French physician Fodéré, and "The Complete System of Police Medicine" by the German medical expert Johann Peter Franck.

In 1775, Swedish chemist Carl Wilhelm Scheele devised a way of detecting arsenous oxide, simple arsenic, in corpses, although only in large quantities. This investigation was expanded, in 1806, by German chemist Valentin Ross, who learned to detect the poison in the walls of a victim's stomach, and by English chemist James Marsh, who used chemical processes to confirm arsenic as the cause of death in an 1836 murder trial.

Two early examples of English forensic science in individual legal proceedings demonstrate the increasing use of logic and procedure in criminal investigations. In 1784, in Lancaster, England, John Toms was tried and convicted for murdering Edward Culshaw with a pistol. When the dead body of Culshaw was examined, a pistol wad (crushed paper used to secure powder and balls in the muzzle) found in his head wound matched perfectly with a torn newspaper found in Toms' pocket. In Warwick, England, in 1816, a farm laborer was tried and convicted of the murder of a young maidservant. She had been drowned in a shallow pool and bore the marks of violent assault. The police found footprints and an impression from corduroy cloth with a sewn patch in the damp earth near the pool. There were also scattered grains of wheat and chaff. The breeches of a farm laborer who had been threshing wheat nearby were examined and corresponded exactly to the impression in the earth near the pool.

FORENSIC SCIENCE IN THE MEDIA

Sherlock Holmes, the fictional character created by Sir Arthur Conan Doyle in works produced from 1887 to 1915, used forensic science as one of his investigating methods. Conan Doyle credited the inspiration for Holmes on his teacher at the medical school of the University of Edinburgh, the gifted surgeon and forensic detective Joseph Bell.

Decades later, the comic strip, Dick Tracy also featured a detective using a considerable number of forensic methods, although sometimes the methods were more fanciful than actually possible. Popular television series focusing on crime detection, including CSI: Crime Scene Investigation, CSI: Miami, CSI: NY, NCIS and Bones depict glamorized versions of the activities of 21st Century forensic scientists. These related TV shows have changed individuals' expectations of forensic science, an influence termed the "CSI effect".

In the video game Phoenix Wright: Ace Attorney, forensic science is used in various cases.

The second incarnation of the comic book character The Flash also worked as a forensic scientist in his civilian identity.

8

Cultural and Social Anthropology

Cultural anthropology, also called socio-cultural anthropology or social anthropology, is a field (one of four that are commonly recognized in the United States) of anthropology, the holistic study of humanity. It is the branch of anthropology that has developed and promoted "culture" as a meaningful scientific concept; it is also the branch of anthropology that studies cultural variation among humans. The anthropological concept of "culture" reflects in part a reaction against earlier Western discourses based on an opposition between "culture" and "nature", according to which some human beings lived in a "state of nature". Anthropologists argue that culture is "human nature," and that all people have a capacity to classify experiences, encode classifications symbolically, and teach such abstractions to others.

Since humans acquire culture through learning (the processes of enculturation and socialization), people living in different places or different circumstances may develop different cultures. Anthropologists have also pointed out that through culture people can adapt to their environment in non-genetic ways, so people living in different environments will often have different cultures. Much of anthropological theory has originated in an appreciation of and interest in the tension between the local (particular cultures) and the global (a universal human nature, or the web of connections between people in distinct places/circumstances).

A BRIEF HISTORY

Modern socio-cultural anthropology has its origins in 19th century "ethnology", which involves the organized comparison of human societies. Scholars like E.B. Tylor and J.G. Frazer in England worked mostly with materials collected by others-usually missionaries, explorers, or colonial officials-this earned them their current sobriquet of "arm-chair anthropologists". Ethnologists had an especial interest in why people living in different parts of the world sometimes had similar beliefs and practices. In addressing this question, ethnologists in the 19th century divided into two schools of thought. Some, like Grafton Elliot Smith, argued that different groups must somehow have learned from one another, however indirectly; in other words, they argued that cultural traits spread from one place to another, or "diffused". Other ethnologists argued that different groups had the capability of inventing similar beliefs and practices independently. Some of those who advocated "independent invention", like Lewis Henry Morgan, additionally supposed that similarities meant that different groups had passed through the same stages of cultural evolution.

20th century anthropologists largely reject the notion that all human societies must pass through the same stages in the same order. Some 20th century ethnologists, like Julian Steward, have instead argued that such similarities reflected similar adaptations to similar environments. Others, like Claude Lévi-Strauss, have argued that apparent patterns of development reflect fundamental similarities in the structure of human thought.

In the 20th century most socio-cultural anthropologists turned to the study of ethnography, in which an anthropologist actually lives among another society for a considerable period of time, simultaneously participating in and observing the social and cultural life of the group. Bronislaw Malinowski (who conducted fieldwork in the Trobriand Islands and taught in England) developed this method, and Franz Boas (who conducted fieldwork in Baffin Island and taught in the United States) promoted it. Boas´s students drew on his conception of culture and cultural relativism to develop cultural anthropology in the United States. Simultaneously, Malinowski and A.R. Radcliffe Brown´s students were developing social anthropology in the United Kingdom. Whereas cultural anthropology focused on symbols and values, social anthropology focused on social groups and institutions. Today socio-cultural anthropologists attend to all these elements.

Although 19th century ethnologists saw "diffusion" and "independent invention" as mutually exclusive and competing theories, most ethnographers quickly reached a consensus that both processes occur, and that both can plausibly account for cross-cultural similarities. But these ethnographers pointed out the superficiality of many such similarities, and that even traits that spread through diffusion often changed their meaning and functions as they moved from one society to another. Accordingly, these anthropologists showed less interest in comparing cultures, generalizing about human nature, or discovering universal laws of cultural development, than in understanding particular cultures in those cultures' own terms. Such ethnographers and their students promoted the idea of "cultural relativism", the view that one can only understand another person's beliefs and behaviors in the context of the culture in which he or she lived.

In the early 20th century socio-cultural anthropology developed in different forms in Europe and in the United States. European "social anthropologists" focused on observed social behaviors and on "social structure", that is, on relationships among social roles (e.g. husband and wife, or parent and child) and social institutions (e.g. religion, economy, and politics). American "cultural anthropologists" focused on the ways people expressed their view of themselves and their world, especially in symbolic forms (such as art and myths). These two approaches frequently converged (kinship, for example, and leadership function both as symbolic systems and as social institutions), and generally complemented one another. Today almost all socio-cultural anthropologists refer to the work of both sets of predecessors, and have an equal interest in what people do and in what people say.

CONTEMPORARY THEORY AND METHODS

Today ethnography continues to dominate socio-cultural anthropology. Nevertheless, many contemporary socio-cultural anthropologists have rejected earlier models of ethnography that treated local cultures as bounded and isolated. These anthropologists continue to concern themselves with the distinct ways people in different locales experience and understand their lives, but they often argue that one cannot understand these particular ways of life solely in the local context; one must analyze them (they say) in the context of regional or even global political and economic relations. Notable proponents of this approach include Arjun Appadurai, James Clifford, George Marcus, Sidney Mintz, Michael Taussig and Eric Wolf.

A growing trend in anthropological research and analysis is the use of multi-sited ethnography, discussed in George Marcus's article "Ethnography In/Of the World System: the Emergence of Multi-Sited Ethnography". Looking at culture as embedded in macro-constructions of a global social order, multi-sited ethnography uses traditional methodology in various locations both spatially and temporally. Through this methodology greater insight can be gained when examining the impact of world-systems on local and global communities. Also emerging in multi-sited ethnography are greater inter-disciplinary approaches to fieldwork, bringing in methods from cultural studies, media studies, science and technology studies, and others. In multi-sited ethnography research tracks a subject across spatial and temporal boundaries.

For example, a multi-sited ethnography may follow a "thing," such as a particular commodity, as it transfers through the networks of global capitalism. Multi-sited ethnography may also follow ethnic groups in diaspora, stories or rumours that appear in multiple locations and in multiple time periods, metaphors that appear in multiple ethnographic locations, or the biographies of individual people or groups as they move through space and time. It may also follow conflicts that transcend boundaries. Multi-sited ethnographies, such as Nancy Scheper-Hughes's ethnography of the international black market for the trade of human organs. In this research she follows organs as they transfer through various legal and illegal networks of capitalism, as well as the rumours and urban legends that circulate in impoverished communities about child kidnapping and organ theft.

Sociocultural anthropologists have increasingly turned their investigative eye on to "Western" culture. For example, Philippe

Bourgois won the Margaret Mead Award in 1997 for In Search of Respect, a study of the entrepreneurs in a Harlem crack-den. Also growing more popular are ethnographies of professional communities, such as laboratory researchers, Wall Street investors, law firms, or IT computer employees.

Interestingly, the title a college gives it introductory anthropology course can be used as a measure of that department's anthropological focus. Some departments are inspired by the branching developments in social anthropology, often with a British or European influence, and may title an introductory course accordingly. Departments influenced by American thinking, which takes a more holistic approach, frequently title their introductory course "cultural anthropology."

SOCIAL ANTHROPOLOGY

Social anthropology was founded in Britain following World War I through a methodological revolution pioneered by Bronislaw Malinowski's meticulous process-oriented fieldwork in the Trobriand Islands of Melanesia between 1915 and 1918 and through Alfred Radcliffe-Brown's theoretical program for systematic comparison that was based on a conception of rigorous fieldwork and the structure-functionalist conception of Durkheim's sociology. Other intellectual founders include W. H. R. Rivers and A. C. Haddon, whose orientation reflected the contemporary Volkerpsychologie of Wilhelm Wundt and Adolph Bastian, and Sir E. B. Tylor, who defined anthropology as a positivistic science following Auguste Comte. Edmund Leach (1962) defined social anthropology as a kind of comparative micro-sociology based on intensive fieldwork studies. There was never a settled theoretical orthodoxy on the nature of science and society but always a tension between several views that were seriously opposed.

Following World War II, sociocultural anthropology as comprised by the fields of ethnography and ethnology diverged into an American school of cultural anthropology while social anthropology diversified in Europe by challenging the principles of structure-functionalism, absorbing ideas from Claude Levi-Strauss's structuralism and from Max Gluckman's Manchester school, and embracing the study of conflict, change, urban anthropology, and networks. A European Association of Social Anthropologists (EASA) was founded in 1989 as a society of scholarship at a meeting of founder members from fourteen European countries, supported by the Wenner-Gren Foundation for Anthropological Research. The Association seeks to advance anthropology in Europe by organizing biennual conferences and by editing its academic journal, Social Anthropology/ Anthropologie Sociale.

Other universities outside Britain do have departments of Social Anthropology, including in the United States (e.g., Stanford University, Harvard University, University of Chicago) and many non-European anthropologists identify themselves as social anthropologists, and often in ways not anticipated by the founders of the field, as for example in the subfield of structure and dynamics.

DISCOURSE

Discourse is a term used in semantics and discourse analysis, but it also refers to a social conception of discourse, often linked with the work of French philosopher Michel Foucault (1926-1984) and Jürgen Habermas' The Theory of Communicative Action (1985). Each thinker had personal conceptions of discourse which are thought to be incompatible with the other. They remain two important figures in this field; Habermas trying to find the transcendent rules upon which speakers could agree on a groundworks consensus, while Foucault was developing a battle-type of discourse which opposed the classic marxist definition of ideology as part of the superstructure.

Discourse Analysis

The Social Conception of Discourse

In the social sciences, a discourse is considered to be an institutionalized way of thinking, a social boundary defining what can be said about a specific topic, or, as Judith Butler puts it, "the limits of acceptable speech"-or possible truth. Discourses are seen to affect our views on all things; it is not possible to escape discourse. For example, two notably distinct discourses can be used about various guerrilla movements describing them either as "freedom fighters" or "terrorists". In other words, the chosen discourse delivers the vocabulary, expressions and perhaps also the style needed to communicate. Discourse is closely linked to different theories of power and state, at least as long as defining discourses is seen to mean defining reality itself. According to Foucault's definition, discourse must be heard rather as synonym of his concept of episteme, notwithstanding important theoretical displacements (episteme was first thought as the condition of possibility of discourses).

In other words, Foucault's discourse must both be understood as a singular discourse, as defined above, and as a more general discourse, meaning the boundaries given to any particular discourse. In this more general sense, discourse is not composed only of words, which would be to limit oneself to a dualist conception: as he demonstrated in Discipline and Punish, discourse is also composed of architectural dispositifs, such as Jeremy Bentham's panopticon or the map of a classroom, etc. A dispositif is "a resolutely heterogeneous assemblage, containing discourses, institutions, architectural buildings, reglementary decisions, scientific statements, philosophical, moral, philanthropic propositions, in one word: said as well as non-said, those are the dispositif's elements. The dispositif in itself is the network that we can establish between those elements."

According to Foucault, discourse can't be reduced to an ideological reflexion, it is to be thought as itself a Kampfplatz or battlefield. Against Kant's conception, Foucault argues that truth is not the objective bounty that the winners can take; truth is not an absolute, it is on the contrary produced in this battle with strategic aims. This conception of truth may be related to Althusser's theory on the "epistemological break" between science and ideology (the "epistemological break" is not an event, but a process; "science" always has to fight for its truth against ideology, which keeps coming back).

Since knowledge and power are intrinsically related, according to Foucault, he can thus say that power relations are immanent to discourses, whereas in the classic marxist conception, the discourse is conceived as the ideological superstructure-which, of course, interacts with the base, as Marx wrote, but this does not impede the power relations being essentially located in the economic base, afterward reflected in the superstructure. Furthermore, as he showed in Society Must Be Defended (1976-77), discourse is not anyone's property and thus has no essentialist meaning. The same discourse may change political sides quite often, being reappropriated and endlessly modified, as did Foucault show in his analysis of the historical and political discourse; there is a "polymorphic tactics" of discourses. In other words, specific discourses are not tied to the subject; rather, the subject is a social construction of the discourse, or, as Nietzsche said, a "grammatical fiction". Judith Butler would maintain this ambivalency of discourse, which can be performed in various contexts by different subjectivities. In psychology critical perspectives on discourse have been developed in relation to developmental psychology by Erica Burman and in relation to social theory and psychoanalysis by Ian Parker (psychologist), and a critical research group, the Discourse Unit, was founded by these two. This perspective has also then had an influential bearing on critical psychology.

Philosophy and religion are often closely interwoven in Eastern thought. Many Asian religious and philosophical traditions originated in India and China and spread across Asia through cultural diffusion and the migration of peoples. Hinduism is the wellspring of Buddhism, the Mahayana branch of which spread north and eastwards from India into Tibet, China, Mongolia, Japan and Korea and south from China into Vietnam. Theravada Buddhism spread throughout Southeast Asia, including Sri Lanka, parts of southwest China, Cambodia, Laos, Myanmar, and Thailand.

Indian philosophy includes Hindu philosophy. They contain elements of nonmaterial pursuits, whereas another school of thought from India, Carvaka, preached the enjoyment of material world. Confucianism and Taoism, both of which originated in China have had pervasive influence on both religious and philosophical traditions, as well as statecraft and the arts throughout Asia.

During the 20th century, in the two most populous countries of Asia, two dramatically different political philosophies took shape. Gandhi gave a new meaning to Ahimsa, a core belief of both Hinduism and Jainism, and redefined the concepts of nonviolence and nonresistance. During the same period, Mao Zedong's communist philosophy became a powerful secular belief system in China.

Folk Religions

Folk religions practiced by tribal groups are common in Asia, Africa and the Americas. Their influence can be considerable; may pervade the culture and even become the state religion, as with Shintoism. Like the other major religions, folk religion answers human needs for reassurance in times of trouble, healing, averting misfortune and providing rituals that address the major passages and transitions in human life.

The "American Dream"

The American Dream is a belief, held by many in the United States, that through hard work, courage, and self-determination, regardless of social class, a person can gain a better life. This notion is rooted in the belief that the United States is a "city upon a hill, a light unto the nations," which were values held by many early European settlers and maintained by subsequent generations.

Marriage

Most Christian churches give some form of blessing to a marriage; the wedding ceremony typically includes some sort of pledge by the community to support the relationship. In marriage, Christians draw a parallel with the relationship between Jesus Christ and His Church. The Roman Catholic Church believes it is morally wrong to divorce, and divorcées cannot remarry in a church marriage (without a formal annulment of the previous marriage).

Cultural Studies

Cultural studies developed in the late 20th century, in part through the re-introduction of Marxist thought into sociology, and in part through the articulation of sociology and other academic disciplines such as literary criticism. This movement aimed to focus on the analysis of subcultures in capitalist societies. Following the non-anthropological tradition, cultural studies generally focus on the study of consumption goods (such as fashion, art, and literature). Because the 18th-and 19th-century distinction between "high" and "low" culture seems inappropriate to apply to the mass-produced and mass-marketed consumption goods which cultural studies analyses, these scholars refer instead to "popular culture".

Today, some anthropologists have joined the project of cultural studies. Most, however, reject the identification of culture with consumption goods. Furthermore, many now reject the notion of culture as bounded, and consequently reject the notion of subculture. Instead, they see culture as a complex web of shifting patterns that link people in different locales and that link social formations of different scales. According to this view, any group can construct its own cultural identity.

Currently, a debate is underway regarding whether or not culture can actually change fundamental human cognition. Researchers are divided on the question.

Cultural Change

Cultures, by predisposition, both embrace and resist change, depending on culture traits. For example, men and women have complementary roles in many cultures. One gender might desire changes that affect the other, as happened in the second half of the 20th century in western cultures. Thus there are both dynamic influences that encourage acceptance of new things, and conservative forces that resist change. Three kinds of influence cause both change and resistance to it:

1. forces at work within a society
2. contact between societies
3. changes in the natural environment.

Cultural change can come about due to the environment, to inventions (and other internal influences), and to contact with other cultures. For example, the end of the last ice age helped lead to the invention of agriculture, which in its turn brought about many cultural innovations.

In diffusion, the form of something (though not necessarily its meaning) moves from one culture to another. For example, hamburgers, mundane in the United States, seemed exotic when introduced into China. "Stimulus diffusion" refers to an element of one culture leading to an invention in another. Diffusion of innovations theory presents a research-based model of why and when individuals and cultures adopt new ideas, practices, and products.

"Acculturation" has different meanings, but in this context refers to replacement of the traits of one culture with those of another, such as happened to certain Native American tribes and to many indigenous peoples across the globe during the process of colonization. Related processes on an individual level include assimilation (adoption of a different culture by an individual) and transculturation.

Cultural invention has come to mean any innovation that is new and found to be useful to a group of people and expressed in their behavior but which does not exist as a physical object. Humanity is in a global "accelerating culture change period", driven by the expansion of international commerce, the mass media, and above all, the human population explosion, among other factors. The world's population now doubles in less than years.

Culture change is complex and has far-ranging effects. Sociologists and anthropologists believe that a holistic approach to the study of cultures and their environments is needed to understand all of the various aspects of change. Human existence may best be looked at as a "multifaceted whole." Only from this vantage can one grasp the realities of culture change.

9

Anthropology and Nature

Nature, in the broadest sense, is equivalent to the natural world, physical universe, material world or material universe. "Nature" refers to the phenomena of the physical world, and also to life in general. The term generally does not include manufactured objects and human interaction unless qualified in ways such as, e.g., "human nature" or "the whole of nature". Nature is also generally distinguished from the supernatural. It ranges in scale from the subatomic to the galactic.

The word "nature" derives from the Latin word natura, or "the course of things, natural character." Natura was a Latin translation of the Greek word physis, which originally related to the intrinsic characteristics that plants, animals, and other features of the world develop of their own accord. This is well shown in the first written use of the word, in connection with a plant.

The concept of nature as a whole, the physical universe, is one of several expansions of the original notion; it began with certain core applications of the word by pre-Socratic philosophers, and has steadily gained currency ever since. This usage was confirmed during the advent of modern scientific method in the last several centuries.

Within the various uses of the word today, "nature" may refer to the general realm of various types of living plants and animals, and in some cases to the processes associated with inanimate objects-the way that particular types of things exist and change of their own accord, such as the weather and geology of the Earth, and the matter and energy of which all these things are composed. It is often taken to mean the "natural environment" or wilderness-wild animals, rocks, forest, beaches, and in general those things that have not been substantially altered by human intervention, or which persist despite human intervention. This more traditional concept of natural things which can still be found today implies a distinction between the natural and the artificial, with the latter being understood as that which has been brought into being by a human or human-like consciousness or mind.

Earth

Earth (or, "the earth") is the fifth largest planet in the solar system, third in order of distance from the Sun. It is the largest of its planetary system's terrestrial planets and the only place in the universe known to support life.

The most prominent features of the earth's climate are its two large polar regions, two relatively narrow temperate zones, and a wide equatorial tropical to subtropical region. Precipitation patterns vary widely according to location, ranging from several metres of water per year to less than a millimetre. About 70 percent of the surface is covered by salt-water oceans. The remainder consists of continents and islands, with the vast majority of the inhabited land in the Northern Hemisphere.

Earth has evolved through geological and biological processes that have left traces of the original conditions. The outer surface is divided into several tectonic plates that gradually migrate across the surface over geologic time spans, which at least several times have changed relatively quickly. The interior of the planet remains active, with a thick layer of molten Earth mantle and an iron-filled core that generates a magnetic field.

The atmospheric conditions have been significantly altered from the original conditions by the presence of life forms, which create an ecological balance that stabilizes the surface conditions. Despite the wide regional variations in climate by latitude and other geographic factors, the long-term average global climate is quite stable during interglacial periods, and variations of a degree or two of average global temperature have historically had major effects on the ecological balance, and on the actual geography of the Earth.

HISTORICAL PERSPECTIVE

Based on the available evidence, scientists have reconstructed detailed information about the planet's past. Earth is believed to have formed about 4.55 billion years ago out of the solar nebula, along with the Sun and other planets. The moon formed relatively soon afterwards (roughly 20 million years later, or 4.53 billion years ago).

Initially molten, the outer layer of the planet cooled, resulting in the solid crust. Outgassing and volcanic activity produced the primordial atmosphere. Condensing water vapor, augmented by ice delivered by comets, produced the oceans. The highly energetic chemistry is believed to have produced a self-replicating molecule around 4 billion years ago.

Continents formed, then broke up and re-formed as the surface of Earth reshaped itself over the course of hundreds of millions of years, occasionally combining to make a supercontinent. Roughly 750 million years ago, the earliest known supercontinent Rodinia, began to break apart. The continents later recombined to form Pannotia which broke apart about 540 million years ago, then finally Pangaea, which broke apart about 180 million years ago.

There is significant evidence, still being discussed among scientists, that a severe glacial action during the Neoproterozoic era covered much of the planet in a sheet of ice. This hypothesis has been termed the "Snowball Earth", and it is of particular interest as it precedes the Cambrian explosion in which multicellular life forms began to proliferate about 530-540 million years ago.

Since the Cambrian explosion there have been five distinctly identifiable mass extinctions. The last mass extinction occurred some 65 million years ago, when a meteorite collision probably triggered the extinction of the non-avian dinosaurs and other large reptiles, but spared small animals such as mammals, which then resembled shrews. Over the past 65 million years, mammalian life diversified.

Several million years ago, a species of small African ape gained the ability to stand upright. The subsequent advent of human life, and the development of agriculture and further civilization allowed humans to affect the Earth more rapidly than any previous life form, affecting both the nature and quantity of other organisms as well as global climate. (By comparison, the Oxygen Catastrophe, produced by the proliferation of algae during the Siderian period, required about 300 million years to culminate.)

The present era is classified as part of a mass extinction event, the Holocene extinction event, the fastest ever to have occurred. Some, such as E. O. Wilson of Harvard University, predict that human destruction of the biosphere could cause the extinction of one-half of all species in the next 100 years. The extent of the current extinction event is still being researched, debated and calculated by biologists.

WEATHER AND CLIMATE

The atmosphere of the Earth serves as a key factor in sustaining the planetary ecosystem. The thin layer of gases that envelops the Earth is held in place by the planet's gravity. Dry air consists of 78% nitrogen, 21% oxygen, 1% argon and other inert gases, carbon dioxide, etc.; but air also contains a variable amount of water vapor. The atmospheric pressure declines steadily with altitude, and has a scale height of about 8 kilometres at the Earth's surface: the height at which the atmospheric pressure has declined by a factor of e (a mathematical constant equal to 2.71...). The ozone layer of the Earth's atmosphere plays an important role in depleating the amount of ultraviolet (UV) radiation that reaches the surface. As DNA is readily damaged by UV light, this serves to protect life at the surface. The atmosphere also retains heat during the night, thereby reducing the daily temperature extremes.

Terrestrial weather occurs almost exclusively in the lower part of the atmosphere, and serves as a convective system for redistributing heat. Ocean currents are another important factor in determining climate, particularly the major underwater thermohaline circulation which distributes heat energy from the equatorial oceans to the polar regions. These currents help to moderate the differences in temperature between winter and summer in the temperate zones. Also, without the redistributions of heat energy by the ocean currents and atmosphere, the tropics would be much hotter, and the polar regions much colder.

Weather can have both beneficial and harmful effects. Extremes in weather, such as tornadoes or hurricanes and cyclones, can expend large amounts of energy along their paths, and produce devastation. Surface vegetation has evolved a dependence on the seasonal variation of the weather, and sudden changes lasting only a few years can have a dramatic effect, both on the vegetation and on the animals dependent on its growth for their food.

The planetary climate is a measure of the long-term trends in the weather. Various factors are known to influence the climate, including ocean currents, surface albedo, greenhouse gases, variations in the solar luminosity, and changes to the planet's orbit. Based on historical records, the Earth is known to have undergone drastic climate changes in the past, including ice ages. The climate of a region depends on a number of factors, especially latitude. A latitudinal band of the surface with similar climatic attributes forms a climate region. There are a number of such regions, ranging from the tropical climate at the equator to the polar climate in the northern and southern extremes. Weather is also influenced by the seasons, which result from the Earth's axis being tilted relative to its orbital plane. Thus, at any given time during the summer or winter, one part of the planet is more directly exposed to the rays of the sun. This exposure alternates as the Earth revolves in its orbit. At any given time, regardless of season, the northern and southern hemispheres experience opposite seasons.

Weather is a chaotic system that is readily modified by small changes to the environment, so accurate weather forecasting is currently limited to only a few days. Overall, two things are currently happening worldwide: (1) temperature is increasing on the average; and (2) regional climates have been undergoing noticeable changes.

LIFE

Although there is no universal agreement on the definition of life, scientists generally accept that the biological manifestation of life is characterized by organization, metabolism, growth, adaptation, response to stimuli and reproduction. Life may also be said to be simply the characteristic state of organisms.

Properties common to terrestrial organisms (plants, animals, fungi, protists, archaea and bacteria) are that they are cellular, carbon-and-water-based with complex organization, having a metabolism, a capacity to grow, respond to stimuli, and reproduce. An entity with these properties is generally considered life. However, not every definition of life considers all of these properties to be essential. Human-made analogs of life may also be considered to be life.

The biosphere is the part of Earth's outer shell-including air, land, surface rocks and water-within which life occurs, and which biotic processes in turn alter or transform. From the broadest geophysiological point of view, the biosphere is the global ecological system integrating all living beings and their relationships, including their interaction with the elements of the lithosphere (rocks), hydrosphere (water), and atmosphere (air). Currently the entire Earth contains over 75 billion tons (150 trillion pounds or about 6.8 x 1013 kilograms) of biomass (life), which lives within various environments within the biosphere.

Over nine-tenths of the total biomass on Earth is plant life, on which animal life depends very heavily for its existence. More than 2 million species of plant and animal life have been identified to date, and estimates of the actual number of existing species range from several million to well over 50 million. The number of individual species of life is constantly in some degree of flux, with new species appearing and others ceasing to exist on a continual basis. The total number of species is presently in rapid decline.

EVOLUTION

Life, as we understand it, is currently only known to exist on the planet Earth. The origin of life is still a poorly understood process, but it is thought to have occurred about 3.9 to 3.5 billion years ago during the hadean or archaeon eons on a primordial earth that had a substantially different environment than is found at present. These life forms possessed the basic traits of self-replication and inheritable traits. Once life had appeared, the process of evolution by natural selection resulted in the formation of ever-more diverse life forms. Species that were unable to adapt to the changing environment and competition from other life forms became extinct. However, the fossil record retains evidence of many of these older species. Current fossil and DNA evidence shows that all existing species can trace a continual ancestry back to the first primitive life forms. The advent of photosynthesis in very basic forms of plant life worldwide allowed the sun's energy to be harvested to create conditions allowing for more complex life. The resultant oxygen accumulated in the atmosphere and gave rise to the ozone layer. The incorporation of smaller cells within larger ones resulted in the development of yet more complex cells called eukaryotes. Cells within colonies became increasingly specialized, resulting in true multicellular organisms. With the ozone layer absorbing harmful ultraviolet radiation, life colonized the surface of Earth.

MICROBES

The first form of life to develop on the Earth were microbes, and they remained the only form of life on the planet until about a billion years ago when multi-cellular organisms began to appear. Microorganisms are single-celled organisms that are generally smaller than the human eye can see. They include Bacteria, Fungi, Archaea and Protista.

These life forms are found in almost every location on the Earth where there is liquid water, including the interior of rocks within the planet. Their reproduction is both rapid and profuse. The combination of a high mutation rate and a horizontal gene transfer ability makes them highly adaptable, and able to survive in new environments, including outer space. They form an essential part of the planetary ecosystem. However some microorganisms are pathogenic and can post health risk to other organisms.

PLANTS AND ANIMALS

The distinction between plant and animal life is not sharply drawn, with some categories of life that stand between or across the two. Originally Aristotle divided all living things between plants, which generally do not move, and animals. In Linnaeus' system, these became the Kingdoms Vegetabilia (later Plantae) and Animalia. Since then, it has become clear that the Plantae as originally defined included several unrelated groups, and the fungi and several groups of algae were removed to new kingdoms. However, these are still often considered plants in many contexts. Bacterial life is sometimes included in flora, and some classifications use the term bacterial flora separately from plant flora.

Among the many ways of classifying plants are by regional floras, which, depending on the purpose of study, can also include fossil flora, remnants of plant life from a previous era. People in many regions and countries take great pride in their individual arrays of characteristic flora, which can vary widely across the globe due to differences in climate and terrain.

Regional floras commonly are divided into categories such as native flora and agricultural and garden flora, the latter of which are intentionally grown and cultivated. Some types of "native flora" actually have been introduced centuries ago by people migrating from one region or continent to another, and become an integral part of the native, or natural flora of the place to which they were introduced. This is an example of how human interaction with nature can blur the boundary of what is considered nature.

Another category of plant has historically been carved out for weeds. Though the term has fallen into disfavor among botanists as a formal way to categorize "useless" plants, the informal use of the word "weeds" to describe those plants that are deemed worthy of elimination is illustrative of the general tendency of people and societies to seek to alter or shape the course of nature. Similarly, animals are often categorized in ways such as domestic, farm animals, wild animals, pests, etc. according to their relationship to human life.

Animals as a category have several characteristics that generally set them apart from other living things, though not traced by scientists to having legs or wings instead of roots and leaves. Animals are eukaryotic and usually multicellular, which separates them from bacteria, archaea and most protists. They are heterotrophic, generally digesting food in an internal chamber, which separates them from plants and algae. They are also distinguished from plants, algae, and fungi by lacking cell walls.

With a few exceptions, most notably the sponges (Phylum Porifera), animals have bodies differentiated into separate tissues. These include muscles, which are able to contract and control locomotion, and a nervous system, which sends and processes signals. There is also typically an internal digestive chamber. The eukaryotic cells possessed by all animals are surrounded by a characteristic extracellular matrix composed of collagen and elastic glycoproteins. This may be calcified to form structures like shells, bones, and spicules, a framework upon which cells can move about and be reorganized during development and maturation, and which supports the complex anatomy required for mobility.

ECOSYSTEMS

All forms of life interact with the environment in which they exist, and also with other life forms. In the 20th century this premise gave rise to the concept of ecosystems, which can be defined as any situation where there is interaction between organisms and their environment.

Ecosystems are composed of a variety of abiotic and biotic components that function in an interrelated way. The structure and composition is determined by various environmental factors that are interrelated. Variations of these factors will initiate dynamic modifications to the ecosystem. Some of the more important components are: soil, atmosphere, radiation from the sun, water, and living organisms.

Each living organism has a continual relationship with every other element that makes up its environment. Within the ecosystem, species are connected and dependent upon one another in the food chain, and exchange energy and matter between themselves as well as with their environment.

Every species has limits of tolerance to factors that affect its survival, reproductive success and ability to continue to thrive and interact sustainably with the rest of its environment, which in turn may have effects on these factors for many other species or even on the whole of life. The concept of an ecosystem is thus an important subject of study, as such study provides information needed to make decisions about how human life may interact in a way that allows the various ecosystems to be sustained for future use rather than used up or otherwise rendered ineffective. For the purpose of such study, a unit of smaller size is called a microecosystem. For example, an ecosystem can be a stone and all the life under it. A macroecosystem might involve a whole ecoregion, with its drainage basin.

The following ecosystems are examples of the kinds currently under intensive study:

- "continental ecosystems", such as "forest ecosystems", "meadow ecosystems" such as steppes or savannas), or agro-ecosystems,
- systems in inland waters, such as lentic ecosystem"s such as lakes or ponds; or lotic ecosystems such as rivers,
- oceanic ecosystems.

Another classification can be made by reference to its communities, such as in the case of a human ecosystem. Regional groupings of distinctive plant and animals best adapted to the region's physical natural environment, latitude, altitude, and terrain are known as biomes. The broadest classification, today under wide study and analysis, and also subject to widespread arguments about its nature and validity, is that of the entire sum of life seen as analogous to a self-sustaining organism; a theory studied as earth system science (less formally known as Gaia theory).

HUMAN INTERRELATIONSHIP

The secluded valleys along the Na Pali Coast in Hawaii are the residence of tribes that make only small changes in the natural beauty surrounding them.

Although humans currently comprise only about one-half of one percent of the total living biomass on Earth, the human effect on nature is disproportionately large. Because of the extent of human influence, the boundaries between what we regard as nature and "made environments" is not clear cut except at the extremes. Even at the extremes, the amount of natural environment that is free of discernible human influence is presently diminishing at an increasingly rapid pace, or, according to some, has already disappeared.

The development of technology by the human race has allowed the greater exploitation of natural resources and has helped to alleviate some of the risk from natural hazards. In spite of this progress, however, the fate of human civilization remains closely linked to changes in the environment. There exists a highly complex feedback-loop between the use of advanced technology and changes to the environment that are only slowly becoming understood. Manmade threats to the Earth's natural environment include pollution, deforestation, and disasters such as oil spills. Humans have contributed to the extinction of many plants and animals.

Humans employ nature for both leisure and economic activities. The acquisition of natural resources for industrial use remains a primary component of the world's economic system. Some activities, such as hunting and fishing, are used for both sustenance and leisure, often by different people. Agriculture was first adopted around the 9th millennium BCE. Ranging from food production to energy, nature influences economic wealth.

Although early humans gathered uncultivated plant materials for food and employed the medicinal properties of vegetation for healing, most modern human use of plants is through agriculture. The clearance of large tracts of land for crop growth has led to a significant reduction in the amount available of forestation and wetlands, resulting in the loss of habitat for many plant and animal species as well as increased erosion.

WILDERNESS

Wilderness is generally defined as a natural environment on Earth that has not been directly modified by human activity. Ecologists consider wilderness areas to be an integral part of the planet's self-sustaining natural ecosystem (the biosphere). The word, "wilderness", derives from the notion of wildness; in other words that which is not controllable by humans. The word's etymology is from the Old English wildeornes, which in turn derives from wildeor meaning wild beast (wild + deor = beast, deer). From this point of view, it is the wildness of a place that makes it a wilderness. The mere presence or activity of people does not disqualify an area from being "wilderness." Many ecosystems that are, or have been, inhabited or influenced by activities of people may still be considered "wild." This way of looking at wilderness includes areas within which natural processes operate without very noticeable human interference.

Looked at through the lens of the visual arts, nature and wildness have been important subjects in various epochs of world history. An early tradition of landscape art occurred in the Tang Dynasty (618-907). The tradition of representing nature as it is became one of the aims of Chinese painting and was a significant influence in Asian art. Artists learned to depict mountains and rivers "from the perspective of nature as a whole and on the basis of their understanding of the laws of nature ... as if seen through the eyes of a bird." In the 13th century, Shih Erh Chi listed "scenes lacking any places made inaccessible by nature," as one of the 12 things to avoid in painting.

In the Western world the idea of wilderness having intrinsic value emerged in the 1800s, especially in the works of the Romantic movement. British artists John Constable and JMW Turner turned their attention to capturing the beauty of the natural world in their paintings. Before that, paintings had been primarily of religious scenes or of human beings. William Wordsworth's poetry described the wonder of the natural world, which had formerly been viewed as a threatening place. Increasingly the valuing of nature became an aspect of Western culture.

BEAUTY

Beauty in nature is a common theme in modern life and in art, and books emphasizing beauty in nature fill large sections of libraries and bookstores. That nature has been depicted and celebrated by so much art, photography, poetry and other literature shows the strength with which many people associate nature and beauty. Why this association exists, and what the association consists of, is studied by the branch of philosophy called aesthetics. Beyond certain basic characteristics that many philosophers agree about to explain what is seen as beautiful, the opinions are virtually endless.

Many scientists, who study nature in more specific and organized ways, also share the conviction that nature is beautiful; the French mathematician, Jules Henri Poincaré (1854-1912) said:

The scientist does not study nature because it is useful; he studies it because he delights in it, and he delights in it because it is beautiful.

If nature were not beautiful, it would not be worth knowing, and if nature were not worth knowing, life would not be worth living. Of course I do not here speak of that beauty which strikes the senses, the beauty of qualities and of appearance; not that I undervalue such beauty, far from it, but it has nothing to do with science; I mean that profounder beauty which comes from the harmonious order of the parts and which a pure intelligence can grasp.

A common classical idea of beautiful art involves the word mimesis, the imitation of nature. Also in the realm of ideas about beauty in nature is that the perfect is implied through symmetry, equal division, and other perfect mathematical forms and notions.

MATTER AND ENERGY

Some fields of science see nature as matter in motion, obeying certain laws of nature which science seeks to understand. For this reason the most fundamental science is generally understood to be "physics"-the name for which is still recognizable as meaning that it is the study of nature.

Matter is commonly defined as the substance of which physical objects are composed. It constitutes the observable universe. According to the theory of special relativity, there is no unchangeable distinction between matter and energy, because matter can be converted to energy, and vice versa. The visible components of the universe are now believed to compose only 4 percent of the total mass. The remainder is believed to consist of 23 percent cold dark matter and 73 percent dark energy. The exact nature of these components is still unknown and is currently under intensive investigation by physicists.

The behavior of matter and energy throughout the observable universe appears to follow well-defined physical laws. These laws have been employed to produce cosmological models that successfully explain the structure and the evolution of the universe we can observe. The mathematical expressions of the laws of physics employ a set of twenty physical constants that appear to be static across the observable universe. The values of these constants have been carefully measured, but the reason for their specific values remains a mystery.

NATURE BEYOND EARTH

Outer space, also simply called space, refers to the relatively empty regions of the universe outside the atmospheres of celestial bodies. Outer space is used to distinguish it from airspace (and terrestrial locations). There is no discrete boundary between the Earth's atmosphere and space, as the atmosphere gradually attenuates with increasing altitude. Outer space within the solar system is called interplanetary space, which passes over into interstellar space at what is known as the heliopause. Although outer space is certainly spacious, it is far from empty. Outer space is sparsely filled with several dozen organic molecules discovered to date by microwave spectroscopy, blackbody radiation left over from the big bang and the origin of the universe, and cosmic rays, which include ionized atomic nuclei and various subatomic particles. There is also some gas, plasma and dust, and small meteors. Additionally, there are signs of human life in outer space today, such as material left over from previous manned and unmanned launches which are a potential hazard to spacecraft. Some of this debris re-enters the atmosphere periodically.

The planet Earth is currently the only known body within the solar system to support life. However, current evidence suggests that in the distant past the planet Mars possessed bodies of liquid water on the surface. For a brief period in Mars' history, it may have also been capable of forming life. At present though, most of the water remaining on Mars is frozen. If life exists at all on Mars, it is most likely to be located underground where liquid water can still exist.

Conditions on the other terrestrial planets, Mercury and Venus, appears to be too harsh to support life as we know it. But it has been conjectured that Europa, the fourth-largest moon of Jupiter, may possess a sub-surface ocean of liquid water and could potentially host life.

DEVELOPMENT ANTHROPOLOGY

Development anthropology refers to the application of anthropological perspectives to the multidisciplinary branch of development studies. It take international development and international aid as primary object. In this branch of anthropology, the term development refers to the social action made voluntary by different agents (institutions, business, enterprise, state, independent volunteer) who are trying to modify the economic, technical, political or/and social life of a given place in the world, especially in developing nation.

For development anthropology, development is neither a goal, an ideal nor a failure. It is an object of study. With researches on the field, the anthropologist can describe, analyze and understand the different actions of development that took and take place in a given place. The various impacts on the local population, environment, social and economic life are to be examined.

DEVELOPMENT CRITICISM

Most of the development anthropologists severely criticize what had been done before in development effort since 1960. They blame the different agents to have only considered a small aspect of the local people's lives without analyzing the consequences on a larger scale. Again, international development is often seen in anthropology as an extension of the colonialism era or as post-colonialism. Some author, like Arturo Escobar even see international development as a means for the occident to keep control over the resources of the former colonies. In fact, between 1945 and 1960, the former colonies were going through the decolonization era, and the development plan helped to maintain dependency from the formers colonies to the old metropole. This point of view is largely supported by the dependency theory. Mainly, the development project is seen as an effort of modernization and an eradication of the indigenous culture.

Applied Anthropology in Development

On the other side, some anthropologist while contribute directly on the field to some projects development. They'll put in use their perspective of development. This method differ from economists in some areas in which this is evaluated. Economists look at aggregate measures like gross national product and per capita income, as well as measures of income distribution and inequality in a society. Anthropology can provide a more fine-grained analysis of the qualitative information behind these numbers, such as the nature of the social groups involved and the social significance of the composition of income. Thus, development anthropologists often deal with assessing the important qualitative aspects of development sometimes ignored by an economic approach.

DIFFUSION (ANTHROPOLOGY)

The diffusion of innovations within a single culture applies, for example, to the acceptance of new technological products like the wristwatch and the personal computer, foods like tomato sauce and California sushi, music styles like opera and bossa nova, dressing styles like the top hat and blue jeans, ideals like democracy or feminism, and so on.

Diffusion across cultures, too, is a well-attested and uncontroversial phenomenon. For example, the practice of agriculture is widely believed to have diffused from somewhere in the Middle East to all of Eurasia, less than 10,000 years ago, having been adopted by many pre-existing cultures. Other established examples of diffusion include the spread of the war chariot and iron smelting in ancient times, and the use of cars and Western business suits in the 20th century.

Mechanisms for Inter-cultural Diffusion

Inter-cultural diffusion can happen in many ways. Migrating populations will carry their culture with them. Ideas can be carried by trans-cultural visitors, such as merchants, explorers, soldiers, diplomats, slaves, and hired artisans.

Technology diffusion has often occurred by one society luring skilled scientists or workers by payments or other inducement. Trans-cultural marriages between two neighboring or interspersed cultures have also contributed. Among literate societies, diffusion can happen through letters or books (and, in modern times, through other media as well).

Diffusion Theories

The many models that have been proposed for inter-cultural diffusion are:

- Heliocentric diffusionism--the theory that all cultures originated from one culture.
- Culture circles diffusionism (Kulturkreise)--the theory that cultures originated from a small number of cultures.
- Evolutionary diffusionism--the theory that societies are influenced by others and that all humans share psychological traits that make them equally likely to innovate, resulting in development of similar innovations in isolation.
- Biblical diffusionism--all culture started with Adam; during the Renaissance, this theory was formalized as the great chain of being.

A concept that has often been mentioned in this regard, which may be framed in the evolutionary diffusionism model, is that of "an idea whose time has come"-whereby a new cultural item appears almost simultaneously and independently in several widely separated places, after certain prerequisite items have diffused across the respective communities.

This concept has been invoked, for example, with regard to the development of calculus by Newton and Leibnitz, or the inventions of the airplane and of the electronic computer.

The Theory Applied to Middle Ages Europe

One of the most remarkable examples of diffusion theory is the massive technology addition into Europe in the period 1000 to 1700 AD. In the prior Dark Ages period, Byzantine and Asian cultures were far more advanced than Europe: however, this era beginning in the High Middle Ages reversed that balance and resulted in a Europe which greatly surpassed Asian, Byzantine and Muslim cultures in pre-industrial technology.

In the Dark Ages, many important basic inventions had their roots elsewhere, notably: gunpowder, clock mechanisms, shipbuilding, paper and the windmill; however, in each of these cases Europeans not only adopted the technologies, but improved the manufacturing scale, inherent technology and applications to a point clearly surpassing the evolution of the original invention in its country of origin.

For example, by the late fourteenth century, European fleets. Armed with advanced cannons, decimated Arab and Chinese fleets, paving the way for unfettered domination of the seas that led to the colonial era.

Diffusion Disputes

While the concept of diffusion is well accepted in general, conjectures about the existence or the extent of diffusion in some specific contexts have been hotly disputed.

An example of such disputes is the proposal by Thor Heyerdahl that similarities between the culture of Polynesia and the pre-Columbian civilizations of the Andes are due to diffusion from the latter to the former-a theory that currently has few supporters among professional anthropologists.

Attempts to explain similarities between two cultures by diffusion are often criticized for being ethnocentric, since they imply that the supposedly "receptors" would not be capable of innovation. In fact, some authors made such claims explicitly-for example, to argue for pre-Columbian trans-oceanic contact as the "only possible explanation" for the origin of the great civilizations in the Andes and of Central America.

Those disputed are fueled in part by the overuse of cultural diffusion, starting in the late 19th century, as a blanket explanation for all similarities between widely dispersed cultures. The most famous proponent of this theory was William Graham Sumner, who argued that civilization first formed in Ancient Egypt and then diffused to other places.

Diffusion theories also suffer from being inherently speculative and hard to prove or disprove; especially for relatively simple cultural items like "pyramid-shaped buildings", "solar deity", "row of standing stones", or "animal paintings in caves". After all, the act of diffusion proper is a purely mental (or at most verbal) phenomenon, that leaves no archaeological trace.

Therefore, diffusion can be deduced with some certainty only when the similarities involve a relatively complex and partly arbitrary collection of items-such as a writing system, a complex myth, or a pantheon of several gods.

Another criticism that has been leveled at many diffusion proposals is the failure to explain why certain items were not diffused. For example, attempts to "explain" the New World civilizations by diffusion from Europe or Egypt should explain why basic concepts like wheeled vehicles or the potter's wheel did not cross the ocean, while writing and stone pyramids did.

KINSHIP

Kinship is the most basic principle of organizing individuals into social groups, roles, and categories. It was originally thought to be determined by biological descent, a view that was challenged by David M. Schneider in his work on Symbolic Kinship (1984, A Critique of The Study of Kinship).

The crux of his argument was that anthropologists had founded the domain of "kinship" on the notions of human reproduction and the biologically defined relatedness of their own Euro-American culture. Human reproduction and notions of biological relatedness cannot be presumed to structure people's social relationships in other cultural contexts.

The word kinship can refer more broadly to any emotional relationship. This can also refer to ideas which are mathematically related.

In its most general sense, kinship can be used in reference to similarity; for instance, a car is akin to a truck. In some cultures, the formal establishment of kinship involves various customs and obligations.

Anthropologists have studied different systems of kinship in a wide variety of cultures.

Many codes of ethics consider the bond of kinship as creating obligations between the related persons stronger than those between strangers, as in Confucian filial piety and the Christian injunction that charity begins at home.

10

Linguistic Anthropology

Linguistic anthropology is that branch of anthropology that brings linguistic methods to bear on anthropological problems, linking the analysis of semeiotic and particularly linguistic forms and processes (on both small and large scales) to the interpretation of sociocultural processes (again on small and large scales).

HISTORICAL DEVELOPMENT

As Duranti (2003) has noted (and the next paragraphs summarize his article), three paradigms have emerged over the history of the subdiscipline.

ANTHROPOLOGICAL LINGUISTICS

The first paradigm was originally referred to as "linguistics", although as it and its surrounding fields of study matured it came to be known as "anthropological linguistics". The field was devoted to themes unique to the subdiscipline-linguistic documentation of languages then seen as doomed to extinction (these were the languages of native North America on which the first members of the subdiscipline focused) such as:

- Grammatical description,
- Typological classification, and
- The unresolved issue of linguistic relativity (associated with Edward Sapir and Benjamin Lee Whorf but actually developed by Franz Boas and, before him, by a long line of European thinkers from Vico to Herder to Humboldt).

Dell Hymes was largely responsible for launching the second paradigm that fixed the name "linguistic anthropology" in the 1960s, though he also coined the term "ethnography of speaking" (or "ethnography of communication") to describe the agenda he envisioned for the field. It would involve taking advantage of new developments in technology, including new forms of mechanical recording.

A new unit of analysis was also introduced by Hymes. Whereas the first paradigm focused on ostensibly distinct "languages" (scare quotes indicate that contemporary linguistic anthropologists treat the concept of "a language" as an ideal construction covering up complexities within and "across" so-called linguistic boundaries), the unit of analysis in the second paradigm was new-the "speech event." (The speech event is an event defined by the speech occurring in it--a lecture, for example--so that a dinner is not a speech event, but a speech situation, a situation in which speech may or may not occur.) Much attention was devoted to speech events in which performers were held accountable for the form of their linguistic performance as such (Bauman 1977, Hymes 1981 [1975]).

Hymes also pioneered a linguistic anthropological approach to ethnopoetics.

Hymes had hoped to link linguistic anthropology more closely with the mother discipline. The name certainly stresses that the primary identity is with anthropology, whereas "anthropological linguistics" conveys a sense that the primary identity of its practitioners was with linguistics, which is a separate academic discipline on most university campuses today (not in the days of Boas and Sapir). However, Hymes' ambition in a sense backfired; the second paradigm in fact marked a further distancing of the subdiscipline from the rest of anthropology.

ANTHROPOLOGICAL ISSUES STUDIED VIA LINGUISTIC METHODS AND DATA

In the current paradigm, which has emerged since the late 1980s, instead of continuing to pursue agendas that come from a discipline alien to anthropology, linguistic anthropologists have systematically addressed themselves to problems posed by the larger discipline of anthropology-but using linguistic data and methods.

AREAS OF INTEREST

Identity: So, for example, they investigate questions of sociocultural identity *linguistically*. Linguistic anthropologist Don Kulick has done this in relation to identity, for example, in a series of settings, first in a village called Gapun in Papua New Guinea (Kulick 1992). Kulick explored how the use of two languages with and around children in Gapun village-the traditional language (Taiap) not spoken anywhere but in their own village and thus primordially "indexical" of Gapuner identity, and Tok Pisin (the widely circulating official language of New Guinea). (Linguistic anthropologists use "indexical" to mean indicative, though some indexical signs create their indexical meanings on the fly, so to speak Silverstein 1976.) To speak the Taiap language is associated with one identity-not only local but "Backward" and also an identity based on the display of *hed* (personal autonomy). To speak Tok Pisin is to index a Modern, Christian (Catholic) identity, based not on *hed* but on *save*, that is an identity linked with the will and the skill to cooperate. In later work (Kulick and Klein 2003), Kulick demonstrates that certain loud speech performances called *um escândalo*, Brazilian travesti (roughly, 'transvestite') sex workers shame clients. The travesti community, the argument goes, ends up at least making a powerful attempt to transcend the shame the larger Brazilian public might try to foist off on them-again, through loud public discourse and other modes of performance.

Socialization: Linguistic anthropologists Elinor Ochs and Bambi Schieffelin, in a remarkable series of studies (Ochs and Schieffelin 1984; Ochs 1988; Ochs and Taylor 2001; Schieffelin 1990) addressed the important anthropological topic of socialization (the process by which infants, children, and foreigners become members of a community, learning to participate in its culture), using linguistic as well as ethnographic methods. They discovered that the processes of enculturation and socialization do not occur apart from the process of language acquisition, but that children acquire language and culture together in what amounts to an integrated process. Ochs and Schieffelin demonstrated that baby talk is not universal, that the direction of adaptation (whether the child is made to adapt to the ongoing situation of speech around it or vice versa) was a variable that correlated, for example, with the direction it was held vis-a-vis a caregiver's body. In many societies caregivers hold a child facing outward so as to orient it to a network of kin whom it must learn to recognize early in life.

Ochs and Schieffelin demonstrated that members of all societies socialize children both to and through the use of language. Ochs and Taylor uncovered how, through naturally occurring stories told during dinners in white middle class households in southern California, both mothers and fathers participated in replicating male dominance (the "father knows best" syndrome) by the distribution of participant roles such as protagonist (often a child but sometimes mother and almost never the father) and "problematizer" (often the father, who raised uncomfortable questions or challenged the competence of the protagonist). When mothers collaborated with children to get their stories told they unwittingly set themselves up to be subject to this process.

Schieffelin's more recent research (1995, 2000, 2002, 2006) has uncovered the socializing role of pastors and other fairly new Bosavi converts in the Southern Highlands, Papua New Guinea community she studies. Pastors have introduced new ways of conveying knowledge-i.e. new linguistic epistemic markers (1995)-and new ways of speaking about time (2002). And they have struggled with and largely resisted those parts of the Bible that speak of being able to know the inner states of others (e.g. the gospel of Mark, chapter 2, verses 6-8; Schieffelin 2006).

IDEOLOGIES

In a third example of the current (third) paradigm, since Roman Jakobson's student, Michael Silverstein (1979) opened the way, there has been an efflorescence of work done by linguistic anthropologists on the major anthropological theme of ideologies-in this case "linguistic ideologies," sometimes defined as "shared bodies of commonsense notions about the nature of language in the world" (Rumsey 1990:346). Silverstein (1985) has demonstrated that these ideologies are not mere false consciousness but actually influence the evolution of linguistic structures, including the dropping of "thee" and "thou" from everyday English usage. Woolard (2004), in her overview of "code switching," or the systematic practice of alternating linguistic varieties within a conversation or even a single utterance, finds the underlying question anthropologists ask of the practice-Why do they do that?-reflects a dominant linguistic ideology. It is the ideology that people should "really" be monoglot and efficiently targeted toward referential clarity rather than diverting themselves with the messiness of multiple varieties in play at a single time.

Attitudes toward codes such as Spanish and English in the U.S. are certainly informed by linguistic ideologies. This extends to the widespread impression, created by statements such as that by U.S. Senator Lamar Alexander, Republican of Tennessee (in regards to a recently passed measure making English the "official" language of the U.S.), that English is "part of our blood." To Horwitz, this invocation of blood implies that English reflects the deepest vein of the nation's ancestry, i.e., the oldest language spoken in what is now the United States. Such a claim, if made openly, would be doubly absurd, ignoring a) all of the Native American languages severely impacted by the arrival of Europeans, but also b) Spanish, the language of a rather sizable number of European explorers and settlers across the length and breadth of what is now the United States (Horwitz 2006). Thus Alexander is attempting to "naturalize" language and national identity via the metaphor of "blood."

Much research on linguistic ideologies probes subtler influences on language, such as the pull exerted on Tewa-a Kiowa-Tanoan language spoken in certain New Mexico Pueblos as well as on the Hopi Reservation in Arizona.

Social spaces: In a final example of this third paradigm, a group of linguistic anthropologists has done very creative work on the idea of social space. Duranti published a ground breaking article on Samoan greetings and their use and transformation of social space (1992). Prior to that, Indonesianist Joseph

Errington (1988)-making use of earlier work by Indonesianists not necessarily concerned with language issues per se-brought linguistic anthropological methods (and semeiotic theory) to bear on the notion of the "exemplary center," or the center of political and ritual power from which emanated exemplary behavior. Errington demonstrated how the Javanese *priyayi*, whose ancestors served at the Javanese royal courts, became emissaries, so to speak, long after those courts had ceased to exist, representing throughout Java the highest example of 'refined speech.' The work of Joel Kuipers further develops this theme vis-a-vis on the island of Sumba, Indonesia. And, even though it pertains to Tewa Indians in Arizona rather than Indonesians, Paul Kroskrity's argument that speech forms originating in the Tewa kiva (or underground ceremonial space) forms the dominant model for all Tewa speech can be seen as a rather direct parallel.

Silverstein (2004) tries to find the maximum theoretical significance and applicability in this idea of exemplary centers. He feels, in fact, that the exemplary center idea is one of linguistic anthropology's three most important findings. He generalizes the notion in the following manner, arguing that "there are wider-scale institutional 'orders of interactionality,' historically contingent yet structured. Within such large-scale, macrosocial orders, in-effect ritual centers of semiosis come to exert a structuring, value-conferring influence on any particular event of discursive interaction with respect to the meanings and significance of the verbal and other semeiotic forms used in it" (2004: 623; compare Wilce in press). Current approaches to such classic anthropological topics as ritual by linguistic anthropologists emphasize not static linguistic structures but the unfolding in realtime of a "'hypertrophic' set of parallel orders of iconicity and indexicality that seem to cause the ritual to create its own sacred space through what appears, often, to be the magic of textual and nontextual metricalizations, synchronized".

LINGUISTICS

Linguistics is the scientific study of language. Someone who engages in this study is called a linguist. Linguistics can be theoretical or applied. Theoretical (or general) linguistics encompasses a number of sub-fields, such as the study of language structure (grammar), and meaning (semantics). The study of grammar encompasses morphology (formation and alteration of words) and syntax (the rules that determine the way words combine into phrases and sentences). Phonology, the study of sound systems and abstract sound units, and phonetics, which is concerned with the actual properties of speech sounds (phones) as well as those of non-speech sounds, and how they are produced and perceived, also form part of this field.

Linguistics compares languages (comparative linguistics) and explores their histories, in order to find universal properties of language and to account for its development and origins (historical linguistics).

Applied linguistics puts linguistic theories into practice in areas such as foreign language teaching, speech therapy, translation and speech pathology.

Linguistic inquiry is pursued by a wide variety of specialists, who may not all be in harmonious agreement; as Russ Rymer put it:

- Linguistics is arguably the most hotly contested property in the academic realm. It is soaked with the blood of poets, theologians, philosophers, philologists, psychologists, biologists, anthropologists, and neurologists, along with whatever blood can be got out of grammarians.

DIVISIONS, SPECIALTIES, AND SUBFIELDS

The central concern of theoretical linguistics is to characterize the nature of human language ability, or competence: to explain what it is that an individual knows when said to know a language; and to explain how it is that individuals come to know languages.

All humans (setting aside extremely pathological cases) achieve competence in whatever language is spoken (or signed, in the case of sign language) around them when they are growing up, with apparently little need for conscious instruction. Non-humans do not. Therefore, there is some basic innate property of humans that causes them to be able to use language. There is no discernible genetic process responsible for differences between languages: an individual will acquire whatever language(s) they are exposed to as a child, regardless of their parentage or ethnic origin.

Linguistic structures are pairings of meaning and sound (or other externalization). Linguists may specialize in some subpart of the linguistic structure, which can be arranged in the following terms, from sound to meaning:

- Phonetics, the study of the sounds of human language
- Phonology (or phonemics), the study of patterns of a language's basic sounds
- Morphology, the study of the internal structure of words
- Syntax, the study of how words combine to form grammatical sentences
- Semantics, the study of the meaning of words (lexical semantics) and fixed word combinations (phraseology), and how these combine to form the meanings of sentences
- Pragmatics, the study of how utterances are used (literally, figuratively, or otherwise) in communicative acts
- Discourse analysis, the study of sentences organised into texts

Many linguists would agree that the divisions overlap considerably, but the independent significance of each of these areas is not universally acknowledged. Regardless of any particular linguist's position, each area has core concepts that foster significant scholarly inquiry and research. Intersecting with these specialty domains are fields arranged around the kind of external factors that are considered. For example:

- Language acquisition, the study of how language is acquired
- Historical linguistics or Diachronic linguistics, the study of languages whose historical relations are recognizable through similarities in vocabulary, word formation, and syntax

- Psycholinguistics, the study of the cognitive processes and representations underlying language use
- Sociolinguistics, the study of social patterns of linguistic variability
- Clinical linguistics, the application of linguistic theory to the area of Speech-Language Pathology
- Neurolinguistics, the study of the brain networks that underly grammar and communication
- Biolinguistics, the study of natural as well as human taught communication systems in animals compared to human language
- Computational linguistics, the study of computational implementations of linguistics structures
- Applied linguistics, the study of language related issues applied in every day life, notably language policies and language education.

VARIATIONS IN LANGUAGES

A substantial part of linguistic investigation is into the nature of the differences among the languages of the world. The nature of variation is very important to an understanding of human linguistic ability in general: if human linguistic ability is very narrowly constrained by biological properties of the species, then languages must be very similar. If human linguistic ability is unconstrained, then languages might vary greatly.

But there are different ways to interpret similarities among languages. For example, the Latin language spoken by the Romans developed into Spanish in Spain and Italian in Italy. Similarities between Spanish and Italian are in many cases due to both being descended from Latin. So in principle, if two languages share some property, this property might either be due to common inheritance or due to some property of the human language faculty. Of course, there is always the possibility of random chance being at the root of the similarity, such as with Spanish 'mucho' and English 'much', which are not related historically in any way, though they mean essentially the same thing and sound similar.

Often, the possibility of common inheritance can be essentially ruled out. Given the fact that learning language comes quite easily to humans, it can be assumed that languages have been spoken at least as long as there have been biologically modern humans, probably at least fifty thousand years. Independent measures of language change (for example, comparing the language of ancient texts to the daughter languages spoken today) suggest that change is rapid enough to make it impossible to reconstruct a language that was spoken so long ago; as a consequence of this, common features of languages spoken in different parts of the world are not normally taken as evidence for common ancestry.

Even more striking, there are documented cases of sign languages being developed in communities of congenitally deaf people who could not have been exposed to spoken language. The properties of these sign languages have been shown to conform generally to many of the properties of spoken languages, strengthening the hypothesis that those properties are not due to common ancestry but to more general characteristics of the way languages are learned.

Loosely speaking, the collection of properties, which all languages share, can be referred to as "universal grammar" (or UG), which is a much debated topic. Linguists and non-linguists also use this term in several different ways.

Universal properties of language may be partly due to universal aspects of human experience; for example all humans experience water, and the fact that all human languages have a word for water is probably not unrelated to this fact. The challenging questions regarding universal grammar generally require one to control this factor. Clearly, experience is part of the process by which individuals learn languages. But experience by itself is not enough, since animals raised around people learn extremely little human language, if any at all.

A more interesting example is this: suppose that all human languages distinguish nouns from verbs (this is generally believed to be true). This would require a more sophisticated explanation, since nouns and verbs do not exist in the world, apart from languages that make use of them.

In general, a property of UG could be due to general properties of human cognition, or due to some property of human cognition that is specific to language. Too little is understood about human cognition in general to allow a meaningful distinction to be made. As a result, generalizations are often stated in theoretical linguistics without a stand being taken on whether the generalization could have some bearing on other aspects of cognition.

PROPERTIES OF LANGUAGE

It has been understood since the time of the ancient Greeks that languages tend to be organized around grammatical categories such as noun and verb, nominative and accusative, or present and past. The vocabulary and grammar of a language are organized around these fundamental categories.

In addition to making substantial use of discrete categories, language has the important property that it organizes elements into recursive structures; this allows, for example, a noun phrase to contain another noun phrase (as in the chimpanzee's lips) or a clause to contain a clause (as in I think that it's raining). Though recursion in grammar was implicitly recognized much earlier (for example by Jespersen), the importance of this aspect of language was only fully realized after the 1957 publication of Noam Chomsky's book Syntactic Structures, which presented a formal grammar of a fragment of English. Prior to this, the most detailed descriptions of linguistic systems were of phonological or morphological systems, which tend to be closed and admit little creativity.

Chomsky used a context-free grammar augmented with transformations. Since then, context-free grammars have been written for substantial fragments of various languages (for example GPSG, for English), but it has been demonstrated that human languages include cross-serial dependencies, which cannot be handled adequately by Context-free grammars. This requires increased power, for example transformations.

An example of a natural-language clause involving a cross-serial dependency is the Dutch.

Ik denk dat Jan Piet de kinderen zag helpen zwemmen.

I think that Jan Piet the children saw help swim.

'I think that Jan saw Piet help the children swim'.

The important point is that the noun phrases before the verb cluster (Jan, Piet, de kinderen) are identified with the verbs in the verb cluster (zag, helpen, zwemmen) in left-right order.

This means that natural language formalisms must be relatively powerful in terms of generative capacity. The models currently used (LFG, HPSG, Minimalism) are very powerful, in general too powerful to be computationally tractable in principle. Implementations of them are scaled down.

DETAILS ON SELECTED DIVISIONS AND SUBFIELDS

Contextual linguistics

Contextual linguistics may include the study of linguistics in interaction with other academic disciplines. While in core theoretical linguistics language is studied independently, the interdisciplinary areas of linguistics consider how language interacts with the rest of the world.

Sociolinguistics, anthropological linguistics, and linguistic anthropology are social sciences that consider the interactions between linguistics and society as a whole.

Critical discourse analysis is where rhetoric and philosophy interact with linguistics.

Psycholinguistics and neurolinguistics combine medical science and linguistics.

Other cross-disciplinary areas of linguistics include language acquisition, evolutionary linguistics, computational linguistics and cognitive science.

APPLIED LINGUISTICS

Theoretical linguistics is concerned with finding and describing generalities both within particular languages and among all languages. Applied linguistics takes the results of those findings and applies them to other areas. Often applied linguistics refers to the use of linguistic research in language teaching, but results of linguistic research are used in many other areas, as well.

Many areas of applied linguistics today involve the explicit use of computers. Speech synthesis and speech recognition use phonetic and phonemic knowledge to provide voice interfaces to computers. Applications of computational linguistics in machine translation, computer-assisted translation, and natural language processing are extremely fruitful areas of applied linguistics which have come to the forefront in recent years with increasing computing power. Their influence has had a great effect on theories of syntax and semantics, as modelling syntactic and semantic theories on computers constrains the theories to computable operations and provides a more rigorous mathematical basis.

DIACHRONIC LINGUISTICS

Whereas the core of theoretical linguistics is concerned with studying languages at a particular point in time (usually the present), diachronic linguistics examines how language changes through time, sometimes over centuries. Historical linguistics enjoys both a rich history (the study of linguistics grew out of historical linguistics) and a strong theoretical foundation for the study of language change.

In universities in the United States, the non-historic perspective seems to have the upper hand. Many introductory linguistics classes, for example, cover historical linguistics only cursorily. The shift in focus to a non-historic perspective started with Saussure and became predominant with Noam Chomsky.

Explicitly historical perspectives include historical-comparative linguistics and etymology.

PRESCRIPTION AND DESCRIPTION

Research currently performed under the name "linguistics" is purely descriptive; linguists seek to clarify the nature of language without passing value judgements or trying to chart future language directions. Nonetheless, there are many professionals and amateurs who also prescribe rules of language, holding a particular standard out for all to follow.

Prescriptivists tend to be found among the ranks of language educators and journalists, and not in the actual academic discipline of linguistics. They hold clear notions of what is right and wrong, and may assign themselves the responsibility of ensuring that the next generation use the variety of language that is most likely to lead to "success," often the acrolect of a particular language. The reasons for their intolerance of "incorrect usage" may include distrust of neologisms, connections to socially-disapproved dialects (i.e., basilects), or simple conflicts with pet theories. An extreme version of prescriptivism can be found among censors, whose personal mission is to eradicate words and structures which they consider to be destructive to society.

Descriptivists, on the other hand, do not accept the prescriptivists' notion of "incorrect usage." They might describe the usages the other has in mind simply as "idiosyncratic," or they may discover a regularity (a rule) that the usage in question follows (in contrast to the common prescriptive assumption that "bad" usage is unsystematic). Within the context of fieldwork, descriptive linguistics refers to the study of language using a descriptivist approach. Descriptivist methodology more closely resembles scientific methodology in other disciplines.

SPEECH VERSUS WRITING

Most contemporary linguists work under the assumption that spoken language is more fundamental, and thus more important to study than written language. Reasons for this perspective include:

- Speech appears to be a human universal, whereas there have been many cultures and speech communities that lack written communication;
- People learn to speak and process spoken languages more easily and much earlier than writing;
- A number of cognitive scientists argue that the brain has an innate "language module", knowledge of which is thought to come more from studying speech than writing, particularly since language as speech is held to be an evolutionary adaptation, whereas writing is a comparatively recent invention.

Of course, linguists agree that the study of written language can be worthwhile and valuable. For linguistic research that uses the methods of corpus linguistics and computational linguistics, written language is often much more convenient for processing large amounts of linguistic data. Large corpora of spoken language are difficult to create and hard to find, and are typically transcribed and written. Additionally, linguists have turned to text-based discourse occurring in various formats of computer-mediated communication as a viable site for linguistic inquiry.

The study of writing systems themselves is in any case considered a branch of linguistics.

HISTORY OF LINGUISTICS

Early Indian Vedic texts (Rig Veda 1:164:45; 4:58:3; 10:125) suggest a structure for languages: Language is composed of sentences with four stages of evolution that are expressed in three tenses (past, present and future). The sentences are composed of words that have two distinct forms of existence (vocal form, the word, and perceptional form, the meaning). These words are recognized mainly as verbs that represent real world acts and nouns that take on seven* cases (depending on their mode of participation in real world acts). (*The number, seven, here is not very critical; the message is that the nouns are inflected into appropriate cases to indicate their mode of participation in concerned acts).

The Sanskrit grammarian Panini (c. 520-460 BC) is the earliest known linguist and is often acknowledged as the founder of linguistics. He is most famous for formulating the 3,959 rules of Sanskrit morphology in the text Arnadhyayi, which is still in use today. Panini's grammar of Sanskrit is highly systematised and technical.

Inherent in its analytic approach are the concepts of the phoneme, the morpheme and the root, only recognized by Western linguists some two millennia later. His rules fully describe Sanskrit morphology without any redundancy. A consequence of his grammar's focus on brevity is its highly unintuitive structure, reminiscent of contemporary "machine language" (as opposed to "human readable" programming languages). His sophisticated logical rules and technique have been widely influential in ancient and modern linguistics.

Bhartrihari (c. 450-510) was another important author on Indic linguistic theory. He theorized the act of speech as being made up of four stages: first, conceptualization of an idea, second, its verbalization and sequencing and third, delivery of speech into atmospheric air, all these by the speaker and last, the comprehension of speech by the listener, the interpreter.

The work of Panini, and the later Indian linguist Bhartrihari, had a significant influence on many of the foundational ideas proposed by Ferdinand de Saussure, professor of Sanskrit, who is widely considered the father of modern structural linguistics.

In the Middle East, the Persian linguist Sibawayh made a detailed and professional description of Arabic in 760, in his monumental work, Al-kitab fi al-nahw, bringing many linguistic aspects of language to light. In his book he distinguished phonetics from phonology.

Other early scholars of linguistics include Jakob Grimm, who devised the principle of consonantal shifts in pronunciation known as Grimm's Law in 1822, Karl Verner, who discovered Verner's Law, August Schleicher who created the "Stammbaumtheorie" and Johannes Schmidt who developed the "Wellentheorie" ("wave model") in 1872.

Ferdinand de Saussure was the founder of modern structural linguistics. Edward Sapir, a leader in American structural linguistics, was one of the first who explored the relations between language studies and anthropology. His methodology had strong influence on all his successors. Noam Chomsky's formal model of language, transformational-generative grammar, developed under the influence of his teacher Zellig Harris, who was in turn strongly influenced by Leonard Bloomfield, has been the dominant model since the 1960s.

Chomsky remains by far the most influential linguist in the world today. Linguists working in frameworks such as Head-Driven Phrase Structure Grammar (HPSG) or Lexical Functional Grammar (LFG) stress the importance of formalization and formal rigor in linguistic description, and may distance themselves somewhat from Chomsky's more recent work (the "Minimalist" program for Transformational grammar), connecting more closely to earlier work of Chomsky's. Linguists working in Optimality Theory state generalizations in terms of violable rules, which is a greater departure from mainstream linguistics, and linguists working in various kinds of functional grammar and Cognitive Linguistics tend to stress the non-autonomy of linguistic knowledge and the non-universality of linguistic structures, thus departing importantly from the Chomskyan paradigm.

ETHNOGRAPHY

Ethnography is the genre of writing that presents varying degrees of qualitative and quantitative descriptions of human social phenomena, based on fieldwork. Ethnography presents the results of a holistic research method founded on the idea that a system's properties cannot necessarily be accurately understood independently of each other. The genre has both formal and historical connections to travel writing and colonial office reports. Several academic traditions, in particular the constructivist and relativist paradigms, claim ethnographic research as a valid research method.

Cultural and Social Anthropology

Cultural anthropology and social anthropology were developed around ethnographic research and their canonical texts are mostly ethnographies: e.g. Argonauts of the Western Pacific by Bronislaw Malinowski, The Nuer by E. E. Evans-Pritchard, Coming of Age in Samoa by Margaret Mead, or Naven by Gregory Bateson. Cultural & social anthropologists today place such a high value on actually doing ethnographic research that ethnology-the comparative synthesis of ethnographic information-is rarely the foundation for a career. Within cultural anthropology, there are several sub-genres of ethnography. Beginning in the late 1950s and early 1960s, anthropologists began writing "confessional" ethnographies that intentionally exposed the nature of ethnographic research. Famous examples include Tristes Tropiques by Claude Lévi-Strauss, The High Valley by Kenneth Read, and The Savage and the Innocent by David Maybury-Lewis, as well as the mildly fictionalized Return to Laughter by Elenore Smith Bowen

(Laura Bohannan). Later "reflexive" ethnographies refined the technique to translate cultural differences by representing their effects on the ethnographer. Famous examples include "Deep Play: Notes on a Balinese Cockfight" by Clifford Geertz, Reflections on Fieldwork in Morocco by Paul Rabinow, The Headman and I by Jean-Paul Dumont, and Tuhami by Vincent Crapanzano.

In the 1980s, the rhetoric of ethnography was subjected to intense scrutiny within the discipline, under the general influence of literary theory and post-colonial/post-structuralist thought. "Experimental" ethnographies that reveal the ferment of the discipline include Shamanism, Colonialism, and the Wild Man by Michael Taussig, Debating Muslims by Michael F. J. Fischer and Mehdi Abedi, A Space on the Side of the Road by Kathleen Stewart, and Advocacy after Bhopal by Kim Fortun.

Cultural anthropologists, such as Clifford Geertz and Xavier Andrade, study and interpret cultural diversity through ethnography based on field work. It provides an account of a particular culture, society, or community. The fieldwork usually involves spending a year or more in another society, living with the local people and learning about their ways of life. Ethnographers are participant observers. They take part in events they study because it helps with understanding local behavior and thought.

Other related Fields

Sociology and cultural studies also produce ethnography. Urban sociology and the Chicago School in particular are associated with ethnographic research, although some of the most well-known examples (including Street Corner Society by William Foote Whyte and Black Metropolis by St. Clair Drake and Horace R. Caton) were influenced by an anthropologist, Lloyd Warner, who happened to be in the sociology department at Chicago, and by sociologist Robert Park whose earlier career had included journalism. Symbolic interactionism developed from the same tradition and yielded several excellent sociological ethnographies, including Shared Fantasy by Gary Alan Fine, which documents the early history of fantasy role-playing games. But even though many sub-fields and theoretical perspectives within sociology use ethnographic methods, ethnography is not the sine qua non of the discipline, as it is in cultural anthropology.

Education, Ethnomusicology, Performance Studies, Folklore, and Linguistics are others fields which have made extensive use of ethnography. The American anthropologist George Spindler (Stanford University) was a pioneer in applying ethnographic methodology to the classroom. James Spradley is another well-known ethnographer, especially for his book, The Ethnographic Interview, published in 1979. Ethnographic methods have been used to study business settings. Groups of workers, managers and so on are different social categories participating in common social systems. Each group shows different characteristic attitudes, behavior patterns and values. Increasingly, universities (such as the University of Illinois at Urbana-Champaign) are using ethnographic methods as a technique to encourage undergraduate research in the humanities. For example, the Ethnography of the University (EOTU) program sponsors undergraduate research on UIUC and archives it in web-accessible form for the UIUC community. EOTU also functions as a learning group for students, staff, and faculty interested in what it means to conduct research on universities as institutions.

Anthropologists like Daniel Miller and Mary Douglas have used ethnographic data to answer academic questions about consumers and consumption. Businesses, too, have found ethnographers helpful for understanding how people use products and services, as indicated in the increasing use of ethnographic methods to understand consumers and consumption, or for new product development (sometimes called 'design ethnography'). The recent Ethnographic Praxis in Industry (EPIC) conference is evidence of this. Ethnographers' systematic and holistic approach to real-life experience is valued by product developers, who use the method to understand unstated desires or cultural practices that surround products. Where focus groups fail to inform marketers about what people really do, ethnography links what people say to what they actually do-avoiding the pitfalls that come from relying only on self-reported, focus-group data.

11

Archaeology

Archaeology, archeology, or archæology is the study of human cultures through the recovery, documentation and analysis of material remains and environmental data, including architecture, artifacts, biofacts, human remains, and landscapes.

The goals of archaeology are to document and explain the origins and development of human culture, understand culture history, chronicle cultural evolution, and study human behavior and ecology, for both prehistoric and historic societies. It is considered in North America to be one of the four sub-fields of anthropology.

Archaeology is the study of human culture through material remains from humans in the past. In the Old World, archaeology has tended to focus on the study of physical remains, the methods used in recovering them and the theoretical and philosophical underpinnings in achieving the subject's goals. The discipline's roots in antiquarianism and the study of Latin and Ancient Greek provided it with a natural affinity with the field of history. In the United States and, increasingly, in other parts of the world, archaeology is more commonly devoted to the study of human societies and is regarded as one of the four branches of anthropology. The other three branches are cultural anthropology, which studies behavioural, symbolic, and material dimensions of culture; linguistics, which studies language, including the origins of language and language groups; and physical anthropology, which includes the study of human evolution and physical and genetic characteristics. Other disciplines also supplement archaeology, including paleontology, paleozoology, paleoethnobotany, paleobotany, geography, geology, art history, and classics. Archaeology has been described as a craft that enlists the sciences to illuminate the humanities. According to American archaeologist Walter Taylor in A Study of Archeology (American Anthropological Association 1948), "Archaeology is neither history nor anthropology. As an autonomous discipline, it consists of a method and a set of specialised techniques for the gathering, or 'production' of cultural information".

Archaeology is an approach to understanding human culture through its material remains regardless of chronology. In England, archaeologists have uncovered the long-lost layouts of medieval villages abandoned after the crises of the 14th century and the equally lost layouts of 17th century parterre gardens swept away by a change in fashion. In downtown New York City archaeologists have exhumed the 18th century remains of the Black burial ground. Traditional archaeology is viewed as the study of pre-historical human cultures, that is, cultures that existed before the development of writing for that culture. Historical archaeology is the study of cultures with some form of writing.

In the study of relatively recent cultures by Western scholars, archaeology is closely allied with ethnography. This is the case in large parts of North America, Oceania, Siberia, and other places where the study of archaeology mingles with the living traditions of the cultures being studied. Kennewick Man is an example of archaeology interacting with modern culture. In the study of cultures that were literate or had literate neighbours, history and archaeology supplement one another for broader understanding of the complete cultural context, as at Hadrian's Wall.

IMPORTANCE AND APPLICABILITY

Often archaeology provides the only means to learn of the existence and behaviors of people in the past. Many thousands of cultures and societies and millions of people have come and gone across the millennia of which there simply is little or no written record-no history-or for which written records may be misrepresentative or incomplete. Writing as it is known and understood today did not exist anywhere in the world until about 5000 years ago, and only spread among a relatively small number of technologically advanced civilisations. In contrast Homo sapiens have existed for at least 200,000 years, and other species of Homo for millions of years. These civilisations are, not coincidentally, the best-known; they have been open to the inquiry of historians for centuries, while the study of prehistoric cultures has arisen only recently. Even within a civilisation that is literate at some levels, many important human practices are not officially recorded. Any knowledge of the formative early years of human civilisation-the development of agriculture, cult practices of folk religion, the rise of the first cities-must come from archaeology.

Even where written records do exist, they are invariably incomplete or biased to some extent. In many societies, literacy was restricted to the elite classes, such as the clergy or the bureaucracy of court or temple. The literacy even of an aristocracy has sometimes been restricted to deeds and contracts. The interests and world-view of elites are often quite different from the lives and interests of the rest of the populace. Writings that were produced by people more representative of the general population were unlikely to find their way into libraries and be preserved there for posterity. Thus, written records tend to reflect the biases, assumptions, cultural values and possibly deceptions of a limited range of individuals, usually only a fraction of the larger population. As such, written records cannot be trusted as a sole source. The material record is nearer to a fair representation of society, though it is subject to its own inaccuracies, such as sampling bias and differential preservation.

In addition to their scientific importance, archaeological remains sometimes have political significance to descendants of the people who produced them, monetary value to collectors, or simply strong aesthetic appeal. Many people identify archaeology with the recovery of such aesthetic, religious, political, or economic treasures rather than with the reconstruction of past societies.

This view is often espoused in works of popular fiction, such as Raiders of the Lost Ark, The Mummy, and King Solomon's Mines. When such unrealistic subjects are treated more seriously, accusations of pseudoscience are invariably levelled at their proponents. However, these endeavours, real and fictional, are not representative of the modern state of archaeology.

GOALS

There is still a tremendous emphasis in the practice of archaeology on field techniques and methodologies. These include the tasks of surveying areas in order to find new sites, excavating sites in order to unearth the cultural remains therein, and classification and preservation techniques in order to analyse and keep these remains. Every phase of this process can be a source of information.

The academic goals of archaeology are not universally agreed upon, and there are at least three broad, distinct theories of exactly what archaeological research should do. Nevertheless, there is much common ground.

ACADEMIC SUB-DISCIPLINES

As with most academic disciplines, there are a very large number of archaeological sub-disciplines characterised by a specific method or type of material (e.g. lithic analysis, music, archaeobotany), geographical or chronological focus (e.g. Near Eastern archaeology, Medieval archaeology), other thematic concern (e.g. maritime archaeology, landscape archaeology, battlefield archaeology), or a specific archaeological culture or civilisation (e.g. Egyptology).

CULTURAL RESOURCES MANAGEMENT

Cultural resources management (CRM) (also called heritage management in Britain) is a branch of archaeology that accounts for most research done in the United States and much of that in western Europe as well. In the United States, CRM archaeology has been a growing concern since the passage of the National Historic Preservation Act of 1966 and most of the archaeology done in that country today proceeds from either direct or related requirements of that measure. In the United States, the vast majority of taxpayers, scholars, and politicians believe that CRM has helped to preserve much of that nation's history and prehistory that would have otherwise been lost in the expansion of cities, dams, and highways. Along with other statutes, this mandates that no construction project on public land or involving public funds may damage an unstudied archaeological site.

The application of CRM in the United Kingdom is not limited to government-funded projects. Since 1990 PPG 16 has required planners to consider archaeology as a material consideration in determining applications for new development. As a result, numerous archaeological organisations undertake mitigation work in advance of (or during) construction work in archaeologically sensitive areas, at the developer's expense.

Among the goals of CRM are the identification, preservation, and maintenance of cultural sites on public and private lands, and the removal of culturally valuable materials from areas where they would otherwise be destroyed by human activity, such as proposed construction. This study involves at least a cursory examination to determine whether or not any significant archaeological sites are present in the area affected by the proposed construction. If these do exist, time and money must be allotted for their excavation. If initial survey and/or test excavation indicates the presence of an extraordinarily valuable site, the construction may be prohibited entirely. CRM is a thriving entity, especially in the United States and Europe where archaeologists from private companies and all levels of government engage in the practice of their discipline.

Cultural resources management has, however, been criticized. CRM is conducted by private companies that bid for projects by submitting proposals outlining the work to be done and an expected budget. It is not unheard-of for the agency responsible for the construction to simply choose the proposal that asks for the least funding. CRM archaeologists face considerable time pressure, often being forced to complete their work in a fraction of the time that might be allotted for a purely scholarly endeavour. Compounding the time pressure is the vetting process of site reports which are required (in the US) to be submitted by CRM firms to the appropriate State Historic Preservation Office (SHPO). From the SHPO's perspective there is to be no difference between a report submitted by a CRM firm operating under a deadline, and a multi-year academic project. The end result is that for a Cultural Resource Management archaeologist to be successful, they must be able to produce academic quality documents at a corporate world pace.

The annual ratio of open academic archaeology positions (inclusive of Post-Doc, temporary, and non tenure track appointments) to the annual number of archaeology MA/MSc and PhD students is grossly disproportionate. This dearth of academic positions causes a predictable excess of well educated individuals who join the ranks of the following year's crop of non-academically employed archaeologists. Cultural Resource Management, once considered an intellectual backwater for individuals with "strong backs and weak minds" has reaped the benefit of this massive pool of well educated professionals. This results in CRM offices increasingly staffed by advance degreed individuals with a track record of producing scholarly articles but who have the notches on their trowels to show they have been in the trenches as a shovelbum.

FIELD METHODS

Survey

A modern archaeological project often begins with a survey. Regional survey is the attempt to systematically locate previously unknown sites in a region. Site survey is the attempt to systematically locate features of interest, such as houses and middens, within a site. Each of these two goals may be accomplished with largely the same methods.

Survey was not widely practiced in the early days of archaeology. Cultural historians and prior researchers were usually content with discovering the locations of monumental sites from the local populace, and excavating only the plainly visible features there. Gordon Willey pioneered the technique of regional settlement pattern survey in 1949 in the Viru Valley of coastal Peru, and survey of all levels became prominent with the rise of processual archaeology some years later.

Survey work has many benefits if performed as a preliminary exercise to, or even in place of, excavation. It requires relatively little time and expense, because it does not require processing large volumes of soil to search out artifacts. (Nevertheless, surveying a large region or site can be expensive, so archaeologists often employ sampling methods.) It avoids ethical issues (of particular concern to descendant peoples) associated with destroying a site through excavation. It is the only way to gather some forms of information, such as settlement patterns and settlement structure. Survey data are commonly assembled into maps, which may show surface features and/or artifact distribution.

The simplest survey technique is surface survey. It involves combing an area, usually on foot but sometimes with the use of mechanised transport, to search for features or artifacts visible on the surface. Surface survey cannot detect sites or features that are completely buried under earth, or overgrown with vegetation. Surface survey may also include mini-excavation techniques such as augers, corers, and shovel test pits.

Aerial survey is conducted using cameras attached to aircraft, balloons, or even kites. A bird's-eye view is useful for quick mapping of large or complex sites. Ariel photographs are used to document the status of the archaeological dig. Aerial imaging can also detect many things not visible from the surface. Plants growing above a buried man made structure, such as a stone wall, will develop more slowly, while those above other types of features (such as middens) may develop more rapidly. Photographs of ripening grain, which changes colour rapidly at maturation, have revealed buried structures with great precision. Aerial photographs taken at different times of day will help show the outlines of structures by changes in shadows. Aerial survey also employs infrared, ground-penetrating radar wavelengths, and thermography.

Archaeological geophysics can be the most effective way to see beneath the ground. Magnetometers detect minute deviations in the Earth's magnetic field caused by iron artifacts, kilns, some types of stone structures, and even ditches and middens. Devices that measure the electrical resistivity of the soil are also widely used. Most soils are moist below the surface, which gives them a relatively low resistivity. Features such as hard-packed floors or concentrations of stone have a higher resistivity.

Although some archaeologists consider the use of metal detectors to be tantamount to treasure hunting, others deem them an effective tool in archaeological surveying. Examples of formal archaeological use of metal detectors include musketball distribution analysis on English Civil War battlefields, metal distribution analysis prior to excavation of a nineteenth century ship wreck, and service cable location during evaluation. Metal detectorists have also contributed to the archaeological record where they have made detailed records of their results and refrained from raising artifacts from their archaeological context. In the UK, metal detectorists have been solicited for involvement in the Portable Antiquities Scheme.

Regional survey in underwater archaeology uses geophysical or remote sensing devices such as marine magnetometer, side-scan sonar, or sub-bottom sonar.

EXCAVATION

Archaeological excavation existed even when the field was still the domain of amateurs, and it remains the source of the majority of data recovered in most field projects. It can reveal several types of information usually not accessible to survey, such as stratigraphy, three-dimensional structure, and verifiably primary context.

Modern excavation techniques require that the precise locations of objects and features, known as their provenance or provenience, be recorded. This always involves determining their horizontal locations, and sometimes vertical position as well. Similarly, their association, or relationship with nearby objects and features, needs to be recorded for later analysis. This allows the archaeologist to deduce what artefacts and features were likely used together and which may be from different phases of activity. For example, excavation of a site reveals its stratigraphy; if a site was occupied by a succession of distinct cultures, artefacts from more recent cultures will lie above those from more ancient cultures. Excavation is the most expensive phase of archaeological research. Also, as a destructive process, it carries ethical concerns. As a result, very few sites are excavated in their entirety. Sampling is even more important in excavation than in survey. It is common for large mechanical equipment, such as backhoes (JCBs), to be used in excavation, especially to remove the topsoil (overburden), though this method is increasingly used with great caution. Following this rather dramatic step, the exposed area is usually hand-cleaned with trowels or hoes to ensure that all features are apparent.

The next task is to form a site plan and then use it to help decide the method of excavation. Features dug into the natural subsoil are normally excavated in portions in order to produce a visible archaeological section for recording. A feature, for example a pit or a ditch, consists of two parts: The cut and the fill. The cut describes the edge of the feature, where the feature meets the natural soil. It is the features boundary. The fill is, understandably, what the feature is filled with, and will often appear quite distinct from the natural soil. The cut and fill are given consecutive numbers for recording purposes. Scaled plans and sections of individual features are all drawn on site, black and white and colour photographs of them are taken, and recording sheets are filled in describing the context of each. All this information serves as a permanent record of the now-destroyed archaeology and is used in describing and interpreting the site.

POST-EXCAVATION ANALYSIS

Once artifacts and structures have been excavated, or collected from surface surveys, it is necessary to properly study them, to gain as much data as possible. This process is known as post-excavation analysis, and is normally the most time-consuming part of the archaeological investigation. It is not uncommon for the final excavation reports on major sites to take years to be published.

At its most basic, the artifacts found are cleaned, catalogued and compared to published collections, in order to classify them typologically and to identify other sites with similar artifact assemblages. However, a much more comprehensive range of analytical techniques are available through archaeological science, meaning that artifacts can be dated and their compositions examined. The bones, plants and pollen collected from a site can all be analysed (using the techniques of zooarchaeology, paleoethnobotany, and palynology), while any texts can usually be deciphered.

These techniques frequently provide information that would not otherwise be known and therefore contribute greatly to the understanding of a site.

HISTORY OF ARCHAEOLOGY

The history of archaeology has been one of increasing professionalisation, and the use of an increasing range of techniques, to obtain as much data on the site being examined as possible.

Excavations of ancient monuments and the collection of antiquities have been taking place for thousands of years, but these were mostly for the extraction of valuable or aesthetically pleasing artifacts.

It was only in the 19th century that the systematic study of the past through its physical remains began to be carried out. A notable early development was the founding in Rome in 1829, by Eduard Gerhard and others, of the Institute for Archaeological Correspondence (Instituto di corrispondenza archeologica or Institut für archäologisches Korrespondenz). Archaeological methods were developed by both interested amateurs and professionals, including Augustus Pitt Rivers and William Flinders Petrie.

This process was continued in the 20th century by such people as Mortimer Wheeler, whose highly disciplined approach to excavation greatly improved the quality of evidence that could be obtained.

During the 20th century, the development of urban archaeology and then rescue archaeology have been important factors, as has the development of archaeological science, which has greatly increased the amount of data that it is possible to obtain.

Another branch, archaeoastronomy, is not as well known as archaeology, but deals with the study of ancient or traditional astronomies in cultural context.

ARCHAEOLOGICAL THEORY

There is no single theory of archaeology, and even definitions are disputed. Until the mid-20th century and the introduction of technology, there was a general consensus that archaeology was closely related to both history and anthropology. The first major phase in the history of archaeological theory is commonly referred to as cultural, or culture, history, which was developed during the late 19th and early 20th centuries.

In the 1960s, a number of young, primarily American archaeologists, such as Lewis Binford, rebelled against the paradigms of cultural history. They proposed a "New Archaeology", which would be more "scientific" and "anthropological", with hypothesis testing and the scientific method very important parts of what became known as processual archaeology.

In the 1980s, a new movement arose led by the British archaeologists Michael Shanks, Christopher Tilley, Daniel Miller, and Ian Hodder. It questioned processualism's appeals to science and impartiality and emphasised the importance of relativism, becoming known as post-processual archaeology. However, this approach has been criticised by processualists as lacking scientific rigour. The validity of both processualism and post-processualism is still under debate.

Archaeological theory now borrows from a wide range of influences, including neo-Darwinian evolutionary thought, phenomenology, postmodernism, agency theory, cognitive science, Functionalism, gender-based and Feminist archaeology, and Systems theory.

PUBLIC ARCHAEOLOGY

Early archaeology was largely an attempt to uncover spectacular artifacts and features, or to explore vast and mysterious abandoned cities. Such pursuits continue to fascinate the public, portrayed in books (such as King Solomon's Mines) and films (such as The Mummy and Raiders of the Lost Ark).

Much thorough and productive research has indeed been conducted in dramatic locales such as Copán and the Valley of the Kings, but the stuff of modern archaeology is not so reliably sensational. In addition, archaeological adventure stories tend to ignore the painstaking work involved in modern survey, excavation, and data processing techniques. Some archaeologists refer to such portrayals as "pseudoarchaeology".

Nevertheless, archaeology has profited from its portrayal in the mainstream media. Many practitioners point to the childhood excitement of Indiana Jones films and Tomb Raider games as the inspiration for them to enter the field. Archaeologists are also very much reliant on public support, the question of exactly who they are doing their work for is often discussed. Without a strong public interest in the subject, often sparked by significant finds and celebrity archaeologists, it would be a great deal harder for archaeologists to gain the political and financial support they require.

In the UK, popular archaeology programmes such as Time Team and Meet the Ancestors have resulted in a huge upsurge in public interest. Where possible, archaeologists now make more provision for public involvement and outreach in larger projects than they once did, and many local archaeological organisations operate within the Community archaeology framework to expand public involvement in smaller-scale, more local projects. However, the move towards being more professional has meant that volunteer places are now often relegated to unskilled labour, and even this is less freely available than before.

Developer-funded excavation necessitates a well-trained staff that can work quickly and accurately, observing the necessary health and safety and indemnity insurance issues involved in working on a modern building site with tight deadlines. Certain charities and local government bodies sometimes offer places on research projects either as part of academic work or as a defined community project. There is also a flourishing industry selling places on commercial training excavations and archaeological holiday tours.

Archaeologists prize local knowledge and often liaise with local historical and archaeological societies, which is one reason why Community archaeology projects are starting to become more common. Anyone looking to get involved in the field without having to pay to do so should contact a local group.

PSEUDOARCHAEOLOGY

Pseudoarchaeology is an umbrella term for all activities that claim to be archaeological but in fact violate commonly accepted archaeological practices. It includes much fictional archaeological work (discussed above), as well as some actual activity. Many non-fiction authors have ignored the scientific methods of processual archaeology, or the specific critiques of it contained in post-processualism.

An example of this type is the writing of Erich von Däniken. His Chariots of the Gods (1968), together with many subsequent lesser-known works, expounds a theory of ancient contacts between human civilisation on Earth and more technologically advanced extraterrestrial civilisations. This theory, known as palaeocontact theory, or Ancient astronaut theory, is not exclusively Däniken's nor did the idea originate with him. Works of this nature are usually marked by the renunciation of well-established theories on the basis of limited evidence, and the interpretation of evidence with a preconceived theory in mind.

LOOTING

Looting of archaeological sites by people in search of hoards of buried treasure is an ancient problem. For instance, many of the tombs of the Egyptian pharaohs were looted in antiquity. The advent of archaeology has made ancient sites objects of great scientific and public interest, but it has also attracted unwelcome attention to the works of past peoples. A brisk commercial demand for artifacts encourages looting and the illicit antiquities trade, which smuggles items abroad to private collectors. Looters damage the integrity of a historic site, deny archaeologists valuable information that would be learnt from excavation, and are often deemed to be robbing local people of their heritage.

The popular consciousness often associates looting with poor Third World countries. Many are former homes to many well-known ancient civilizations but lack the financial resources or political will to protect even the most significant sites. Certainly, the high prices that intact objects can command relative to a poor farmer's income make looting a tempting financial proposition for some local people. However, looting has taken its toll in places as rich and populous as the United States and Western Europe as well. Abandoned towns of the ancient Sinagua people of Arizona, clearly visible in the desert landscape, have been destroyed in large numbers by treasure hunters. Sites in more densely populated areas farther east have also been looted. Where looting is proscribed by law it takes place under cover of night, with the metal detector a common instrument used to identify profitable places to dig.

PUBLIC OUTREACH

Motivated by a desire to halt looting, curb pseudoarchaeology, and to secure greater public funding and appreciation for their work, archaeologists are mounting public-outreach campaigns. They seek to stop looting by informing prospective artifact collectors of the provenance of these goods, and by alerting people who live near archaeological sites of the threat of looting and the danger that it poses to science and their own heritage. Common methods of public outreach include press releases and the encouragement of school field trips to sites under excavation by professional archaeologists.

The final audience for archaeologists' work is the public and it is increasingly realised that their work is ultimately being done to benefit and inform them. The putative social benefits of local heritage awareness are also being promoted with initiatives to increase civic and individual pride through projects such as community excavation projects and better interpretation and presentation of existing sites.

DESCENDANT PEOPLES

In the United States, examples such as the case of Kennewick Man have illustrated the tensions between Native Americans and archaeologists which can be summarised as a conflict between a need to remain respectful towards burials sacred sites and the academic benefit from studying them. For years, American archaeologists dug on Indian burial grounds and other places considered sacred, removing artifacts and human remains to storage facilities for further study. In some cases human remains were not even thoroughly studied but instead archived rather than reburied. Furthermore, Western archaeologists' views of the past often differ from those of tribal peoples. The West views time as linear; for many natives, it is cyclic. From a Western perspective, the past is long-gone; from a native perspective, disturbing the past can have dire consequences in the present. To an archaeologist, the past is long-gone and must be reconstructed through its material remains; to indigenous peoples, it is often still alive.

As a consequence of this, American Indians attempted to prevent archaeological excavation of sites inhabited by their ancestors, while American archaeologists believed that the advancement of scientific knowledge was a valid reason to continue their studies. This contradictory situation was addressed by the Native American Graves Protection and Repatriation Act (NAGPRA, 1990), which sought to reach a compromise by limiting the right of research institutions to possess human remains. Due in part to the spirit of postprocessualism, some archaeologists have begun to actively enlist the assistance of indigenous peoples likely to be descended from those under study.

Archaeologists have also been obliged to re-examine what constitutes an archaeological site in view of what native peoples believe to constitute sacred space. To many native peoples, natural features such as lakes, mountains or even individual trees have cultural significance. Australian archaeologists especially have explored this issue and attempted to survey these sites in order to give them some protection from being developed. Such work requires close links and trust between archaeologists and the people they are trying to help and at the same time study.

While this cooperation presents a new set of challenges and hurdles to fieldwork, it has benefits for all parties involved. Tribal elders cooperating with archaeologists can prevent the excavation of areas of sites that they consider sacred, while the archaeologists gain the elders' aid in interpreting their finds. There have also been active efforts to recruit aboriginal peoples directly into the archaeological profession.

REPATRIATION

A new trend in the heated controversy between First Nations groups and scientists is the repatriation of native artifacts to the original descendants. An example of this occurred June 21, 2005, when community members and elders from a number of the 10 Algonquian nations in the Ottawa area convened on the Kitigan Zibi reservation in Kanawagi, Quebec, to inter ancestral human remains and burial goods-some dating back 6,000 years.

The ceremony marked the end of a journey spanning thousands of years and many miles. The remains and artifacts, including beads, tools and weapons, were originally excavated from various sites in the Ottawa Valley, including Morrison and the Allumette Islands. They had been part of the Canadian Museum of Civilization's research collection for decades, some since the late 1800s. Elders from various Algonquin communities conferred on an appropriate reburial, eventually deciding on traditional redcedar and birchbark boxes lined with redcedar chips, muskrat and beaver pelts.

Now, an inconspicuous rock mound marks the reburial site where close to 90 boxes of various sizes are buried. Although negotiations were at times tense between the Kitigan Zibi community and museum, they were able to reach agreement.

ARCHAEOLOGICAL CULTURE

In archaeology, culture refers to either of two separate but allied concepts:

- An archaeological culture is a pattern of similar artefacts and features found within a specific area over a limited period of time. They are sometimes termed Techno-Complexes (Technology-Complexes) to differentiate them from sociological culture.

By using the term "culture", archeologists indicate that these patterns of assemblages are thought to be indicative of the wider behaviour of a particular society. Where the assemblages consist of only a single artefact type the term is more correctly an industry, although the ideas behind the culture and the industry are the same. Cultures are the basic units of Prehistoric archaeology and were first fully explored by Vere Gordon Childe in the late 1920s. He wrote: We find certain types of remains-pots, implements, ornaments, burial rites and house forms-constantly recurring together. such a complex of associated traits we shall call a "cultural group" or just a "culture". We assume that such a complex is the material expression of what today we would call "a people".

This assumption exemplifies Childe's materialist view of the past which was influenced by his Marxist beliefs. The so-called Culture History approach to archaeology is largely reliant on this rigid concept of material culture and human beings being closely connected. Later archaeologists have questioned this interpretation and its tempting conclusion that a culture is a single group with straightforward aims. As archaeological knowledge has increased, the definitions of what cultures mean have become less clear. For example, cultures are assigned names by archaeologists not the people who originally made the assemblages; the names are arbitrary and normally connected with the modern names for past societies' occupation sites or defining items they used.

Such names can be misleading as in many cases it has transpired that the supposed monolithic culture is in fact a number of different ones following further study. The original name therefore, which was retroactively applied, has little significance. Diffusionist and migrationist interpretations used to explain changes in past societies often rely on the idea of large numbers of people moving great distances and bringing their culture with them. An alternative interpretation is that the so-called culture is in fact just the technological know-how which has travelled through trading for example and that beliefs and practices connected with the material culture are likely to differ from place to place. an example is the Windmill Hill culture which now simply serves as a general label for several different groups occupying southern Britain during the Neolithic. Conversely, some archaeologists have also tried to argue that some supposedly distinctive cultures are really manifestations of a wider culture but with local differences based on environmental factors as with Clactonian man.

When defining an archaeological culture, the archaeologist points to a specific set of findings; few archaeological sites, however, present a 'pure' example, and when assigning finds to a specific culture, the archaeologist either has only partial remains of the 'pure' definition, or has mixed findings. There is also the very real phenomenon of two or more distinct material cultures which may or may not represent different peoples sharing the same geographic extent during the same time period. Which such synchronous findings are often cited as evidence for one or more intrusive cultures, one classic example that cautions us is that of the (now largely extinct) distinction between village Arabs and Bedouin Arabs, where you have radically different material cultures which are in reality part of a much larger unity.

The concept of the culture still remains popular however and as with the three-age system it remains useful in most cases as a shorthand term for time periods, regions and distinctive practices.

Examples of archaeological cultures include:

- Aurignacian culture
- Beaker people
- Wessex culture
- Material culture refers to physical objects from the past, the study of which is the basis of the discipline. Material culture is the counterpart of verbal culture and learned behaviour and together they constitute human activity. Archaeologists seek to study and explain past human activity and the changes that affected it. The term is derived from anthropology and sociology which study distinctive cultures. Archaeologists also try to understand the general articulation of past human societies by inferring what the less permanent aspects of their cultures may have been like from the material record they have left behind and sometimes other sources such as modern anthropological evidence. Examples include William Duncan Strong's direct historical approach.

Material culture consists of:

- artefacts

- features
- ecofacts (also known as biofacts)
- manuports .

EXPERIMENTAL ARCHAEOLOGY

Experimental archaeology employs a number of different methods, techniques, analyses, and approaches in order to generate and test hypotheses or an interpretation, based upon archaeological source material, like ancient structures or artifacts. It should not be confused with primitive technology which is not concerned with any archaeological or historical evidence, living history or historical reenactment, which is generally undertaken as a hobby, for entertainment or to demonstrate a romantic atmosphere of a specific (pre)historic era. Experimental Archaeology is "Within the context of a controllable imitative experiment to replicate past phenomena in order to generate and test hypotheses to provide or enhance analogies for archaeological interpretation" (Mathieu, 12)

One of the main forms of experimental archaeology is the creation of copies of historical structures using only historically accurate technologies.

This is sometimes known as reconstruction archaeology. However, the product of experimental archaeology is data, not the constructed house, axe, pot or whatsoever. A good example is Butser Ancient Farm in the English county of Hampshire which is a working replica of an Iron Age farmstead where long-term experiments in prehistoric agriculture, animal husbandry and manufacturing are held to test ideas posited by archaeologists. In Denmark, the Lejre Experimental Centre carries out even more ambitious work on such diverse topics as artificial Bronze Age and Iron Age burials, prehistoric science and stone tool manufacture in the absence of flint.

Other examples include:

- The Kon-Tiki, a balsa raft built by Thor Heyerdahl and sailed from Peru to Polynesia to demonstrate the possibility of cultural exchange between South America and the Polynesian islands.

- Attempts (so far unsuccessful) to transport large stones like those used in Stonehenge from their probable original location in Pembrokeshire to the site on Salisbury Plain, using only technology that would have been available at the time.
- The reconstruction of part of Hadrian's Wall at Vindolanda, carried out in limited time by local volunteers.
- Greek triremes have been reconstructed by skilled sailors from plans and archaeological remains and have been successfully tried out at sea.
- Attempts to manufacture steel that matches all the characteristics of Damascus steel, whose original manufacturing techniques have been lost for centuries.
- Experiments in Ancient Roman Coin Minting.

In recent years, experimental archeology has been featured in several television productions, such as BBC's "Building the Impossible" and the Discovery Channel's "Secrets of Lost Empires". On television shows, the serious scientific benefits of the techniques are somewhat lessened by imposing strict deadlines on the team.

Other types of experimental archaeology may involve burying modern replica artefacts and ecofacts for varying lengths of time to analyse the post-depositional effects on them. Other archaeologists have built modern earthworks and measured the effects of silting in the ditches and weathering and subsidence on the banks to understand better how ancient monuments would have looked.

The work of Flintknappers is also a kind of experimental archaeology as much has been learnt about the many different types of flint tools through the hands-on approach of actually making them.

Experimental archaeologists have equipped modern professional butchers, archers and lumberjacks with replica flint tools to judge how effective they would have been for certain tasks. Use wear traces on the modern flint tools are compared to similar traces on archaeological artefacts, making probabillity hypotheses on the possible kind of use feasible. Hand axes have been shown to be particularly effective at cutting animal meat from the bone and jointing it.

HISTORICAL ARCHAEOLOGY

Historical archaeology is a branch of archaeology that concerns itself with "historical" societies, i.e. those that had systems of writing. It is distinguished from prehistoric archaeology (also called "ancient archaeology"), which studies societies with no writing, and protohistoric archaeology, which studies societies with very little writing.

The term is also used, especially in North America and Australasia, to describe the archaeology of the most recent past-from approximately AD 1500 to the present, meaning that it is concerned with European settler societies, as distinguished from the archaeology of indigenous inhabitants. The term is increasingly used in Europe to refer to Post-Medieval Archaeology (circa AD 1450-present).

Some archaeologists, especially in the UK, have also begun to engage with archaeologies of the very recent (20th century) and "contemporary past"-leading to the emergence of the field of contemporary archaeology.

While the study of history has uncovered much information on historic societies by studying the written records that those societies left behind, for some, historical archaeology remains an indispensable method of inquiry to supplement, corroborate, and at times overturn the findings inferred from the documentary record.

For others, historical archaeology's distinctive engagement with materiality leads to entirely new accounts of the recent past.

One problem with the written record is that ancient records do not cover all topics equally. Also, the written record is often biased. Literacy was often limited to the upper classes, such as the clergy and aristocracy. The general population produced few records of its own, and those that it did were less likely to be preserved. The literate classes were primarily concerned with recording their own interests. Furthermore, many topics of interest to scholars, such as economic history and religious history, were widely taken for granted and thus not described in records.

Furthermore, not all records written in antiquity have been preserved. For example, much knowledge of the Roman Empire was lost during the early Middle Ages because Europeans had yet to take a renewed interest in their ancestors. Additionally, many of the ancient records that have survived are not primary sources; For example, the works of Aristobulus, the historian who accompanied Alexander the Great on his campaigns, were mostly destroyed within a few centuries and supplanted by the writings of later scholars who used him as a source.

Finally, written sources are not always trustworthy. Those who write history usually have some personal involvement in it, and they may distort the truth (whether consciously or unconsciously) to cast themselves in a more positive light. On the other hand, it is practically impossible to systematically distort the archaeological record so as to imply events that never occurred. This is not to say that historical archaeology is a replacement for historical records; rather the two can be used in conjunction. In fact, the existence of written records allows historical archaeologists opportunities that do not exist in prehistorical archaeology. Historical accounts, inventories and other documents, census records, old maps, and photographs can all be utilized in the interpretation of a site or an artifact assemblage.

ZOOARCHAEOLOGY

Zooarchaeology (or Archaeozoology) is the study of animal remains from archaeological sites. The remains consist primarily of the hard parts of the body such as bones, teeth, and shells. Such remains may represent the food refuse of ancient populations as well as animals used for transportation, farm labor, clothing, decoration, or pets.

The study of these remains helps archaeologists understand past human subsistence strategies and economic interactions, and completes our picture of the kind of environments humans have inhabited.

Naming the Discipline

The multi-disciplinary nature of this field is reflected in the disagreements over its name. One of the first clear references to this area of study was by Lubbock (1865) who used the term zoologico-archaeologist. The modern derivatives, such as zooarchaeology, zooarcheologie, or zooarchaeologia are probably the most commonly used terms in the Americas and reflect the anthropological perspective prevalent in their research. In Eurasia and Africa the term archaeozoology is more commonly seen, and this emphasises the biological nature of the animal remains. Other terms that are occasionally used are osteoarchaeology, bioarchaeology and ethnozoology. While these disputes may seem trivial, they reflect differences in the approach and perception of the same material (Reitz and Wing, 1999: 2-6).

12

Applied Anthropology

Applied anthropology refers to the application of method and theory in anthropology to the analysis and solution of practical problems. Inasmuch as anthropology proper comprises four subdisciplines--biological, cultural, linguistic, and archeological anthropology--the practical application of any of these subdisciplines may properly be designated "applied anthropology. Indeed, some practical problems may invoke all subdisciplines. For example, a Native American community development program may involve archeological research to determine legitimacy of water rights claims, ethnography may involve assessing the current and recent historical cultural characteristics of the community, linguistics may be applied to restoring language competetence, and biological, or more specifically "medical" anthropology may be applied to determine the factors contributing to dietary deficiency diseases, etc.

Some regard applied anthropology to be a fifth subdiscipline of anthropology that applies anthropological data, perspectives, theory, and methods to identify, assess and solve contemporary social problems.

Applied anthropologists often work for nonacademic clients such as governments, development agencies, nongovernmental organizations (NGOs), tribal and ethnic associations, interest groups, social-service and educational agencies, and businesses. Ethnography and participant observation are the applied anthropologist's primary research tools. They also use textual analysis, survey research and other empirical methods to inform policy or to market products. An applied anthropologist is often likely to be employed in a non-academic setting.

This is a contrast to more academic sociocultural anthropology, which may be more concerned with creating theoretical models which correspond to its units of analysis, e.g. social inequality, performance, exchange, meaning, and so forth. Sometimes the research that falls within the applied field is referred to as "applied" in contrast to academic research, which is referred to as "basic."

Examples of questions that an applied anthropologist would attempt to solve might be:

- If an American buys diapers at 2AM on a Saturday in a grocery store, what is likely to be his/her next purchase?
- How can public health authorities promote condom use amongst members of a particular subculture?
- What measures could be taken to make sponge diving safer for Greek sponge divers?
- Why do people migrate to XYZ place or from PQR place?

The premiere journal in the US of applied anthropology is Human Organization published by the Society for Applied Anthropology.

Under the directorship of the RAI, Jonathan Benthall, author of The Best of Anthropology Today, created the annual The Lucy Mair Medal of Applied Anthropology. This recognizes excellence in using anthropology "for the relief of poverty or distress, or for the active recognition of human dignity."

ANTHROPOLOGY IN PUBLIC HEALTH

Public health is often described as having the population or community as its patient, in contrast to the individual-level focus of clinical medicine. This focus on community creates a natural foundation for partnership between public health and anthropology, which takes as its primary focus the study of people in groups, and especially in local communities. Anthropology has four major subfields: cultural anthropology, physical or biological anthropology, archeology, and linguistics. Crosscutting the subfields are several subdisciplinary foci that have much to contribute to the achievement of public health objectives. The most important for public health is medical anthropology, a field that first emerged as a coherent subdiscipline in the 1950s and has rapidly grown to become one of the largest areas of research and practice within anthropology. The richness of this subdiscipline is apparent in the range of theoretical perspectives encompassed by it.

Anthropology has also made important methodological contributions to public health, especially with regard to the use of ethnography for the systematic collection of field data; qualitative methods for the collection and analysis of descriptive, interpretative, and formative data; and the integration of qualitative and quantitative approaches. The ability to translate scientific knowledge into effective practice at the community level is a third area where anthropological approaches have much to offer public health.

THEORETICAL CONTRIBUTIONS

As with anthropology and public health, the basic unit of study in ecology is the population. The medical-ecological approach links biomedicine with biological and cultural anthropology, resulting in important contributions to understanding health and disease as dynamic, adaptive, population-based processes. The ecological model builds on three key assumptions:

1. There are no single causes of disease; rather, disease is ultimately due to a chain of factors related to ecosystem imbalances.
2. Health and disease are part of a set of physical, biological, and cultural subsystems that continually affect one another.
3. The ecological model provides a framework for the study of health in an environmental context, but it does not specify what factors maintain health within any given local system.

Critical medical anthropology raises important questions about the impact of global political and economic structures and processes on health and disease. It expands the context within which medical anthropology operates and brings it closer to the perspective of public health practice by explicitly seeking to contribute to the creation of global health systems that "serve the people." Critical medical anthropology focuses on health care systems and how they function at multiple levels, including the individual level of patient experience, the microlevel of physician-patient relationships, the intermediate level of local health care systems, particularly hospitals and clinics, and the macrosocial level of global political-economic systems. At each of these levels, the goal is to understand how existing social relations structure the relationships among the participants in the systems. In particular, critical medical anthropologists study the way health care is embedded within dominant relations such as those of class, race, and gender.

The individual level of patient experience has been the focus of interpretative anthropology approaches. A. Kleinman (1997) introduced the cultural interpretative model to provide a means of balancing the externalized, objective view of disease with the subjective experience of illness. M. Lock and N. Scheper-Hughes (1990), in turn, developed the concept of "sufferer experience" as an important dimension to the study of health. They developed a metaphorical framework of "the three bodies" to facilitate understanding of the multiple layers of health and illness. The individual body constitutes the layer of lived experience, with an explicit rejection of Cartesian mind-body dualism. The social body encompasses the way in which the individual body becomes a kind of canvas upon which nature, society, and culture is represented. The body politic refers to "the regulation, surveillance, and control of bodies (individual and collective) in reproduction and sexuality, work, leisure, and sickness" (Lock and Scheper-Hughes 1990, p.51). Sickness, in this framework, is understood as a "form of communication" among all three levels, a kind of individual-level expression of social truths and social contradictions. It then follows that, in order to effectively treat the individual expression of sickness, the role of social and political factors in generating sickness must also be considered.

The microlevel of physician-patient relationships and the intermediate level of local health care systems have been the focus of clinical anthropology. M. Konner (1993) provides a global overview of the many political and economic factors that impact the way doctors are trained and socialized, as well as how they shape the way medical care is enacted in clinics and hospitals. P. Farmer (1999) examines inequalities in the distribution and outcome of infectious diseases such as tuberculosis, AIDS (acquired immunodeficiency syndrome), Ebola, and malaria, as well as social responses such as quarantine and accusations of sorcery that often are associated with infectious diseases. His particular concern is with the emergence of disease from socially produced phenomena such as poverty and political upheaval, which he describes as the "biological reflections of social fault lines" (p. 5). Farmer also critiqued simplistic models of disease causality that fail to incorporate dynamic, systematic global factors and, therefore, slight the need for preventive models that target the social determinants of health.

In a similar mode, M. Singer (1994) proposed a synthesis of two key concepts from the ecological model-that health and disease are ultimately due to a chain of factors, and that they are part of a set of interacting subsystems-with the broader global perspective of critical medical anthropology to describe and explain the dynamics of the AIDS pandemic. Singer coined the term "syndemic" to describe the synergistic interaction of social factors, especially local and global inequities, with the epidemiological risk factors for HIV (human immunodeficiency virus), TB, hepatitis, and substance abuse. The syndemic model provides an important intermediate model that frames the investigation of community-level outcomes in terms of individual behavior, local processes, and higher level processes. This model raises difficult questions, and it challenges public health to address the root causes of health disparities. By introducing a multilevel, dynamic epidemiological perspective, it points toward the need to develop and evaluate systems-and community-level interventions that target linked processes.

METHODOLOGICAL CONTRIBUTIONS

The application of anthropological methods to public health problems has been another important area of contribution. The use of systematic, descriptive, and qualitative methods has proven effective in identifying context-specific factors that contribute to health and disease outcomes. Another important methodological contribution is the use of triangulation, or the systematic application of multiple methods in order to reduce bias in situations where controlled comparison is not feasible. For example, anthropologists typically use natural observation of behavior along with self-report data and descriptions of normative expectations to obtain highly accurate descriptions of events and social relationships.

The development of rapid assessment techniques, variously called rapid appraisal, rapid assessment, and rapid rural appraisal, is a prime example of anthropological contributions to the public health methodological toolkit. As described by J. Beebe (1995) this is a multidisciplinary team-based approach designed to generate reasonably valid, reliable, and qualitative results within a short time frame. Rapid assessments can provide the contextual information needed to design in-depth community-level and community-based public health research and to guide decisions about implementing programs in local settings.

J. A. Trostle and J. Sommerfeld (1996) describe a number of mutual methodological benefits to be gained from combining anthropological and epidemiological approaches, including:

- Anthropological knowledge of cross-cultural variability can be used to improve the development and measurement of epidemiologic variables.
- Research results can be communicated more effectively to policymakers and to a public audience when both anthropological and epidemiological descriptions are employed.
- Conceptual and experimental work can be undertaken to determine the best measures of complex cultural and behavioral variables.
- Ethnographic and epidemiological information can be used to design health surveillance systems that return data to communities in more comprehensible forms, creating new meanings for the "popular epidemiology."

The authors also provide a useful overview of the way anthropologists and epidemiologists have approached key social and cultural concepts relevant to the study of health and disease, including culture change and stress; social stratification; risk vulnerability; behavior; and illness constructs. They also review a number of areas of mutual methodological interest. They propose the label of "cultural epidemiology" to describe "cross-cultural analyses of the distribution and determinants of disease and illness and with unpacking variables (e.g., race, class, religion, time) to illustrate and specify their theoretical context and meaning" (p. 266).

TRANSLATING KNOWLEDGE INTO ACTION

Anthropological theory and methods have much to offer public health in the area of translating public health knowledge into effective action. Contributions range from basic issues of cultural sensitivity to enhance the acceptability and effectiveness of proven practices in clinic settings to the development of policy for the provision of complex treatment regimens for emerging epidemics under conditions of inequity in access to health care. As such, anthropologists are asking questions about the root causes of public health's toughest problems. These problems are not often amenable to study using controlled clinical trials or cross-sectional survey designs. Rather, they are dynamic, systems-level problems that require fieldbased observation and the use of multiple methods that are both qualitative and quantitative.

CULTURAL ECOLOGY

Cultural ecology is ecology including humans. It studies the relationship between a given society and its natural environment-the life-forms and ecosystems that support its lifeways. This may be carried out diachronically (examining entities that existed in different epochs), or synchronically (examining a present system and its components).

The central argument is that the natural environment, in small scale or subsistence societies dependent in part upon it-is a major contributor to social organisation and other human institutions. Particularly those concerned with the distribution of wealth and power in a society, and how that affects such behaviour as hoarding or gifting, e.g. the Haida tradition of the potlatch on the Canadian west-coast. In the academic realm, when combined with study of political economy, the study of economies as polities, it becomes political ecology-another academic subfield. It also helps interrogate historical events like the Easter Island Syndrome.

Anthropologist Julian Steward (1955) is associated with the term. In his "Theory of Culture Change; The Methodology of Multilinear Evolution", cultural ecology is the: "..study of the adaptive processes by which the nature of society, and an unpredictable number of features of culture, are affected by the basic adjustment through which man utilizes a given environment."

It is this assertion-that the physical environment affects culture-that had proved controversial, because it implies an element of environmental determinism over human actions. Cultural ecology is, indeed, inflicted with mild environmental determinism, but the approach has value in the types of situations inwhich it was developed. Less so in connected and globalised societies.

Steward's method was to:

(1) document the technologies & methods used to exploit the environment-to get a living from it.

(2) look at patterns of human behavior/culture associated with using the environment.

(3) assess how much these patterns of behavior influenced other aspects of culture (e.g., how, in a drought-prone region, great concern over rainfall patterns meant this became central to everyday life, and led to the development of a religious belief system in which rainfall and water figured very strongly.

This belief system may not appear in a society where good rainfall for crops can be taken for granted, or where irrigation was practiced).

Steward's ideas of cultural ecology became widespread among anthropologists and archaeologists of the mid-20th century, though they would later be critiqued for their environmental determinism. Cultural ecology was one of the central tenets and driving factors in the development of processual archaeology in the 1960s, as archaeologists understood cultural change through the framework of environmental adaptation.

CULTURAL ECOLOGY IN GEOGRAPHY

In geography, cultural ecology developed in response to the "landscape morphology" approach of Carl O. Sauer. Sauer's school was criticized for being unscientific and holding an inaccurate "superorganic" theory of culture.

The first form of cultural ecology applied ideas from ecology and systems theory to understand the adaptation of humans to their environment. These cultural ecologists focused on flows of energy and materials, examining how beliefs and institutions in a culture regulated its interchanges with the natural ecology that surrounded it. In this perspective humans were as much a part of the ecology as any other organism. Important practicioners of this form of cultural ecology include Karl Butzer and David Stoddard.

The second form of cultural ecology introduced decision theory from agricultural economics, particularly inspired by the works of Alexander Chayanov and Ester Boserup. These cultural ecologists were concerned with how human groups made decisions about how they use their natural environment. They were particularly concerned with the question of agricultural intensification, refining the competing models of Thomas Malthus and Boserup. Notable cultural ecologists in this second tradition include Harold Brookfield and B. L. Turner II.

Starting in the 1980s, cultural ecology came under criticism from political ecology. Political ecologists charged that cultural ecology ignored the connections between the local-scale systems they studied and the global political economy. Today few geographers self-identify as cultural ecologists, but ideas from cultural ecology have been adopted and built on by political ecology, land change science, and sustainability science.

CONCEPTUAL VIEWS OF CULTURE AND ECOLOGY

We will seek in vain for text books entitled cultural ecology, but with regard to books about culture and ecology, they began to emerge in the 1950s and 60s. One of the first to be published in the UK was 'The Human Species' by a zoologist, Anthony Barnett. It came out in 1950-subtitled 'The biology of man' but was actually about a much narrower subset of topics. It really dealt with the cultural bearing of some outstanding areas of environmental knowledge about health and disease, food, the sizes and quality of human populations, and the diversity of human types and their abilities. Barnett's view was that his selected areas of information '....are all topics on which knowledge is not only desirable, but for a twentieth-century adult, necessary'. On the second page he went on to say:

"This treatment of biology, centred on man and based on the usefulness of biological knowledge, is the opposite of the conventional one. Even the relatively few who have studied biology at school will find most of the facts in this book unfamiliar. In the schools we may learn in detail about a sea-weed called Fucus, which is not even edible, let alone important; but often little is heard of man's biggest industry, agriculture, on which we depend for food. In the animal kingdom we may begin with the study of an obscure microscopic organism called Amoeba, but perhaps learn nothing of the related malarial parasite, although malaria is probably the worst of all the infectious diseases. The earthworm is studied in detail, but the important part it plays in making soil fertile may go unmentioned. Among insects attention is usually concentrated on the cockroach, which happens to be a minor pest though this fact is often not to be found in the textbooks; the many serious insect pests are ignored. When we come to the group to which man belongs, the vertebrates, the chosen example is commonly the frog, a vertebrate of many highly unusual characteristics, and of negligible economic importance. Some teachers are trying to change all this, and not all biology courses ignore the practical significance of the subject, but many must leave the impression that biology is largely an academic study, of interest only to those concerned with knowledge for its own sake."

In other words, the text pointed some of the concepts underpinning human ecology towards the social problems facing his readers in the 1950s. The second chapter, on nature and nurture (or heredity and environment) defined a topic that underlies much of the rest of the book. This deals with the assertion that human nature cannot change, what this statement could mean, and whether it is true. The third chapter deals in more detail with some aspects of human genetics. The author felt that these two chapters would be, being an academic exposition of the facts, the most difficult ones for readers who were not scientists to comprehend. Chapter 4 completes the story of human reproduction and development (topic of 'heredity and reproduction').

Then come five chapters on the evolution of man, and the differences between groups of men (or races) and between individual men and women today in relation to population growth (topic of 'human diversity'). "Most people know that men are descended from ape-like ancestors, but few know what the evidence for this statement is, or how the process has taken place. Everyone knows that man exists in many shapes and colours; that some men are stupid, others intelligent; some criminal, others virtuous. These facts raise a number of urgent social problems, to some of which biological knowledge can suggest a solution.

Finally, there is a series of chapters on various aspects of human populations (topic of 'life and death'). Like other animals man must, in order to survive, overcome the dangers of starvation and infection; at the same time he must be fertile. Four chapters therefore deal with food, disease and the growth and decline of human populations".

Barnett anticipated that his personal scheme might be criticised on the grounds that it omits an account of those human characteristics, which distinguish humankind most clearly, and sharply from other animals. That is to say, the point might be expressed by saying that human behaviour is ignored; or some might say that human psychology is left out, or that no account is taken of the human mind. He justified his limited view, not because little importance was attached to what was left out, but because the omitted topics were so important that each needed a book of similar size even for a summary account. In other words, the author was embedded in a world of academic specialists and therefore somewhat worried about taking a partial conceptual, and idiosyncratic view of the zoology of Homo sapiens. Moves to produce prescriptions for adjusting human culture to ecological realities were also afoot in North America. Paul Sears, in his 1957 Condon Lecture at the University of Oregon, titled "The Ecology of Man," he mandated "serious attention to the ecology of man" and demanded "its skillful application to human affairs." Sears was one of the few prominent ecologists to successfully write for popular audiences. One of his popular books, Deserts on the March, first published in 1935, has become a minor American classic. Sears documents the mistakes American farmers made in creating conditions that led to the disastrous Dust Bowl. This book gave momentum to the soil conservation movement in the United States. As we shall see later, soil conservation is the key to understanding the fundamental message of cultural ecology to urbanised humanity.

However, teachers had to wait until the late 60s and early 70s for books that were aimed directly at connecting culture with ecology. The social biologist, W.M.S. Russel's publication 'Man Nature and History' appeared in 1967. It formed part of the Aldus Books' Library of Modern Knowledge. The series was backed by Sir Julian Huxley, who writes on the dust cover:

"I find this new venture full of promise. Its main purpose is to present important and exciting features of twentieth-century knowledge and to interpret them in a forceful and visually distinctive manner". The astronomer Fred Hoyle saw the series as: "Exciting in its scope, range of subjects and imaginative use of illustration. The facts are handled with a directness and clarity that should win the approval of everyone who responds to the challenge and complexities of our modern world. What I would have given to have had such books when I was young!"

Another Aldus book of this time was J.A. Lauwerys 'Man's Impact on Nature', which was part of a series on 'Interdependence in Nature' published in 1969. Both Russel's and Lauwerys' books were about cultural ecology, although not titled as such. People still had difficulty in escaping from their labels. Even 'Beginnings and Blunders', produced in 1970 by the polymath zoologist Lancelot Hogben, with the sub title 'Before Science Began', clung to anthropology as a traditional reference point. However, its slant makes it clear that 'cultural ecology' would be a more apt title to cover his wide-ranging description of how early societies adapted to environment with tools, technologies and social groupings. In 1973 the physicist Jacob Brownowski produced 'The Ascent of Man', which summarised a magnificent thirteen part BBC television series about all the ways in which humans have moulded the Earth and its future.

By the 1980s the human ecological-functional view had prevailed. It had become a conventional way to present scientific concepts in the ecological perspective of human animals dominating an overpopulated world, with the practical aim of producing a greener culture. This is exemplified by I. G. Simmons book 'Changing the Face of the Earth', with its telling subtitle 'Culture, Environment History' which was published in 1989. Simmons was a geographer, and his book was a tribute to the influence of W.L Thomas' edited collection, 'Man's role in 'Changing the Face of the Earth' that came out in 1956.

Simmons' book was one of many interdisciplinary culture/ environment publications of the 70s and 80s, which triggered a crisis in geography with regards its subject matter, academic sub-divisions, and boundaries. This was resolved by officially adopting conceptual frameworks as an approach to facilitate the organisation of research and teaching that cuts cross old subject divisions. As we have seen, cultural ecology is in fact a conceptual arena that has, over the past six decades allowed sociologists, physicists, zoologists and geographers to enter common intellectual ground from the sidelines of their specialist subjects.

At this point it is appropriate to define what is meant by 'conceptual'. A concept is a word or group of words that summarizes or classifies certain facts, events or ideas into one category. Conceptual frameworks are adopted to hold the conceptual parts (i.e. the concepts) together as mind maps, for theories or sub-sets of subjects. Frameworks or scaffolds are constructed by linking concepts representing different attributes, or which belong to different classes, and also by developing sets of interrelated statements concerning the relationship(s) between such concepts. The resultant map structure serves to hold the conceptual parts together within which it can be seen graphically that routes exist between ideas, facts, principles, insights and circumstances of the subject, which are all related to each other. Another analogy is that of an ideational scaffold where concepts or topics and subtopics are the bricks from which a coherent body of knowledge is constructed. "Conceptualization" is now a well-established process of thinking and organizing ideas across disciplines. Mind maps grow from the learning of facts and events to form clusters of concepts and to development of theories (i.e. the development of explanation). The actual business of making the maps is aided with mind-mapping programmes.

The graphical mapping of information to make it easier to assimilate may be traced back to Otto Neurath and his invention of ISOTYPE (International System Of TYpographic Picture Education) in the 1930s. One of the first people to use mind-maps was the political economist Henry Hamilton in his book that combined concepts from history and economics. 'History of the Homeland' was written during the Second World War and published in 1947 with mind maps based on interconnected concepts on a common timeline. He introduced his topic network as follows: "This book deals with a very small slab of human history, small in two dimensions. The period it traverses is a minute fraction of the millennia which have elapsed since talkative animals with the trick of using tools began to people our planet, and the patch of earth to which its narrative refers more especially is a small island off the coast of the smallest of the five continents. To know something about its comparatively recent past is a paltry substitute for knowledge of the historic record in its entirety; but for those of us who belong to the Anglo-American speech community, the record has a peculiar interest. We are bound to it in a special sense, which extends beyond its laws, its conquests, its trade or even its inventions. Its story is the clue to why we do things in our own way. History of the Homeland must therefore take within its scope and treat fully many topics which are dealt with not at all or but meagrely in more conventional history texts".

His crossing from economics to history is encapsulated in descriptions of the impact of mass utilisation of natural resources on European rural culture that was more or less in a centuries-old equilibrium with their natural resources.

"Sleepy hamlets, long marooned from the main stream of social and cultural activities were brought within a wider scheme of things. Their mode of living, their food, their dress, their social outlook was transformed as their inhabitants were swept within a vaster and more complicated organisation."

Now, in the first decade of the 21st century, there is a plethora of publications dealing with the ways in which we humans can develop a more acceptable cultural relationship with the environment that supports us. A recently created example is 'sacred ecology', a sub-topic of cultural ecology, produced by Fikret Berkes in 1999. It seeks lessons from traditional ways of life in Northern Canada to shape a new environmental perception for urban dwellers. This particular conceptualisation of people and environment comes from various cultural levels of local knowledge about species and place, resource management systems using local experience, social institutions with their rules and codes of behaviour, and a world view through religion, ethics and broadly defined belief systems.

Faced with the seemingly endless combinations and permutations of concepts to elucidate cultural ecology we may ask is there a common core scaffold that presents what might represent the pillars of a subject. Despite the differences in information concepts, all of the publications carry the message that culture is a balancing act between the mindset devoted to the exploitation of natural resources and that, which conserves them. Perhaps the best model of cultural ecology in this context is, paradoxically, the mismatch of culture and ecology that have occurred when Europeans suppressed the age-old native methods of land use and have tried to settle European farming cultures on soils manifestly incapable of supporting them. Lauwerys expressed this in his story of the wise farmer.

"The wise farmer is concerned not only with the immediate problem of raising a good crop this year but also with ensuring his future prosperity. Assuming that he does not try to raise crops or stock in an unsuitable environment, his main problem lies in maintaining the fertility of his soil. If he succeeds in this-by the use of rotations, by replenishing the soil's organic content with manure or fertilizers, by suitable ploughing methods, and so on-his soil may remain productive indefinitely. But if he fails, the soil will gradually become exhausted. If the farmer is lucky, fertility may return if the land is allowed to lie fallow for a few years. But if the process of deterioration has gone too far, the very structure of the soil will have been destroyed, and the soil will almost certainly fall prey to erosion."

Here are the two central pillars of cultural ecology presented as two modes of production. There is a culture of exploitative ecological management of planetary resources, originally only for survival, but now to support a global consumerism, and a culture of conservation management of ecological assets to control factors, that if ignored, would lead to the exhaustion of Earth's stock of resources. This was certainly the message of the latest of the cultural ecology conceptualisers, Fikret Berkes, who defined cultural ecology as an ethnological approach that sees the modes of production of societies around the world as adaptations to their local environments. His message of how to apply the lessons of cultural ecology was:

"Traditional systems inspire a new resource management science open to the participation of resource users in management, one that uses locally grounded alternatives to top-down centralized resource management. The point is important not only for humanizing resource management, but also for making sure that local needs are addressed and that relevant local knowledge, practice, and values are part of management decision making. In regard to common property resource management and co-management, the general principle, also called the subsidiarity principle, may be stated as, "using as much local-level management as possible; only so much government regulation as necessary"

It is in this sense that there is a sacred ecology associated with environmental awareness, and the task of cultural ecology as an educational scaffold, is to inspire urban dwellers to develop a more acceptable sustainable cultural relationship with the environment that supports them.

CRADLE OF HUMANITY

All human cultures contain myths about the origin of humankind, and attempt to anchor these stories through reference to historic times and places, known to them. These myths must be recognised as culturally important "truths", (from the Greek word "muthos", meaning "truth"), which aim to give "meaning" to life and the world.

For example, amongst the people of Southern Iraq, amongst the early Sumerians the semi-mythical land "Dilmun" was the site of creation, and these stories may have contributed to the later Biblical stories about Eden. In Ancient Egypt in the Memphite theology of Ptah the creation occurred with the appearance of the benben with the act of the God Atum. Amongst the ancient Greeks, various conceptions of creation of Humankind were entertained, often associated with the appearance of the Goddess Gaia. This creation was implicitly associated with the story of the omphalos, or the navel of the world, located at Delphi. In India, the creation of Humanity is associated with the semi-mythical homeland of the Aryan peoples, located somewhere in the vicinity of Mount Meru, located to the north of the Himalaya Mountains. Traditional Chinese mythology associates the cradle of humanity with the Yellow River of Northern China, the confluence of the Huang Ho and the Wei River.

The evangelical Protestants of the 19th century, considered the inventors of the term Cradle of Humanity, made generalized but undocumented claims that the term originated in Mesopotamia in the 2nd century, and that it was used by early non-christian Arabs, to refer to a geographic area that falls within a 1,000 mile radius of the spot they believed to be the birthplace of humankind. No documentation of such a historical use has been forthcoming. Nevertheless, the term has been used not only in religious, but also in secular contexts, and may therefore refer to different locations, depending on the views of the user.

EVOLUTIONARY VIEW

Scientists have also sought to locate the "Cradle of Humanity". In the European Enlightenment, the general view was that modern Humanity first appeared in Central Asia, and this remained the dominant view of science, until the publication of two books by Charles Darwin-"On the Origin of Species" and the "Descent of Man". Scientific evidence for the origin of humankind was discovered a little earlier with the beginnings of paleoanthropology in August 1856, with the discovery of what we now recognise as the fossil of Homo neanderthalensis, which was found in Valley of the Neander River i.e. the Neanderthal, Germany. The discovery was announced in 1857, two years before the publication of Charles Darwin's book On the Origin of Species. Despite this early fossil, this did not challenge the earlier views of the contemporary scientific establishment that the Cradle of Humanity was to be found in Asia.

This view was challenged by Charles Darwin. Based upon the fact that amongst the Great Apes, Chimpanzees and Gorillas are found in Africa, whilst only the Orangutan is found in Asia, Charles Darwin considered that Africa, rather than Asia, may be the Cradle of Humanity.

Darwin's view of Africa was challenged by Ernst Haeckel, who believed that Humanity evolved from the primates in Lemuria, a hypothetical geological "land bridge", which prior to the acceptance of continental drift which was believed to link Africa, India and South East Asia.

In 1891, Eugène Dubois, who accepted Haeckel's views, discovered a group of hominid fossils at the site of Trinil, on the banks of the Bengawan Solo River in Java island|Java, Indonesia. The find was originally named Pithecanthropus erectus, and popularly known as Java Man, Dubois later renaming it Homo erectus in 1894. This was the first discovery of early hominid remains outside of Europe, and led to a revival of the theories that Asia was the homeland of humankind.

But evidence was quickly forthcoming of early human "ape-men" elsewhere. In 1907, at the Mauer sand pits in Germany, a quarry worker found an almost complete mandible, which was designated Homo heidelbergensis by Otto Schoetensack. Since then fossilized remains attributable to Homo erectus have been found also in South Africa, Asia, England and China. But where did these Homo erectus come from?

The 1924 South African discovery of Australopithecus africanus at Taung by Raymond Dart, a pioneer of African paleontology, resurrected Darwin's hypothesis by suggesting that the material was a hominid. Later finds showed that it had a brain capacity little more than a chimpanzee (about 480 cc compared to Modern men 1300 cc) Nevertheless, his use of both Latin ("australo") and Greek ("pithecus") in naming the specimen resulted in the creation of a new genera other than "Homo" in the human lineage. Since then, the new genus-label created by Dart has become accepted as the designation to be used for the entire group of early hominids found in Africa.

By 1939, in the light of other new discoveries in Southern Africa, of the Australopithecus africanus the question of human origins was reevaluated and a number of paleontologists reconsidered South Africa as the possible option for the "cradle of humanity". A find made by a young schoolboy named Gert Terblanche at Kromdraai, South Africa, in 1938, led the eminent scientist Dr. Robert Broom to suggest a second Australopithecus species-Australopithecus robustus. Broom later found several more cranial and mandibular fragments that came to be associated with A. robustus. Broom published the results of his extensive research on the australopithecines in 1946, which marked a crucial turning point for South Africa in the eyes of the global evolutionary community establishing it as the new African "cradle of humanity".

The 1959 discovery by Mary Leakey of a specimen known as OH5 or "Zinj" in Olduvai Gorge, Tanzania is considered by many the watershed in paleoanthropological history. First named Zinjanthropus boisei, later classified as Australopithecus boisei, and now as Paranthropus boisei, this find did not affect prevailing views regarding the location of the "cradle of humanity" the way Homo habilis did only a year later.

Estimated at the time of its discovery in 1960 to be approximately one million years older than Australopithecus robustus, the Homo habilis find at first created a bit of a problem: The name given to it literally means "handy man", and was chosen because of the collection of stone tools that were discovered near the specimens. Further, its height and brain size were larger than those of the australopithecines, and it appeared to be less robust. In other words, this older Homo habilis specimen seemed more advanced than comparatively recent ones.

While the rôle of Homo habilis in human evolution is still not settled, its discovery by the distinguished team of Louis Leakey, John Napier, and Phillip Tobias did result in Tanzania being regarded as the "cradle of humanity" for the following two or three decades.

In 1974 Donald Johanson found the famous "Lucy", the most complete skeleton of an australopithecine to date, that firmly established the group as an intermediate between apes and humans. Together with anthropologist Timothy White, Johanson named the specimen Australopithecus afarensis. Mary Leakey discovered a set of human footprints at Laetoli, which were later thought to be Afarensis prints and by the end of 1980, the heated dispute seems to have been settled and Australopithecus afarensis was widely accepted as a new first human ancestor.

Dated at almost four million years old, A. afarensis, Found in the Afar Triangle of Ethiopia became the oldest hominid fossil yet on record, granting Ethiopia the position as the new "cradle of humanity".

The French magazine 'Science et Vie' made the displacement of Lucy its cover story in its May 1999 edition. The magazine considered Lucy, regarded as the most important fossil specimen of the species Australopithecus afarensis to date, under the caption 'Adieu Lucy' ('Farewell Lucy') and wrote that the apes from the Australopithecus species did not represent the origin of man and should be removed as the earliest Hominid ancestor. (Isabelle Bourdial, "Adieu Lucy", Science et Vie, May 1999, no. 980, pp. 52-62)

The discovery of a fossil temporarily called "Toumaï" (or hope of life in the South Chad language, Goran), estimated at an age of seven million years, the oldest hominid found to date, in the catchment of Lake Chad, has led some to question the African Rift Valley as the Cradle of the evolution of Hominids. A team of researchers led by paleontologist Michel Brunet uncovered an almost complete cranium and lower facial bones of this ancestor that appears to have lived at the point of transition between apes and hominids and for which they have suggested the name Sahelanthropus tchadensis. The location of the find in the Sahel region, a semiarid zone of mid-west Africa that separates the Sahara from the southern tropical forests, has led to the suggestion that the "cradle of humanity", the point at which the eventual human lineage separated from that of the Apes, may have been more in central or western Africa.

While accepting an African origin of the hominids, debate still rages over the site of origin of anatomically modern human beings. The earlier view, presented by Carlton Coon and other evolutionary scientists (eg Wolpoff, Alan Thorne), considered the possibility that modern humans may have evolved simultaneously in several locations on several continents along parallel evolutionary lines, finally engaging in trans-continental migration and interbreeding at the stage of Homo erectus or even later. Known as the "Multi Regional Hypothesis", proponents of these theories consider the discussion on a single evolutionary "cradle of humanity" is not useful.

Others led by Chris Stringer, based upon the fact that the earliest evidence of anatomically modern Homo sapiens is found at Kibbish Omo, and accepting the genomic evidence of Mitochondrial Eve and Y chromosome Adam, consider East Africa to have been once again the specific location as the "cradle of humanity".

Today, the accepted scientific viewpoint among biologists and paleoanthropologists is that mankind evolved through natural selection, and when journalists and popularizers currently usually use the term "Cradle of Humanity", it is intended to refer to Great Rift Valley sites in East Africa, where the oldest hominid fossils have been found. Based upon a range of evidence it is believed that the earliest hominids evolved from apes between 5-7 million years ago, in this area, whilst modern humans (Homo sapiens sapiens) only emerged much later, some time about 150,000-200,000 years ago, possibly in the same region of eastern Africa. Since 2002, however, several groups of prominent paleontologists have begun to challenge East Africa's position as the evolutionary "cradle of humanity", for all hominids, most notably because of the fossil hominid partial skull found in Chad in July 2002. The appearance of the earliest hominids outside Africa focuses on the Liujiang hominid of China, the Dmanisi fossils of Georgia and the Mungo Man fossils in Australia.

CREATIONIST VIEW

Modern fundamentalist Jewish, Christian and Muslim creationists disagree with these evolutionary views and believe that man was created by God in a place called Eden and then placed in a garden located east of Eden. In the Bible, Genesis 2:10-14 it is said that the Garden of Eden was supplied by the Tigris and Euphrates rivers. There is no evidence to support any of these views.

GROUP OF FIFTEEN LANDS

Based on the second century 1,000-mile "limit", the fifteen nations/territories that today comprise the "Cradle of Humanity" are, in alphabetical order: Bahrain, the Gaza Strip, Iran, Iraq, Israel, Jordan, Kuwait, Lebanon, Oman, Qatar, Saudi Arabia, Syria, United Arab Emirates, the Palestinian territories, and Yemen.

The radius of 1,000 miles from Eden as the limit of the Cradle of Humanity may have been "fixed" by the Christian authors of Mesopotamia, Syria and Egypt in the pre-Islamic era.

By the arrival of the Ottoman period (1516-1918), the term had become well accepted throughout the majority of the empire, which extended into parts of southern Europe and exerted much cultural influence for over 400 years. Early in the 19th century, Protestant missionaries began to arrive in the region and found that the term provided a common ground for introducing their teachings to the local population.

There is no evidence that the term "cradle of humanity" has widespread use among Jewish or Christian creationists today, although Mesopotamian Christian Arabs seem to have been the ones to develop the term for describing an area roughly within a 1,000 mile radius of the location they believed to be the site of the Garden of Eden, based on the a passage, attributed to Moses, found in the Bible at Genesis 2:8-14:

"A river watering the garden flowed upward from Eden, and from there it divided. It had four headstreams. The name of the first is Pishon. It winds through the entire land of Havilah, where there is gold. The gold of that land is good; aromatic resin and onyx are also there. The name of the second river is Gihon; it winds through the entire land of Cush. The name of the third river is Tigris; it runs along the east side of Asshur. And the fourth river is the great river Euphrates."

While two of these names, Tigris and Euphrates, refer to rivers which border and define Mesapotamia, the rivers Gihon and Pishon cannot be identified. Cush refers to an ancient region to the south of Egypt, Nubia, in present-day Sudan. However, second century Christians, in spite of this ambiguity, identified the location of Eden at a point that, today, would be just west of the border between Iraq and Iran and just above the northern shore of the Persian Gulf.

A few isolated Christian denominations still appear to use the term, nowadays, as a nickname for "Eden" and when they do, the expression is usually capitalized as Cradle of Humanity. Despite this apparently "Christian" background, the term "Cradle of Humanity" seems to be more heavily used among Muslims, who tend to accept the 1,000 mile limit from "Eden" as the boundary for the area. This may stem from the popularization of the phrase during the period when these present-day states were all ruled by the Ottoman Empire.

AMONG THOSE OPPOSED TO THE TERM "MIDDLE EAST"

The expression "Cradle of Humanity" is frequently used by persons opposed to the expression "Middle East" when, in their opinion that term would seem too ambiguous. They consider the lands of the "Cradle of Humanity" to be clearly defined within an unmistakable geographic limit. However, depending on the context in which the user applies the term "Middle East", it may or may not include countries in northern Africa, southern Europe and various parts of Eurasia east of the Ural Mountains.

Some cultural historians in the self-described "Cradle of Humanity States" also find the thinking behind the terms Near East, Middle East and Far East offensive, since they are vestiges of British colonialism; a period when such expressions were coined based on the distance between England and the region in question. They often argue that, unlike the West Indies, where the present dominant culture was indeed largely formed under the influence of the colonizing powers, most of the dominant culture in so-called Near, Middle and Far East lands, predated the colonials and has actually survived their sometimes destructive influence.

OTHER DISCIPLINES OF ANTHROPOLOGY

Ecological Anthropology

Ecological anthropology deals with human-environmental (nature-culture) relationships over time and space. It investigates the ways that a population shapes its environment and the subsequent manners in which these relations form the population's social, economic, and political life (Salzman and Attwood 1996:169). Ecological anthropology applies a systems approach (Ellen 1982; Hardesty 1997; McGee 1996) to the study of the interrelationship between culture and the environment. At the heart of contemporary ecological anthropology is "an understanding that proceeds from a notion of the mutualism of person and environment" (Ingold 1992:40) and the reciprocity between nature and culture (Harvey 1996).

In the 1960s, ecological anthropology first appeared as a response to cultural ecology a sub-field of anthropology headed by Julian Steward. Steward focused on studying different modes of subsistence as methods of energy transfer and then analysed how they determine other aspects of culture. Culture became the unit of analysis. The first ecological anthropologists explored the idea of that humans as ecological populations should be the unit of analysis and culture became the means by which that population alters and adapts to the environment. It was characterised by systems theory, functionalism and negative feedback analysis.

From the beginning various scholars criticised the discipline saying it inherently was too focused on static equilibriums which ignored change, that it used circular reasoning, and that it oversimplified systems. One of the current criticisms is that, in its original form, ecological anthropology relies upon cultural relativism as the norm (Kottak 1999). However, in today's world, there are few cultures who are isolated enough to live in a true culturally relative state. Instead, cultures are being influenced and changed by governments, NGOs, businesses, etc. In response the discipline has seen a shift towards applied ecological anthropology, political ecology and environmental anthropology.

One of the leading practitioners within this sub-field of anthropology was Roy Rappaport. He delivered many outstanding works on the relationship between culture and the natural environment in which it grows, especially concerning the role of ritual in the processual relationship between the two. He conducted the majority, if not all of his fieldwork amongst a group known as the Maring, who inhabit an area in the highlands of Papua New Guinea. His magnum opus, Ritual and Religion in the making of humanity (1999), was not published until two years after his death. Rich in content and rigorous in analysis, many feel that this work cannot be fully comprehended upon first blush but needs to be absorbed slowly over time.

Economic Anthropology

Economic anthropology is an approach to the central questions of anthropology through the lens of economics. Thus, it is similar to evolutionary psychology in that it attempts to use one scientific discipline to explain another. There are three major paradigms within the field of economic anthropology: formalism, substantivism and culturalism.

Formalism

The formalist model is the one most closely linked to neoclassical economics, defining economics as the study of utility maximisation under conditions of scarcity. As an attempt to use neoclassical theory to analyze subjects outside of its traditional purview, formalist economic anthropology can be linked with new institutional economics. This approach usually makes the following central assumptions:

- Individuals pursue utility (or preference) maximisation by choosing between alternative means. They will always choose alternatives that maximise their utility (or that yields a given amount of utility for the least possible amount of inputs or effort required), often within specific informational or transaction cost constraints.
- Individuals will do so based on rationality, using all available information to measure the cost and utility of each means and considering the opportunity costs involved compared to spending their time and effort on other utility maximising pursuits. Lack of information can be modelled as information asymmetry or as a transaction cost. Whether by conscious forethought, instincts, or traditions, individuals are able to undertake the relevant calculations. In order to make rational choices individuals will seek to obtain all relevant information up to a point where the opportunity cost of information-gathering equals the additional utility gained from having been able to make better informed choices.
- All individuals live under conditions of scarcity of means while at the same time having unlimited wants.
- Underlying individuals' pursuit of utility maximisation is the principle of diminishing marginal utility, meaning that additional resources allocated towards a particular end will tend to achieve that end less and less efficiently. Rational actors will allocate their resources first towards those opportunities that provide the greatest payoff for them, and as opportunities get used up, allocate them towards progressively less efficient ends.

Some formalists use game theory as a model of rational behavior under specific cultural or interpersonal constraints. Formalists such as Firth and Schneider assert that the neoclassical model of economics can be applied to any society if appropriate modifications are made, arguing that the principles outlined above have universal validity. All human cultures are therefore a collection of "choice making individuals whose every action involves conscious or unconscious selections among alternatives means to alternative ends" (Burling, 1962, quoted from Prattis, 1982:207), whereby the ends are culturally defined goals. Goals refer not only to economic value or financial gain but to anything that is valued by the individual, be it leisure, solidarity or prestige.

In the context of hunter-gatherer and Neolithic cultures, formalist models usually must deal with high transaction costs and are thus sometimes simplified to a model of bilateral monopoly.

Since a formalist model usually states what is to be maximized in terms of preferences, which often but not necessarily include culturally expressed value goals, it is deemed to be sufficiently abstract to be capable of explaining human behavior in any context. A traditional assumption many formalists borrow from neoclassical economics is that the individual will make rational choices based on full information, or information that is incomplete in a specific way, in order to maximize whatever that individual considers being of value. While preferences may vary or change, and information about choices may or may not be complete, the principles of economising and maximising still apply.

The role of the anthropologist may then to analyse each culture in regards to its culturally appropriate means of attaining culturally recognized and valued goals. Individual preferences may differ from culturally recognized goals, and under economic rationality assumptions individual decisions are guided by individual preferences in an environment constrained by culture, including the preferences of others. Such an analysis should uncover the culturally-specific principles that underlie the rational decision-making process. In this way, economic theory has been applied by anthropologists to societies without price-regulating markets (e.g. Firth, 1961; Laughlin, 1973). Besides cultural values, formalists may also use evolutionary psychology to help model preferences.

Substantivism

The substantivist position, first proposed by Karl Polanyi in his work The Great Transformation, argues that the term 'economics' has two meanings: the formal meaning refers to economics as the logic of rational action and decision-making, as rational choice between the alternative uses of limited (scarce) means. The second, substantive meaning, however, presupposes neither rational decision-making nor conditions of scarcity. It simply refers to study of how humans make a living from their social and natural environment. A society's livelihood strategy is seen as an adaptation to its environment and material conditions, a process which may or may not involve utility maximisation. The substantive meaning of 'economics' is seen in the broader sense of 'economising' or 'provisioning'. Economics is simply the way society meets their material needs.

Polanyi's term "great transformation" refers to the divide between modern, market-dominated societies and non-Western, non-capitalist preindustrial societies. Polanyi argues that only the substantive meaning of economics is appropriate for analysing the latter. Without a system of price-making markets formal economic analysis does not apply, for example in centrally planned economies or preindustrial societies. Individual choice in such places is not so much based on the maximisation of economic profit but rather on social relationships, cultural values, moral concerns, politics or religion. Production in most peasant and tribal societies is for the producers, also called 'production for use' or subsistence production, as opposed to 'production for exchange' which has profit maximisation as its chief aim. These types differ so radically that no single theory can describe them all.

According to Polanyi, in modern capitalist economies the concepts of formalism and substantivism coincide since people organise their livelihoods based on the principle of rational choice. However, in non-Capitalist, pre-industrial economies this assumption does not hold. Unlike their Western capitalist counterparts, they are not based on market exchange but on redistribution and reciprocity.

Reciprocity is defined as the mutual exchange of goods or services as part of long-term relationships. Redistribution implies the existence of a strong political centre such as kinship-based leadership, which receives and then redistributes subsistence goods according to culturally-specific principles. In societies that are not market-based reciprocity and redistribution usually occur together. Conversely, market exchange is seen as the dominant mode of integration in modern industrial societies, while reciprocity may continue in family and inter-household relations, and some redistribution is undertaken by the state or by charitable institutions. Each of these three systems of distribution requires a separate set of analytical concepts.

Another key concept in substantivism is that of 'embeddedness'. Rather than being a separate and distinct sphere, the economy is embedded in both economic and non-economic institutions. Exchange takes place within and is regulated by society rather than being located in a social vacuum.

For example, religion and government can be just as important to economics as economic institutions themselves. Socio-cultural obligations, norms and values play a significant role in people's livelihood strategies. Consequently, any analysis of economics as an analytically distinct entity isolated from its socio-cultural and political context is flawed from the outset. A substantivist analysis of economics will therefore focus on the study of the various social institutions on which people's livelihoods are based.

The market is only one amongst many institutions that determine the nature of economic transactions. Polanyi's central argument is that institutions are the primary organisers of economic processes. The substantive economy is an "instituted process of interaction between man and his environment, which results in a continuous supply of want satisfying material means" (1968:126).

The concept of embeddedness has been very influential in the field of economic anthropology. In his study of Chinese ethnic business networks in Indonesia, Granovetter found individual's economic agency embedded in networks of strong personal relations. In processes of clientelization the cultivation of personal relationships between traders and customers assumes an equal or higher importance than the economic transactions involved.

Economic exchanges are not carried out between strangers but rather by individuals involved in long-term continuing relationships. Granovetter describes the neo-liberal view of economic action as separating economics from society and culture, thereby promoting an 'undersocialized account' that atomises human behavior: "Actors do not behave or decide as atoms outside a social context, nor do they adhere slavishly to a script written for them by the particular intersection of social categories that they happen to occupy. Their attempts at purposive action are instead embedded in concrete, ongoing systems of social relations." (1985:487).

Culturalism

For some anthropologists the substantivist position does not go far enough in its criticism of the universal application of Western economic models on societies all around the globe. Gudeman, for example, argues that the central processes of making a livelihood are culturally constructed. Therefore, models of livelihoods and related economic concepts such as exchange, money or profit must be analyzed through the locals' ways of understanding them.

Rather than devising universal models rooting in Western understandings and using Western economic terminologies and then applying them indiscriminately to all societies, one should come to understand the 'local model'. In his work on livelihoods Gudeman seeks to present the "people's own economic construction" (1986:1); that is, not just examining the cultural construction of values as in which products people like to buy and how much they value leisure, but people's own conceptualizations or mental maps of economics and its various aspects, i.e. their understanding of concepts such as exchange, property or profit. His description of a peasant community in Panama reveals that the locals did not engage in exchange with each other in order to make a profit but rather viewed it as an "exchange of equivalents", with the exchange value of a good being defined by the expenses spent on producing it. Only outside merchants made profits in their dealings with the community, and it was a complete mystery to the locals how they managed to do so...

Gudeman not only rejects the formalist notion of the universal 'economic man'; he also criticizes the substantivist position for imposing their universal model of economics on all preindustrial societies and so making the same mistake as the formalists.

While conceding that substantivism rightly emphasises the significance of social institutions in economic processes, Gudeman considers any derivational model that claims to be of universal nature, be it formalist, substantivist or Marxist, to be ethnocentric and essentially tautological. In his view they all model human relationships as mechanistic processes by taking the logic of natural science based on the material world and applying it to the human world.

Rather than to "arrogate to themselves a privileged right to model the economies of their subjects", anthropologists should seek to understand and interpret local models (1986:38). Such local models may differ radically from their Western counterparts. To quote Gudeman: "Gaining a livelihood might be modelled as a causal and instrumental act, as a natural and inevitable sequence, as a result of supernatural dispositions or as a combination of all these." (1986:47). For example, the Iban only use hand knives to harvest rice. Even though the use of sickles would speed up the harvesting process, their concern that the spirit of the rice may flee is greater than their desire to economize the harvesting process.

Gudeman brings post-modern cultural relativism to its logical conclusion. Generally speaking, however, culturalism can also be seen as an extension of the substantivist view, with a stronger emphasis on cultural constructivism, a more detailed account of local understandings and metaphors of economic concepts, and a greater focus on socio-cultural dynamics than the latter (cf. Hann, 2000).

Culturalists also tend to be both less taxonomic and more culturally relativistic in their descriptions while critically reflecting on the power relationship between the ethnographer (or 'modeller') and the subjects of his or her research. While substantivists generally focus on institutions as their unit of analysis, culturalists lean towards detailed and comprehensive analyses of particular local communities. Both views agree in rejecting the formalist assumption that all human behaviour can be explained in terms of rational decision-making and utility maximisation.

Critics of the Approaches

There have been many critics of the formalist position. Its central assumptions about human behavior have been questioned. In particular, it has been argued that the universality of rational choice and utility maximization cannot be assumed across all cultures. But also with regards to modern Western societies the economic reductionism in explaining human behaviour has been critiqued. Prattis notes that the premise of utility maximisation is tautological; whatever a person does, may it be work or leisure, is declared to be utility maximization. If he or she doesn't maximize money then it must be pleasure or some other value.

To quote: "This post hoc reasoning back to a priori assumptions has minimal scientific value as it is not readily subject to falsification." (1989:212). For example, a person may sacrifice his or her own time, finances or even health to help others. Formalists would then pronounce that s/he does so due to placing a high value on helping others, and so sacrificing other goals in order to maximize this value and thereby to gain utility (e.g. meaning, satisfaction of having helped, approval from others etc.).

But this simply an assumption, the motivation of this person may or may not coincide with this inferred explanation pattern. Similarly, Gudeman argues that Western economic anthropologists will invariably "find" the people they study to behave "rationally" since that is what their model leads them to do. Conversely, formalism will consider any behavior that does not maximize utility based on available means as irrational. However, such "non-maximising acts" may seem perfectly rational and logical for the acting individual whose actions may have been motivated by a completely different set of meanings and understandings.

Finally, there is the substantivist point that both economic institutions and individual economic activities are embedded in the socio-cultural sphere and can therefore not be analysed in isolation. Social relationships play an essential role in people's livelihood strategies; consequently, a narrow focus on atomised individual behavior to the exclusion of his or her socio-cultural context is bound to be flawed.

Substantivism has not been without its critics, either. Prattis (1982) argues that the strict distinction between primitive and modern economies in substantivism is problematic. Constraints on transactional modes are situational rather than systemic (he therefore implies that substantivism focuses on social structures at the expensive of analyzing individual agency). Non-maximizing adaptation strategies occur in all societies, not just in "primitive" ones. Similarly, Plattner (1989) argues that some generalization across different societies are still possible, meaning that Western and non-Western economics are not entirely different. In an age of globalization there are probably hardly any "pure" preindustrial societies left. Conditions of resource scarcity can be said to exist anywhere in the world. It is significant to note anthropological fieldwork that demonstrates rational behavior and complex economic choices amongst peasants (cf. Plattner, 1989:15). Also, individuals in e.g. communist societies can still engage in rational utility maximizing behavior, e.g. by building relationships to bureaucrats who control distribution, or by using small plots of land in their garden to supplement official food rations. Cook thinks that there are significant conceptual problems with the substantivists' theorizing: "They define economics as an aspect of everything that provisions society but nothing that provisions society is defined as economic." (1973:809).

While market exchange is dominant in the West, redistribution can also play a very significant role particularly in the more socialist or welfare-state Western societies such as France, Germany or Sweden. State and charity or religious organizations collect donations and then distribute them to needy groups (or use the funds to offer free or inexpensive social services).

Culturalism can also be criticized from various perspectives. Marxists would argue that culturalists are too idealistic in their notion of the social construction of reality and too weak in their analysis of external (i.e. material) constraints on individuals that affect their livelihood choices. If, as Gudeman argues, local models cannot be objectively appraised or held against a universal standard, then there is also no way of deconstructing them in t[illegible] of ideologies propagated by the powerful that serve to ne[illegible]e resistance through hegemony. This is further complicated by the fact that in an age of globalization most cultures are being integrated into the global capitalist system and are influenced to conform to Western ways of thinking and acting. Local and global discourses are mixing and the distinctions between the two are beginning to blur. Even though people will retain aspects of their existing worldviews, universal models can be used to study the dynamics of their integration into the rest of the world.

Ethnobiology

Ethnobiology is the study of the past and present interrelationships between human cultures and the plants, animals, and other organisms in their environment, including relationships with ecosystems as a whole. It is an interdisciplinary subject which draws on knowledge from many different fields of knowledge such as linguistics, anthropology, biology, chemistry.

The field itself focuses on the study of how human societies relate to the biosphere. It is therefore conventionally centered in the use of diverse flora and fauna by indigenous societies. Humans relate to plants and animals both in space and time. Therefore, this relationship encompasses human cultures worldwide and it includes the past and the present human interactions with the living environment.

The term ethnobiology did not come into use until the twentieth century (Sillitoe, 2006). It was originally and is still being referred to as biological anthropology by many scholars in related disciplines. However, unlike the traditional biological anthropology which primarily studies humans and the nonhuman primates as biological organism, ethnobiology is wider in scope, both in academic and practical aspects. Most importantly, ethnobiology makes apparent academic connection between human cultural practices and subdisciplines of biology.

The principal disciplines of enthnobiology include ethnobotany, ethnomycology, ethnolichenology, ethnozoology (e.g. ethnoentomology, ethnoichthyology, ethnoornithology), ethnoecology, paleoethnobotany, and zooarchaeology. The academic and practical aspects of the sub-field ethnobotany are remarkably apparent in its historical review of human cultural evolution right from gathering, gardening and various levels of ethnomedical practices. It also evaluates plant as a medicine and how it got blended into spiritual uses of various cultures. Many ethnobotanists are therefore interested in researching on the use of traditional "plant medicines" and why they are culturally linked to the spirit world.

The subfield ethnozoology generally focuses on the relationship between animals and humans throughout human history. It therefore studies human practices such as hunting, fishing and animal husbandry in space and time. In all its disciplines, ethnobiology satisfies its anthropological aspect by considering classified cultural and cognitive issues. The biological component is manifested by its eminent focus on historical evolution and utilization of the living resource.

Ethnobiology-is an interdisciplinary subject that focuses on the study of how human societies relate to the biosphere. It is therefore conventionally centred in the use of diverse flora and fauna by indigenous societies. Humans' interrelationship with plant and animals can be delineated both in space and time. This relationship therefore encompasses human cultures worldwide and it includes the past and the present human interactions with living environment.

ETHNOBOTANY

Ethnobotany is the study of the relationship between plants and people: From"ethno"-study of people and "botany"-study of plants. Ethnobotany is considered a branch of ethnobiology. Ethnobotany studies the complex relationships between (uses of) plants and cultures. The focus of ethnobotany is on how plants have been or are used, managed and perceived in human societies and includes plants used for food, medicine, divination, cosmetics, dyeing, textiles, for building, tools, currency, clothing, rituals, social life, and music.

History of Ethnobotany

Though the term "ethnobotany" was not coined until 1895 by the US botanist Harshberger, the history of the field begins long before that. In AD 77, the Greek surgeon Dioscorides published "De Materia Medica", which was a catalog of about 600 plants in the Mediterranean. It also included information on how the Greeks used the plants, especially for medicinal purposes. This illustrated herbal contained information on how and when each plant was gathered, whether or not it was poisonous, its actual use, and whether or not it was edible (it even provided recipes). Dioscorides stressed the economic potential of plants. For generations, scholars learned from this herbal, but did not actually venture into the field until after the Middle Ages.

In 1542 Leonhart Fuchs, a Renaissance artist, lead the way back into the field. His "De Historia Stirpium" cataloged 400 plants native to Germany and Austria.

John Ray (1686-1704) provided the first definition of "species" in his "Historia Plantarum": a species is a set of individuals who give rise through reproduction to new individuals similar to themselves.

In 1753 Carl Linnaeus wrote "Species Plantarum", which included information on about 5,900 plants. Linnaeus is famous for inventing the binomial method of nomenclature, in which all species (mineral, vegetable or animal) get a two part name (genus, species).

The 19th century saw the peak of botanical exploration. Alexander von Humboldt collected data from the new world, and the famous Captain Cook brought back information on plants from the South Pacific. At this time major botanical gardens were started, for instance the Royal Botanic Gardens, Kew.

Edward Palmer collected artifacts and botanical specimens from peoples in the North American West (Great Basin) and Mexico from the 1860s to the 1890s. Once enough data existed, the field of "aboriginal botany" was founded. Aboriginal botany is the study of all forms of the vegetable world which aboriginal peoples use for food, medicine, textiles, ornaments, etc.

The first individual to study the emic perspective of the plant world was a German physician working in Sarajevo at the end of 19th Century: Leopold Glueck. His published work on traditional medical uses of plants done by rural people in Bosnia (1896) has to be considered the first modern ethnobotanical work.

Other scholars analysed uses of plants under an indigenous/local perspective in the early 20th century: e.g. Matilda Coxe Stevenson, Zuni plants (1915); Frank Cushing, Zuni foods (1920); and the team approach of Wilfred Robbins, JP Harrington, and Barbara Freire-Marreco, Tewa pueblo plants (1916).

Modern Ethnobotany

Beginning in the 20th century, the field of ethnobotany experienced a shift from the raw compilation of data to a greater methodological and conceptual reorientation. This is also the beginning of academic ethnobotany.

Today the field of ethnobotany requires a variety of skills: botanical training for the identification and preservation of plant specimens; anthropological training to understand the cultural concepts around the perception of plants; linguistic training, at least enough to transcribe local terms and understand native morphology, syntax, and semantics.

13

Generative Anthropology

Generative Anthropology is a new science of the human based on the idea that the origin of language is a singular event and that the history of the culture is a genetic or "generative" development of that event. In contrast to fashionable methodologies that dissolve the human in the fractal complexity of cultural differences, Generative Anthropology (GA) attempts to understand cultural phenomena in the simplest terms possible: all things human are traced back to their source in the hypothetical scene of origin in which human beings as sign-using creatures first emerged.

Origins

Generative Anthropology (GA) originated with Professor Eric Gans of UCLA who has developed his ideas in series of books and articles beginning with The Origin of Language: A Formal Theory of Representation (1981). Gans builds on the ideas of René Girard, notably mimetic desire, but Generative Anthropology also departs from and goes beyond Girard in many ways. Generative Anthropology stands as an independent and strikingly original way of understanding the human species, our origin, culture, history, and development.

Gans founded (and edits) the web-based journal Anthropoetics: The Journal of Generative Anthropology as a scholarly forum for research into human culture and origins based on Generative Anthropology and the closely related Fundamental Anthropology of René Girard. In his web-based Chronicles of Love and Resentment Gans applies the principles of GA to a wide variety of fields including popular culture, film, post-modernism, economics, contemporary politics, the Holocaust, philosophy, religion, and paleo-anthropology.

Origin of the Hypothesis

The core of Generative Anthropology is Eric Gans' "originary hypothesis." The originary hypothesis is a hypothesis about the origin of language. Gans claims that an originary hypothesis in some form is the necessary basis for humanistic inquiry. If the study of human culture and language is to be truly rigorous and scientific, Gans reasons, it must begin by defining its object of study. For Gans, what defines the human is language, which he sees as qualitatively different from animal communication systems. Unlike animal communication systems, language has syntax, allowing for unlimited new combinations and content, and language is symbolic in nature, not limited to empirical reference. Language also implies a capacity for history, the memorializing of specific historical events.

The origin of language marks off a new stage in human evolution, the beginning of culture, including art, desire, and the sacred. In addition, language makes possible new forms of social organization which are radically different from animal "pecking order" hierarchies dominated by an alpha male. Because language is so radically different from animal communication systems, its origin must have been a singular event, and the principle of parsimony requires that language originated only once. This is the central claim of Generative Anthropology: the origin of language was an event. Since language entails the capacity for memory and history, that is, language serves as a more or less durable record of its own history, the best way to define language is through a hypothesis of its origin based on our knowledge of culture including religious and literary texts. Since this event leaves no fossil record, we can only hypothesize about the conditions of its origin. As with any scientific hypothesis, its value is in its capacity to account for the known facts of human history and culture including the fossil records of human origins.

What connects proto-hominid species with the human species is mimetic behavior: imitation is an adaptive learning behavior, a form of intelligence favored by natural selection.

Imitation, however, as René Girard observes, leads to conflict, when two individuals imitate each other in their attempt to appropriate a desired object. The problem is to explain the transition from one form of mimesis, imitation, to another, qualitatively different form, representation. Many anthropologists have assumed that language evolved in order to mediate our relationship to the environment, that is, to describe the world. But this ignores the fact that humans are the species for whom the main danger to our existence is posed by other humans, intra-species violence, not the environment. Human representation, according to Gans, is not simply a "natural" evolutionary development of animal communication systems, as many anthropologists have assumed. The human sign is a radical break from animal signs and gestures. The signifier implies a symbolic dimension that is not reducible to empirical referents.

At the originary scene, in evolutionary terms, we have a hominid species which is gradually becoming more mimetic, presumably in response to environmental pressures including climate changes and competition for limited resources. We know that the higher primates have dominance hierarchies which serve to limit and prevent destructive conflict within the social group. But as individuals within the proto-human group become more mimetic, the dominance system breaks down; it becomes inadequate to control the threat of violence posed by conflictual mimesis.

Gans envisions an "originary event" along the following lines. It is important to remember that this hypothesis is intended as a reconstruction of the minimal conditions for the emergence of the sign, rather than a naturalistic description of the event, the details of which must remain inaccessible.

A group of hominids have surrounded an appetitive object, such as the slain body of a large mammal following a hunt. The attraction of the object, however, exceeds the limits of simple appetite due to the operation of group mimesis, which, in the Girardian sense, is essentially an expression of competition or rivalry. The object becomes more attractive simply because each member of the group is attending to it as attractive: each individual mimics the attention given to the object by the others. Appetite is thus artificially "inflated" through this mutual reinforcement. It is not appropriate to speak of desire at this point, since desire, strictly speaking, as a cultural relation, only comes into being with the sign. The power of appetitive mimesis (in conjunction with the threat of violence) is such that the central object begins to assume that aura we call "sacred": infinitely desirable and infinitely dangerous.

Mimesis thus gives rise to a pragmatic paradox: the double imperative to appropriate and to refrain from appropriation (to avoid conflict). In other words, imitating the rival means not imitating the rival, because imitation leads to conflict, the attempt to destroy rather than imitate (Gans, Signs of Paradox 18). We can assume that a similar scenario plays itself out many times without necessarily giving birth to the sign. But when the mimetic instinct becomes so powerful that it endangers the survival of the group, we have an intra-species pressure which would favor the emergence of the sign.

Continuing now with our scenario, the power of mimesis compels each member of the group to reach out to appropriate the object in defiance of the dominance hierarchy. At the same time, the overwhelming possibility of violence makes appropriation impossible. The object seems to possess a sacred force which resists human control. The gesture to appropriate the object is therefore aborted, and at least one member of the group intends this aborted gesture as a sign designating the central object and is successful in communicating this meaning to the group. The sign focuses attention on the sacred power of the central object, which is conceived as the source of its own power.

The object which compels attention yet prohibits consumption can only be represented. The basic advantage of the sign over the object is that "The sign is an economical substitute for its inaccessible referent. Things are scarce and consequently objects of potential contention; signs are abundant because they can be reproduced at will" (Gans, Originary Thinking 9). The desire for the object is mediated by the sign, which paradoxically both creates desire, by attributing significance to the object, yet also defers desire, by designating the object as sacred or taboo. The mimetic impulse is sublimated, expressed in a different form, as the act of representation. Individual self-consciousness is also born at this moment, in the recognition of alienation from the sacred center. The primary value/function of the sign in this scenario is ethical, as the deferral of violence, but the sign is also referential. What the sign refers to, strictly speaking, is not the physical object, but rather the mediated object of desire as realized in the imagination of each individual.

The emergence of the sign on the originary scene is only a temporary deferral of violence. The emission of the sign is immediately followed by the sparagmos, the discharge of the mimetic tension created by the sign in the violent dismemberment and consumption of the worldly incarnation of the sign, the central appetitive object. The violence of the sparagmos is mediated by the sign and thus directed towards the central object rather than the other members of the group. By including the sparagmos in the originary hypothesis, Gans intends to incorporate Girard's insights into scapegoating and the sacrificial.

The "scene of representation" is fundamentally social or interpersonal. The act of representation always implies the presence of an other or others. The usage of a sign evokes the (communal) scene of representation, structured by a sacred center and a human periphery. The significance of the sign seems to emerge from the sacred center (in its resistance to appropriation), but the pragmatic significance of the sign is realized in the peaceful presence of the group to itself, that is, the relationship between the humans on the periphery. The sign allows for the evolution of new forms of social organization. The minimal basis of the uniquely flexible and dynamic human social order is the sign itself. The usage of the sign identifies one as a member of the community, and, qua sign-user, in principle equal to every other member of the community. The intuition of fundamental human equality, as expressed for example in "the golden rule," is based on the equal capacity for language.

The scene of representation is a triangular structure including a human periphery and a sacred (or simply significant) center. The sign functions as a means of communication, but always in reference to a third term, originally the sacred center. All signs, in one way or another, point to the sacred, that which is significant to the community (the original form of significance is the sacred). At the same time, the sacred cannot be signified directly, since it is essentially an imaginary or ideal construction of mimetic desire. The significance is realized in the human relationships as mediated by the sign. When an individual refers to an object or idea, the reference is fundamentally to the significance of that object or idea for the human community. Language attempts to reproduce the non-violent presence of the community to itself, even though it may attempt to do so sacrificially, by designating a scapegoat victim.

Generative Anthropology is "generative" because human culture is understood as a "genetic" development of the originary event. The scene of representation is a true cultural universal, but it must be analyzed in terms of its dialectical development. The conditions for the generation of significance are subject to historical evolution, so that the formal articulation of the sign always includes a dialogical relationship to past forms.

HUMAN ECOSYSTEM

Human ecosystems are complex cybernetic systems that are increasingly being used by ecological anthropologists and other scholars to examine the ecological aspects of human communities in a way that integrates multiple factors as economics, socio-political organization, psychological factors, and physical factors related to the environment. The term 'ecosystem' was coined in 1930 by Roy Clapham, to denote the physical and biological components of an environment considered in relation to each other as a unit. British ecologist Arthur Tansley later refined the term, describing it as the interactive system established between biocoenosis (a group of living creatures) and their biotope (the environment in which they live).

Central to the ecosystem concept is the idea that living organisms are continually engaged in a set of relationships with every other element constituting the environment in which they exist. The human ecosystem concept is then grounded in the deconstruction of the human/nature dichotomy, and the emergent premise that all species are ecologically integrated with each other, as well as with the abiotic constituents of their biotope. Ecosystems can be bounded and discussed with tremendous variety of scope, and describe any situation where there is relationship between organisms and their environment. A system as small as a household or university, or as large as a nation state, may then be suitably discussed as a human ecosystem. While they may be bounded and individually discussed, (human) ecosystems do not exist independently, but interact in a complex web of human and ecological relationships connecting all (human) ecosystems to make up the biosphere. As virtually no surface of the earth today is free of human contact, all ecosystems can be more accurately considered as human ecosystems.

The human ecosystem concept draws from disciplines such as ecology, anthropology, sociology, philosophy, political science, cybernetics, and psychology, seeking to understand the complex system of relationships in which humans interact. These relationships exist within nested hierarchies of context with which individuals and human aggregates interact with differentially.

Most analysis of human ecosystems focuses on particular contexts of relationship, such as biological, individual, socio-cultural, environmental et cetera. World Systems Theory, as proposed by Immanuel Wallerstein, is an example of a systemic analysis of the socio-political and economic dimensions of the global network of human ecosystems. The human ecosystem unit of analysis is perhaps most often used by ecological anthropologists, and is apparent in the work of scholars such as Roy Rappaport, who has explored ritual cycles and communication within human ecosystems (Rappaport, 1999). Gregory Bateson, E.N. Anderson, Mary Douglas, Keith Basso, and Paul Nadasdy are some other anthropologists who have employed the human ecosystem as a unit of analyses.

CYBERNETICS

Through the emergence and subsequent evolution of cybernetics human ecosystems are increasingly recognized as complex cybernetic systems. Cybernetics, the study of communication and control in living beings and machines, was established as a cohesive discipline in the 1940s by Norbert Weiner (who coined the term), Warren McCulloch and others. The discipline is not grounded in any one empirical field, but is concerned with the study of systems and control in an abstracted sense. The emphasis is on the functional relations that hold between the different parts of a system, rather than the parts themselves. This is directly applicable to any inquiry involving human ecosystems, which emphasize the relationships between humans and the biotic and abiotic constituents of the environments they inhabit. Such relationships include the transfer of information, nested hierarchies of context and meaning, feedback, emergent phenomena, self-organization and autopoiesis. These phenomena are perhaps most holistically identified and interpreted by means of cybernetic analysis.

INFORMATION

The transmission and transformation of information is central to the inquiry of human ecosystems. As scholars such as E.N. Anderson illustrate (1996), humans certainly appear to be specialized information processors. In the context of human ecosystems, information is viewed as a type of input to or output from an organism or designed device. This idea stems from information theory, the foundations of which were laid by Claude Shannon, who published an influential paper titled "A Mathematical Theory of Communication" in 1948. Throughout the 1940s and 1950s cognitive psychology became concerned with information processing, in attempt to understanding human thinking. This approach considers cognition as being essentially computational. During this time cybernetics was emerging, also concerned with the nature and transmission of information.

Information processing is generally considered as the changing (processing) of information in any manner detectable by the observer. It can be described as either sequential or parallel, both of which can be either centralized or decentralized (distributed). Cyberneticians have argued that it is a process which describes everything that happens (changes) in the universe, from the falling of a rock (a change in position) to the printing of a text file from a digital computer system. In the 1960s and 1970s cybernetic theory began to permeate anthropology, through the work of Roy Rappaport and Gregory Bateson in particular.

HUMAN ECOSYSTEMS AS COMPLEX CYBERNETIC SYSTEMS

Work by scholars such as Roy Rappaport, Gregory Bateson, and E.N Anderson has focused of transfer and transformation of information in human ecosystems. Inquiries as such have focused on the ecological and informational aspects of relationships in human ecosystems. In Steps to an Ecology of Mind (1972) Bateson discusses information as pattern and difference within complex cybernetic systems.

In the 1990s Edwin Hutchins developed a school of psychology known as distributed cognition, which draws heavily from anthropology and sociology, emphasizing the social aspects of cognition. Distributed cognition is directly applicable to studies of human ecosystems, considering systems as sets of representations, and modeling the interchange of information between these representations. These representations can be either in the mental space of the participants or external representations available in the environment. In Cognition in the Wild (1994) Hutchins considers information processing within a bounded human ecosystem in a discussion of distributed cognition on board a naval vessel.

HUMAN GEOGRAPHY

Human geography is a branch of geography that focuses on the systematic study of patterns and processes that shape human interaction with the environment, with particular reference to the causes and consequences of the spatial distribution of human activity on the Earth's surface. Geography is concentrated on the question "where". Human geography, however, focuses on answering the "why" of "where".

Scope

It encompasses human, political, cultural, social, and economic aspects of the social sciences. While the major focus of human geography is not the physical landscape of the Earth it is hardly possible to discuss human geography without referring to the physical landscape on which human activities are being played out, and environmental geography is emerging as an important link between the two. Human geography is methodologically diverse using both qualitative methods and quantitative methods, including case studies, survey research, statistical analysis, and model building among others.

Human Height

Adult human height generally varies little between people compared to other anthropometric measures. Exceptional height (variation from the average of around 20%) is usually due to gigantism or dwarfism. Adult height for one sex in a particular ethnic group follows more or less a Gaussian distribution.

Changes in Human Height

In Western countries, height has varied significantly in the past few millennia. During the Industrial Revolution, Westerners were three inches shorter than their ancestors from the 11th century. The European Middle Ages was an era of tallness with men of above six feet (1.83 m) considered unremarkable. Average height decreased again in Britain in the early nineteenth century, then began to rise again mid-century.

In the 18th and 19th centuries, Europeans in North America were far taller than those in Europe-in fact they were the tallest in the world. The original indigenous population of Plains Indians was also among the tallest populations of the world at the time. Several nations, including many nations in Europe, have now surpassed the US, particularly the Netherlands, and the Scandinavian nations.

The Netherlands was in the late nineteenth century a land renowned for its short population, but today it has the 2nd tallest average in the world, with young men averaging 6 ft (1.83 m) tall and only shorter than the peoples of the Dinaric Alps (Serbia, Montenegro, Bosnia), where males average 6 ft 1.08 in (1.856 m) tall. The Dinarians and Dutch are now well known in Europe for extreme tallness. The increase has been so dramatic that various things have been redesigned to fit the much taller frames.

Average male height in impoverished Vietnam and North Korea remains comparatively small at 5 ft 4 in (1.63 m) and 5 ft 5 in (1.65 m) respectively. Currently, young North Korean males are actually significantly shorter. This contrasts greatly with the extreme growth occurring in surrounding Asian populations with correlated increasing standards of living. Young South Koreans are about 3 inches (8 cm) taller than their North Korean counterparts, on average. There is also an extreme difference between older North Koreans and young North Koreans who grew up during the famines of the 1990s-2000s.

Determinants of Growth and Height

The study of human growth is known as auxology. Growth and height have long been recognized as a measure of the health and wellness of individuals, hence part of the reasoning for the use of growth charts. For individuals, as indicators of health problems, growth trends are tracked for significant deviations and growth is also monitored for significant deficiency from genetic expectations.

Genetics is a major factor in determining the height of individuals, though it is far less influential in regard to populations. Average height is increasingly used as a measure of the health and wellness (standard of living and quality of life) of populations. Attributed as a significant reason for the trend of increasing height in parts of Europe is the egalitarian populations where proper medical care and adequate nutrition are relatively equally distributed.

Changes in diet (nutrition) and a general rise in quality of health care and standard of living are the cited factors in the Asian populations. Average height in the United States has remained essentially stagnant since the 1950s. Severe malnutrition is known to cause stunted growth in North Korean, portions of African, certain historical European, and other populations. Diet (in addition to needed nutrients; such things as junk food and attendant health problems such as obesity), exercise, fitness, pollution exposure, sleep patterns, climate, and even happiness (psychological well-being) are other factors that can affect growth and final height.

Height is determined by the complex interactive combination of genetics and environment. Genetic potential plus nutrition minus stressors is a basic formula. Genetically speaking, the heights of mother and son and of father and daughter correlate, suggesting that a short mother will more likely bear a shorter son, and tall fathers will have tall daughters. Humans grow fastest (other than in the womb) as infants and toddlers (birth to roughly age 2) and then during the pubertal growth spurt. A slower steady growth velocity occurs throughout childhood between these periods; and some slow, steady, declining growth after the pubertal growth spurt levels off is common. These are also critical periods where stressors such as malnutrition (or even severe child neglect) have the greatest effect. Conversely, if conditions are optimal then growth potential is maximized; and also there is catch-up growth-which can be significant-for those experiencing poor conditions when those conditions improve.

Moreover, the health of a mother throughout her life, especially during her critical periods, and of course during pregnancy, has a role. A healthier child and adult develops a body that is better able to provide optimal prenatal conditions. The pregnant mother's health is important as gestation is itself a critical period for an embryo/fetus, though some problems affecting height during this period are resolved by catch-up growth assuming childhood conditions are good. Thus, there is an accumulative generation effect such that nutrition and health over generations influences the height of descendants to varying degrees.

The precise relationship between genetics and environment and exact role of genetics itself is complex and uncertain. Human height is both of moderately high phenotypic plasticity and is highly heritable. Height is a multigenic trait. There are substantial relationships in the heights among biological families; the heights of parents and family are a good predictor for the height of their children. Environmental influences are most pronounced if they are highly favorable or unfavorable to growth, especially when occurring during critical periods and when continuing multigenerationally. Genetic profile (genotype) provides potentialities or proclivities which interact with environmental factors throughout the period of growth resulting (phenotype) in final adult height. Essentially, the developing body devotes energy to growth after other bodily functions are satisfied.

Ethnicity and Height

Asian populations were once thought to be inherently shorter, but with the increases in height in East Asian nations such as China and South Korea as diet changes, they have become taller. Many Asians still are on a diet that depresses growth. Diet is also a reason of why Asians are short. A typical Asian diet contains little calcium, little protein, and accommodates a relatively large amount of soybean products, which contain isoflavones, a type of phytoestrogen that acts like a female hormone. Asians take in little iron, Vitamin A and Vitamin D, which causes growth retardation.

It now seems that humans as a species probably possess a roughly similar genetic height potential (excluding permutations like the Pygmies), and that thus a predictive genotypic basis for height differentiation has not yet evolved.

Process of Growth

Growth in stature, determined by its various factors, results from the lengthening of bones via cellular divisions chiefly regulated by somatotropin (human growth hormone (hGH)) secreted by the anterior pituitary gland. Somatotropin also stimulates the release of another growth inducing hormone insulin-like growth factor 1 (IGF-1) mainly by the liver. Both hormones operate on most tissues of the body, have many other functions, and continue to be secreted throughout life; with peak levels coinciding with peak growth velocity, and gradually subsiding with age after adolescence. The bulk of secretion occurs in bursts (especially for adolescents) with the largest during sleep. Exercise promotes secretion. (indeed, adolescents who take steroids can experience stunted growth). A positive net nutrition is also important, with proteins and various other nutrients especially important.

The majority of linear growth occurs as growth of cartilage at the epiphysis (ends) of the long bones which gradually ossify to form hard bone. The legs compose approximately half of adult human height, and leg length is a somewhat sexually dimorphic trait. Height is also attained from growth of the spine, and contrary to popular belief, men are the "leggier" gender with a longer leg to torso ratio, conversely to women's longer torso to leg ratio. (The illusion of the proportion being the other way around is caused by fatty deposits placed high on women's hips.)

Some of this growth occurs after the growth spurt of the long bones has ceased or slowed. The majority of growth during growth spurts is of the long bones. Additionally, the variation in height between populations and across time is largely due to changes in leg length. The remainder of height consists of the cranium. Height is obviously sexually dimorphic and statistically it is more or less normally distributed, but with heavy tails.

Height Abnormalities

Most intra-population variance of height is genetic. Short stature and tall stature are usually not a health concern. If the degree of deviation from normal is significant, hereditary short stature is known as familial short stature and tall stature is known as familial tall stature. Confirmation that exceptional height is normal for a respective person can be ascertained from comparing stature of family members and analyzing growth trends for abrupt changes, among others. There are, however, various diseases and disorders that cause growth abnormalities. Most notably, extreme height may be pathological, such as gigantism (very rare) resulting from childhood hyperpituitarism, and dwarfism which has various causes. Rarely, no cause can be found for extreme height; very short persons may be termed as having idiopathic short stature.

The Food and Drug Administration (FDA) in 2003 approved hGH treatment for those 2.25 standard deviations below the population mean (approximately the lowest 1.2% of the population). An even rarer occurrence, or at least less used term and recognized "problem", is idiopathic tall stature.

If not enough growth hormone is produced and/or secreted by the pituitary gland, then a patient with growth hormone deficiancy can undergo treatment. This treatment involves the injection of pure growth hormone into thick tissue to jump-start the growth process.

Role of an Individual's Height

Tallness has been suggested to be associated with better cardio-vascular health and overall better-than-average health and longevity (Njolstad et al. 1996, McCarron et al 2002). However, height may not be causative of better health and longevity (Miura et al. 2002). Other studies have found no association, or suggest that shorter stature is associated with better health (Samaras & Elrick, 1999). On the other hand, being excessively tall can cause various medical problems, including cardiovascular issues, due to the increased load on the heart to supply the body with blood, and issues resulting from the increased time it takes the brain to communicate with the extremities.

For example, Robert Wadlow, the tallest man known to verifiable history, developed walking difficulties as his height continued to increase throughout his life. In many of the pictures of the later portion of his life, Wadlow can be seen gripping something for support. Late in his life he was forced to wear braces on his legs and to walk with a cane, and he died after developing an infection in his legs because he was unable to feel the irritation and cutting caused by his leg braces (it is important to note that he died in 1940, before the widespread use of modern antibiotics). Height extremities of either excessive tallness or shortness can cause social exclusion and discrimination for both men and women (heightism).

Epidemiological studies have also demonstrated a positive correlation between height and intelligence. The reasons for this association appear to include that height serves as a biomarker of nutritional status or general mental and physical health during development, that common genetic factors may influence both height and intelligence, and that both height and intelligence are affected by adverse early environmental exposures.

In addition, an individual's height can be largely a part of what social clique, or group that they fall in to, though this is usually associated with pre-teens and teenagers. For example, in some schools, students on the basketball team might be "cool", and those with short stature wouldn't likely make the team. Therefore, in some cases, this could contribute to them being classified as "weak" or "uncool", which can be detrimental to that particular individual's self-esteem.

This can also sometimes be translated over into the corporate world. Individuals with short stature can sometimes appear to not have any leadership ability or power, since some people might not take them seriously due to their diminutive nature. However, this is not always the case with most employers.

The Role of Height in Sports

Height often plays a crucial role in sports. For most sports, height is useful as it affects the leverage between muscle volume and bones towards greater speed of movement. It is most valuable in sports like basketball and volleyball, where the "short" players are almost always well above average in height compared to the general population. In some sports, such as horse racing, auto racing, diving, figure skating and gymnastics, a smaller frame is more valuable.

In other sports, the role of height is specific to particular positions. For example, in Football, tall goalkeepers have an advantage because they have greater armspans and can jump higher easily, so one will rarely, if ever, see a short goalkeeper in professional football. However, shorter goalkeepers will have an easier time reaching low shots as they can reach the ground fractionally sooner than taller keepers. In attacking and wide posistions in football height is not always important with some of the best players in the world (i.e. Roberto Carlos and Maradona) being shorter then average, although height positions just as centre-back benifit from tall players. Similarly, in cricket, some good players like Don Bradman and Sachin Tendulkar are/were short. In rugby union, lineout jumpers are usually the tallest players on the pitch, as this increases their chance of winning clean ball, whereas scrum-halves are usually relatively short. In American football, a tall quarterback is at an advantage because it is easier for him to see over the heads of large offensive and defensive linemen while he is in the pocket on a pass play. Tall wide receivers are at an advantage because they can outjump shorter defensive backs to catch high balls. By contrast, shorter running backs are at an advantage because at a lower center of gravity, with increased stride frequency (and thus acceleration), are harder to effectively bring down. In addition, they can get "lost" behind large offensive linemen, making it harder for defenders to react at the beginning of a play. Thus, in the NFL and in NCAA Division I football, running backs under 6 ft 0 in (1.83 m) are more common than running backs over 6 ft 3 in (1.91 m). Former Heisman Trophy winner and Pro Football Hall of Famer Barry Sanders, thought by some to be the greatest running back in history, is a classic example of a running back with an extraordinarily low center of gravity-at only 5 ft 7 1/2 in (1.71 m). However, Jim Brown, another player often considered the greatest running back of all time, was more than 6 ft 2 in (1.88 m) tall, helping display the benefits conferred by the greater leverage which height provides. In baseball, pitchers tend to be taller than position players, since having longer arms tends to mean greater arm speed and harder throws, but while batting means a larger strike zone.

HUMAN WEIGHT

Weight, in the context of human body weight measurements in the medical sciences and in sports is a measurement of mass, and is thus expressed in units of mass, such as kilograms (kg) or pounds (lb). In Britain and Ireland, the unit stone (equivalent to 14 lb or 6.35 kg) is commonly used as well.

A quantity called body mass index (BMI) is often used to express weight relative to height. This is determined by dividing the weight of a person in kilograms by the square of the height in meters.

Health Issues Involving Human Weight

- normal and abnormal growth and development
- the physiological and hormonal control of ingestion and digestion

- hunger and other motivations to eat
- problems in regulating body weight, often resulting in obesity
- eating disorders such as anorexia nervosa and bulimia nervosa
- effects of disease, often resulting in cachexia

Non-health related Issues Involving Human Weight

- leveling the playing field in various sports such as boxing, wrestling, and judo by classifying participants according to their weight
- issues regarding seat sizing and weight limitations on airplanes and other forms of transport

The average weight for all ages, sex and races is rising at an increasing rate in the United States. Adult men and women are roughly an inch (2.5 cm) taller than they were in 1960, but are nearly 30 pounds (14 kg) heavier on average as well. The average weight for men aged 20-74 years rose dramatically from 166.3 pounds (75.4 kg) in 1960 to 191 pounds (86.8 kg) in 2002, while the average weight for women the same age increased from 140 pounds (63.5 kg) in 1960 to 164.3 pounds (74.5 kg) in 2002 Obesity is now often called an epidemic of global proportions.

14

Anthropometry

Anthropometry in physical anthropology, refers to the measurement of living human individuals for the purposes of understanding human physical variation. 2x/2y = 1 Today, anthropometry plays an important role in industrial design, clothing design, ergonomics, and architecture, where statistical data about the distribution of body dimensions in the population are used to optimize products. Changes in life styles, nutrition and ethnic composition of populations lead to changes in the distribution of body dimensions (e.g., the obesity epidemic), and require regular updating of anthropometric data collections.

HISTORY

Bertillon, Galton, and Criminology

The French savant, Alphonse Bertillon (b. 1853), gave this name in 1883 to a system of identification depending on the unchanging character of certain measurements of parts of the human frame. He found by patient inquiry that several physical features and the dimensions of certain bones or bony structures in the body remain practically constant during adult life. He concluded from this that when these measurements were made and recorded systematically every single individual would be found to be perfectly distinguishable from others.

The system was soon adapted to police methods, as the immense value of being able to fix a person's identity was fully realized, both in preventing false personation and in bringing home to any one charged with an offence his responsibility for previous wrongdoing. "Bertillonage," as it was called, became widely popular, and after its introduction into France in 1883, where it was soon credited with highly gratifying results, was applied to the administration of justice in most civilized countries.

England followed tardily, and it was not until 1894 that an investigation of the methods used and results obtained was made by a special committee sent to Paris for the purpose. It reported favourably, especially on the use of the measurements for primary classification, but recommended also the adoption in part of a system of "finger prints" as suggested by Francis Galton, and already practised in Bengal.

There were eleven measurements:

1. Height
2. *Stretch:* Length of body from left shoulder to right middle finger when arm is raised
3. *Bust:* Length of torso from head to seat, taken when seated
4. *Length of Head*: Crown to forehead
5. *Width of Head*: Temple to temple
6. Length of right ear
7. Length of left foot
8. Length of left middle finger
9. *Length of Left Cubit*: Elbow to tip of middle finger
10. Width of cheeks
11. Length of left little finger

From this great mass of details, soon represented in Paris by the collection of some 100,000 cards, it was possible, proceeding by exhaustion, to sift and sort down the cards till a small bundle of half a dozen produced the combined facts of the measurements of the individual last sought.

The whole of the information is easily contained in one cabinet of very ordinary dimensions, and most ingeniously contrived so as to make the most of the space and facilitate the search. The whole of the record is independent of names, and the final identification is by means of the photograph which lies with the individual's card of measurements.

Anthropometrics was first used in the 19th and early 20th century in criminalistics, to identifying criminals by facial characteristics. Francis Galton was a key contributor as well, and it was in showing the redundancy of Bertillon's measurements that he developed the statistical concept of correlation. Bertillon's system originally measured variables he thought were independent-such as forearm length and leg length-but Galton had realized were both the result of a single causal variable (in this case, stature).

Bertillon's goal was to use anthropometry as a way of identifying recidivists-what we would today call "repeat-offense" criminals. Previously, police could only record general descriptions and names, and criminals were fond of using alternative identities. As such, it was a difficult job to identify whether or not certain individuals arrested were "first offenders" or life-long criminals.

Photography of criminals had become commonplace but it had proven ungainly, as there was no coherent way to arrange visually the many thousands of photographs in a fashion which would allow easy use (an officer would have to sort through them all with the hope of finding one). Bertillon's hope was that through the use of measurements of the body, all information about the individual criminal could be reduced to a set of identifying numbers which could be entered into a large filing system.

Bertillon also envisioned the system as being organized in such a way that even if the number of measurements was limited the system could drastically reduce the number of potential matches, through an easy system of body parts and characteristics being labeled as "small", "medium", or "large". For example, if the length of the arm was measured and judged to be within the "medium" range, and the size of the foot was known, this would drastically reduce the number of potential records to compare against. With more measurements of hopefully independent variables, a more precise identification could be achieved, which could then be matched against photographic evidence. Certain aspects of this philosophy would also go into Galton's development of fingerprint identification as well.

Anthropometry, however, gradually fell into disfavour, and it has been generally supplanted by the superior system of finger prints. Bertillonage exhibited certain defects which were first brought to light in Bengal. The objections raised were

1. the costliness of the instruments employed and their liability to become out of order;
2. the need for specially instructed measurers, men of superior education;
3. the errors that frequently crept in when carrying out the processes and were all but irremediable.

Measures inaccurately taken, or wrongly read off, could seldom, if ever, be corrected, and these persistent errors defeated all chance of successful search. The process was slow, as it was necessary to repeat it three times so as to arrive at a mean result. In Bengal, measurements were already abandoned by 1897, when the finger print system was adopted throughout British India. Three years later England followed suit; and as the result of a fresh inquiry ordered by the Home Officc, finger prints were alone relied upon for identification.

ANTHROPOLOGY AND ANTHROPOMETRY

During the early 20th century, anthropometry was used extensively by anthropologists in the United States and Europe. One of its primary uses became the attempted differentiation between differences in the races of man, and it was often employed to show ways in which races were "inferior" to others. The wide application of intelligence testing also became incorporated into a general anthropometric approach, and many forms of anthropometry were used for the advocacy of eugenics policies. During the 1920s and 1930s, though, members of the school of cultural anthropology of Franz Boas also began to use anthropometric approaches to discredit the concept of fixed biological race. Anthropometric approaches to these types of problems became abandoned in the years after the Holocaust in Nazi Germany, who also famously relied on anthropometric measurements to distinguish Aryans from Jews. This school of physical anthropology generally went into decline during the 1940s.

During the 1940s anthropometry was used by William Sheldon when evaluating his somatotypes, according to which characteristics of the body can be translated into characteristics of the mind. He also believed that criminality could be predicted according to the body type. This use of anthropometry is today also outdated. Because of his extensive reliance on photographs of nude Ivy League students for his work, Sheldon ran into considerable controversy when his work became public.

MODERN ANTHROPOMETRY AND BIOMETRICS

Anthropometric studies are today conducted for numerous different purposes. Academic anthropologists investigate the evolutionary significance of differences in body proportion between populations whose ancestors lived in different environmental settings. Human populations exhibit similar climatic variation patterns to other large-bodied mammals, following Bergmann's rule, which states that individuals in cold climates will tend to be larger than ones in warm climates, and Allen's rule, which states that individuals in cold climates will tend to have shorter, stubbier limbs than those in warm climates. On a microevolutionary level, anthropologists use anthropometric variation to reconstruct small-scale population history. For instance, John Relethford's studies of early twentieth-century anthropometric data from Ireland show that the geographical patterning of body proportions still exhibits traces of the invasions by the English and Norse centuries ago.

Outside academia, scientists working for private companies and government agencies conduct anthropometric studies to determine what range of sizes clothing and other items need to be manufactured in. A basically anthropometric division of body types into the categories endomorphic, ectomorphic and mesomorphic derived from Sheldon's somatotype theories is today popular among people doing weight training.

The US Military has conducted over 40 anthropometric surveys of U.S. Military personnel between 1945 and 1988, including the 1988 Army Anthropometric Survey (ANSUR) of men and women with its 240 measures. Statistical data from these surveys, which encompassed over 75,000 individuals, can be found in.

Today people are performing anthropometry with three-dimensional scanners. The subject has a three-dimensional scan taken of their body, and the anthropometrist extracts measurements from the scan rather than directly from the individual. This is beneficial for the anthropometrist in that they can use this scan to extract any measurement at any time and the individual does not have to wait for each measurement to be taken separately.

HUMAN ZOO (ETHNOLOGICAL EXPOSITIONS)

A Human zoo (also called "ethnological expositions" or "Negro Villages") was a 19th and 20th century public exhibit of human beings usually in their natural or "primitive" state. These displays usually emphasized the cultural differences between indigenous and traditional peoples and Western publics. Ethnographic zoos were often predicated on unilinealism, scientific racism, and a version of Social Darwinism. A number of them placed indigenous people (particularly Africans) in a continuum somewhere between the great apes and human beings of European descent. For this reason, ethnographic zoos have since been criticized as highly degrading and racist.

First Human Zoos

One of the first modern public human exhibitions was P.T. Barnum's exhibition of Joice Heth on February 25, 1836 and, subsequently, the Siamese twins Chang and Eng Bunker. However, the notion of the human curiosity has a history at least as long as colonialism. For instance, Columbus brought Indians from his voyage to the New World to the Spanish court in 1493. Another famous example was that of Saartjie Baartman, a member of the Namaqua tribe, better known as the Hottentot Venus, who was displayed in London until her death in 1815. However, human zoos would become common only in the 1870s in the midst of the New Imperialism period.

1870s to World War II

Exhibitions of exotic populations became popular in various countries in the 1870s. Human zoos could be found in Hamburg, Antwerp, Barcelona, London, Milan, New York, and Warsaw with 200,000 to 300,000 visitors attending each exhibition. In Germany, Karl Hagenbeck, a merchant in wild animals and future entrepreneur of many Europeans zoos, decided in 1874 to exhibit Samoan and Sami people (Laplanders) as "purely natural" populations. In 1876, he sent a collaborator to the Egyptian Sudan to bring back some wild beasts and Nubians. The Nubian exhibit was very successful in Europe and toured Paris, London, and Berlin. He also dispatched an agent to Labrador to secure a number of "Esquimaux" (Inuit) from the settlement of Hopedale; these Inuit were exhibited in his Hamburg Tierpark.

Geoffroy de Saint-Hilaire, director of the Parisian Jardin d'acclimatation, decided in 1877 to organize two ethnological spectacles that presented Nubians and Inuit. That year, the audience of the Jardin d'acclimatation doubled to one million. Between 1877 and 1912, approximately thirty ethnological exhibitions were presented at the Jardin zoologique d'acclimatation.

Both the 1878 and the 1889 Parisian World's Fair presented a Negro Village (village nègre). Visited by 28 million people, the 1889 World's Fair displayed 400 indigenous people as the major attraction. The 1900 World's Fair presented the famous diorama living in Madagascar, while the Colonial Exhibitions in Marseilles (1906 and 1922) and in Paris (1907 and 1931) also displayed human beings in cages, often nude or semi-nude. The 1931 exhibition in Paris was so successful that 34 million people attended it in six months, while a smaller counter-exhibition entitled The Truth on the Colonies, organized by the Communist Party, attracted very few visitors-in the first room, it recalled Albert Londres and André Gide's critics of forced labour in the colonies. Nomadic Senegalese Villages were also presented.

Native people of Suriname were displayed in the International Colonial and Export Exhibition in Amsterdam held behind the Rijksmuseum in 1883.

In 1906, socialite and amateur anthropologist Madison Grant, head of the New York Zoological Society, had Congolese pygmy Ota Benga put on display at the Bronx Zoo in New York City alongside apes and other animals. At the behest of Grant, a prominent eugenicist, the zoo director placed Ota Benga in a cage with an orangutan and labeled him The Missing Link, illustrating that in evolutionary terms Africans like Ota Benga were closer to apes than were Europeans.

Although such views had passed far from the mainstream of anthropological thought by the mid-20th century, a Congolese Village was displayed at the Brussels World Fair in 1958.

Analysis of the Human Zoo Phenomenon

Scholars argue that the zoos and the attention they garnered reflected a broader colonialist ambition and also argue that human zoos can be linked to three distinct but interrelated phenomena: the construction of an imaginary Other, the theorization of a hierarchy of races, and the construction of colonial empires. The historian Pascal Blanchard and coauthors write that:

> Human zoos, the incredible symbols of the colonial period and the transition from the nineteenth to twentieth century, have been completely suppressed in our collective history and memory. Yet they were major social events. The French, Europeans and Americans came in their tens of millions to discover the "savage" for the first time in zoos or "ethnographic" and colonial fairs. These exhibitions of the exotic (the future "native") laid the foundations on which, over an almost sixty-year period, was spun the West's progressive transition from a "scientific" racism to a colonial and "mass" racism affecting millions of "visitors" from Paris to Hamburg, London to New York, Moscow to Barcelona...

Between 1890 and World War I, displays of the noble savage turned increasingly toward more sanguinary images as the European powers made military and colonial forays into Africa. Thus, Tuaregs were exhibited after the French conquest of Timbuktu, Malagasy after the occupation of Madagascar, and Amazons of Abomey after Behanzin's 1894 mediatic defeat against the French.

The various so-called "races" were hierarchically disposed in the racist discourse. For example, when the Cossacks were invited to the Jardin zoologique d'acclimatation, the Russian embassy insisted that they should not be confused with the African Negroes; and when Buffalo Bill came with his troupe, he found, without any problem, his place in the exhibition thanks to the presence of Indians. Social Darwinism was thus represented. Anthropometry and phrenology legitimized these inhumane exhibitions which also tend, retroactively, to prove these racialist theories. The exotic (and colonized) populations displayed in these zoos went along with the exhibitions of monsters: dwarves, hunchbacks, giants, or albinos (Negroes as in Paris in 1912). "Doubtlessly eugenics, social Darwinism, and racial hierarchy dialectically answer themselves together... The 'human zoos' thus find themselves in a crossroads between popular racism and scientific objectification of the racial hierarchy, both supported by the colonial expansion." Between 1890 and World War I, a sanguinary image of the savage was created thus destroying the myth of the Noble savage.

As long as they were displayed, the savages were forbidden from showing any sign of assimilation. However, being exhibited for several years, some did force their jailers to pay them-even if the wages were of course ridiculously low. At the time, few were concerned about the health of these prisoners; many Galibis, not used to the cold climate, died in Paris in 1892. "Isn't there the will-deliberate or inconscious-of legitiming [sic] the conqucrants' brutality animalizing the conquested? In this animalization, transgression of the values and norms of what constitutes, for Europe, civilization is a motor element."

A fascination for the body and vigorous sexuality of the savage was also displayed, a theme related to the alleged "Occidental biological degeneration." Until the 1931 Colonial Exhibition in Paris in Vincennes where Kanaks were displayed, images of anthropophagy also become very popular in the mass medias.

To further illustrate the indignities heaped upon the Philippine people following their eventual loss to the Americans, the United States made the Philippine campaign the centrepoint of the 1904 World's Fair held that year in St. Louis, MI [sic]. In what was enthusiastically termed a "parade of evolutionary progress," visitors could inspect the "primitives" that represented the counterbalance to "Civilisation" justifying Kipling's poem

"The White Man's Burden". Pygmies from New Guinea and Africa, who were later displayed in the Primate section of the Bronx Zoo, were paraded next to American Indians such as Apache-warrior Geronimo, who sold his autograph. But the main draw was the Philippine exhibit complete with full size replicas of Indigenous living quarters erected to exhibit the inherent backwardness of the Philippine people. The purpose was to highlight both the "civilising" influence of American rule and the economic potential of the island chains' natural resources on the heels of the Philippine-America War. It was, reportedly, the largest specific Aboriginal exhibit displayed in the exposition. As one pleased visitor commented, the human zoo exhibit displayed "the race narrative of odd peoples who mark time while the world advances, and of savages made, by American methods, into civilized workers."

LEGACY OF HUMAN ZOOS

The concept of the human zoo has not completely disappeared. A Congolese Village was displayed at the Brussels 1958 World's Fair. An African Village was opened in Augsburg's zoo in Germany in July 2005. According to a June 1994 article by Le Monde diplomatique, a human zoo was present in the village of Huang-Haen in Burma, visited by most tourist agencies. In August 2005, London Zoo also displayed human beings wearing fig leaves (though in this case, the humans volunteered). At Plimoth Plantation in Plymouth, Massachusetts, United States, a recreation of a Wampanoag Village can be found adjacent to the reconstructed Plimoth Colony, staffed by Native Americans in traditional garb. In 2007, Adelaide Zoo will be running a Human Zoo exhibit.

Bibliography

Aikens, C. Melvin: *Archaeology of Oregon*, Portland, Bureau of Land Management, 1993.

Andreski, Stanislav: *Social Sciences as Sorcery*, London, Deutsch, 1972.

Badone, Ellen: *The Appointed Hour: Death, Worldview, and Social Change in Brittany*, Berkeley: University of California Press, 1989.

Bailie, Gil: *Violence Unveiled: Humanity at the Crossroads*. New York, Crossroad, 1995.

Bandera, Cesareo: *The Sacred Game: The Role of the Sacred in the Genesis of Modern Literary Fiction*, University Park, Pennsylvania State University Press, 1994.

Barfield, Thomas: *Dictionary of Anthropology*, Oxford, Blackwell, 1997.

Barker, John: *Christianity in Western Melanesian Ethnography. In History and Tradition in Melanesian Anthropology*, Berkeley, University of California, 1992.

Beavert, Virginia: *The Way it Was: Anuku Iwacha*, Yakima, Franklin Press, 1974.

Beidelman, T. O.: *Colonial Evangelism*, Bloomington, Indiana University Press, 1982.

Belshaw, S.: *The Identification of Values in Anthropology*, American Journal of Sociology, 1959.

Bernard, S.: *India: The Social Anthropology of a Civilization*, New Jersey, Prentice-Hall, 1971.

Biolsi, Thomas : *Indians and Anthropologists: Vine Deloria, Jr., and the Critique of Anthropology*, Tuscon, University of Arizona Press, 1997.

Bock, K.: *Handbook of Psychological Anthropology*, Westport, Greenwood Press, 1994.

Bradshaw, Brendan: *The Wild and Wooly West: Early IrishChristianity and Latin Orthodoxy*. Oxford, Basil Blackwell, 1989.

Cancian, Frank: *Economics and Prestige in a Maya Community: A Study of the Religious Cargo System in Zinacantan, Chiapas, Mexico*, Stanford, Stanford University Press, 1965.

Cappieri, Mario: *The Andamanese: Cultural Elements, Elements of Demogenetics, Physical Anthropology, and Radiology*. Miami, Field Research Projects, 1974.

Clifford James : *Writing Culture: The Poetics and Politics of Ethnography*, Berkley, University of California Press, 1986.

Counts, Ayers: *Christianity in Kaliai: Response to Missionization in Northwest New Britain*. Ann Arbor, University of Michigan Press, 1978.

Crane, G. and Michael V. Angrosino: *Field Projects in Anthropology: a Student Handbook*, Prospect Heights, Waveland Press, 1992.

Crump, Thomas: *The Anthropology of Numbers*, England, Cambridge University Press, 1990.

Crumrine, N. Ross: *Symbolic Structure and Ritual Symbolism in Northwest and West Mexico*, Albuquerque, University of New Mexico Press, 1983.

Cyril, S.: *The Identification of Values in Anthropology*, American Journal of Sociology, 1959.

Dahlberg, Andrea: *In Contesting the Sacred: The Anthropology of Christian Pilgrimage*, London, Routledge, 1991.

Dahlberg, Andrea: *The Body as a Principle of Holism: Three Pilgrimages to Lourdes*, London, Routledge, 1991.

Deng, M.: *Dinka Response to Christianity: The Pursuit of Well-Being in a Developing Society*, Oxford, JASO, 1988.

Dennis, Ian: *Nationalism and Desire in Early Historical Fiction*, New York, St. Martin's Press, 1997.

Dorothy, Ayers: *Christianity in Kaliai: Response to Missionization in Northwest New Britain*. Ann Arbor, University of Michigan Press, 1978.

Eade, John: *Contesting the Sacred: Anthropology of Pilgrimage*, London, Routledge, 1991.

Francis, M.: *Dinka Response to Christianity: The Pursuit of Well-Being in a Developing Society*, Oxford, JASO, 1988.

Gaillard, Gerald, : *The Routledge Dictionary of Anthropologists*, London, Routledge, 2003.

Gans, Eric: *Originary Thinking: Elements of Generative Anthropology*, Stanford, Stanford University Press, 1993.

George Marcus: *Writing Culture: The Poetics and Politics of Ethnography*, Berkley, University of California Press, 1986.

George, P.: *Divinity and Experience: The Trance and Christianity in Southern Ghana*, Oxford, JASO, 1988.

Gillies, Eva: *Vernacular Christianity: Essays in the Social Anthropology of Religion Presented to Godfrey Lienhardt*, Oxford, JASO, 1988.

Glazier, D.: *Anthropology of Religion: a Handbook*, Westport, Greenwood Press, 1997.

Goody, Jack: *Production and Reproduction: A Comparative Study of the Domestic Domain*, Cambridge, Cambridge University Press, 1976.

Hagan, P.: *Divinity and Experience: The Trance and Christianity in Southern Ghana*, Oxford, JASO, 1988.

Harper, J. Russell: *Paul Kane's Frontier*, Austin, University of Texas Press, 1971.

Jacobs, Elizabeth: *Nehalem Tillamook Tales*. Eugene, University of Oregon, 1959.

James, Bowman: *The Routledge Dictionary of Anthropologists*, London, Routledge, 2003.

John, M.: *Introduction to Library Research in Anthropology*, Boulder, Westview Press, 1998.

John, T.: *Anthropology Journals and Serials: An Analytical Guide*, New York, Greenwood, 1986.

Josephy, Alvin: *The Nez Perce Indians and the Opening of the Northwest*, Boston, Houghton Mifflin, 1997.

Julia, G. and Michael V. Angrosino: *Field Projects in Anthropology: a Student Handbook*, Prospect Heights, Waveland Press, 1992.

Kay, Paul: *Explorations in Mathematical Anthropology*, Cambridge, MIT Press, 1971.

Kemper, V.: *History of Anthropology: A Research Bibliography*, New York, Garland, 1977.

Krech, Shepard: *Native Canadian Anthropology and History*, Oklahoma, University of Oklahoma Press, 1994.

Larry, J. Zimmerman: *Indians and Anthropologists: Vine Deloria, Jr., and the Critique of Anthropology*, Tuscon, University of Arizona Press, 1997.

Leistritz, F., Murdock, H.: *The Socioeconomic Impact of Resource Development: Methods for Assessment*, Boulder, Westview Press, 1981.

Lison-Tolosana, Carmelo: *The Beatae: Feminie Responses to Christianity in Sixteenth-Century Castile*, Oxford, JASO, 1988.

McKevitt, Christopher: *Contesting the Sacred: The Anthropology of Christian Pilgrimage*, London, Routledge, 1991.

Morinis, Alan: *Sacred Journeys: The Anthropology of Pilgrimage*, Westport, Greenwood Press, 1992.

Philip, K.: *Handbook of Psychological Anthropology*, Westport, Greenwood Press, 1994.

Raymond, L.: *Evolution of Mathematical Concepts: An Elementary Study*, New York, Wilson, 1975.

Richard, L.: *The Church and Healing: Studies in Church History*, Oxford, Basil Blackwell, 1982.

Robert, H.: *Dictionary of Concepts in Cultural Anthropology*, New York, Greenwood Press, 1991.

Robert, J., Talia Ben Zeev: *The Nature of Mathematical Thinking*, New Jersey, Erlbaum, 1996.

Ross, Alexander: *Adventures of the First Settlers on the Oregon or Columbia River*, Corvallis, Oregon State University Press, 2000.

Ruby, Robert: *The Chinook Indians: Traders of the Lower Columbia*, Norman, University of Oklahoma Press, 1988.

Ryle, John: *Miracles of the People: Attitudes to Catholicism in an Afro-Brazilian Religious Centre in Salvador Da Bahia*, Oxford, JASO, 1988.

Silverman, Helaine: *The Ethnography and Archaeology of Two Andean Pilgrimage Centers*, Westport, Greenwood Press, 1991.

Spencer, Frank: *History of Physical Anthropology*, New York: Garland, 1997.

Stephen, D.: *Sacred Journeys: The Anthropology of Pilgrimage*, Westport, Greenwood Press, 1992.

Sternberg, J., Talia Ben Zeev: *The Nature of Mathematical Thinking*, New Jersey, Erlbaum, 1996.

Stirrat L.: *The Church and Healing: Studies in Church History*, Oxford, Basil Blackwell, 1982.

Trautmann, Thomas R.: *Dravidian Kinship, Cambridge Studies in Social Anthropology*, New York, Cambridge University Press, 1981.

Urton, Gary: *The Social Life of Numbers: A Quechua Ontology of Numbers and Philosophy of Arithmetic*, Austin, University of Texas Press, 1997.

Vatuk, Sylvia: *American Studies in the Anthropology of India*, New Delhi, Manohar, 1978.

Weeks, M.: *Introduction to Library Research in Anthropology*, Boulder, Westview Press, 1998.

Wilder, L.: *Evolution of Mathematical Concepts: An Elementary Study*, New York, Wilson, 1975.

Williams, T.: *Anthropology Journals and Serials: An Analytical Guide*, New York, Greenwood, 1986.

Winthrop, H.: *Dictionary of Concepts in Cultural Anthropology*, New York, Greenwood Press, 1991.

Index

C

D

E

F

G

H

❑❑❑